P. M. D. Gray   R. J. Lucas (Eds.)

Advanced Database Systems

10th British National Conference on Databases,
BNCOD 10
Aberdeen, Scotland, July 6-8, 1992
Proceedings

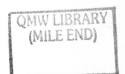

Springer-Verlag
Berlin Heidelberg New York
London Paris Tokyo
Hong Kong Barcelona
Budapest

Series Editors

Gerhard Goos
Universität Karlsruhe
Postfach 69 80
Vincenz-Priessnitz-Straße 1
W-7500 Karlsruhe, FRG

Juris Hartmanis
Department of Computer Science
Cornell University
5149 Upson Hall
Ithaca, NY 14853, USA

Volume Editors

Peter M. D. Gray
Rob J. Lucas
University of Aberdeen, Department of Computing Science, King's College
Aberdeen, AB9 2UB, Scotland, UK

CR Subject Classification (1991): H.2

ISBN 3-540-55693-1 Springer-Verlag Berlin Heidelberg New York
ISBN 0-387-55693-1 Springer-Verlag New York Berlin Heidelberg

Typesetting: Camera ready by author/editor
Printing and binding: Druckhaus Beltz, Hemsbach/Bergstr.
45/3140-543210 - Printed on acid-free paper

Lecture Notes in Computer Science

Edited by G. Goos and J. Hartmanis

Advisory Board: W. Brauer   D. Gries   J. Stoer

Preface

The theme of this book is the potential of new *Advanced Database Systems*. When the first of this series of conferences was held in Aberdeen, back in 1980, the potential of relational databases was clear for all to see, but commercial systems were still a few years off. At that time CODASYL and IMS reigned supreme, whilst the PC did not even exist! During the 80's, relational databases have become an industry standard, but their shortcomings have also become more obvious, many of which were foreseen. In particular, there was a serious shortcoming in data modelling constructs in order to capture complex CAD applications, and a difficulty in extending the model to include new datatypes. This led to an interest in *Object-Oriented Databases,* addressed by three papers.

Following these, we have a paper by an invited speaker *David Gradwell* on how to extend entity-relationship modelling techniques, widely used on relational databases, so that they cope with object-oriented databases. This is an important requirement for their widespread adoption.

Many people have questioned whether relational databases could meet the performance standards of finely-tuned IMS databases. Fortunately there have been developments in the UK in the use of networks of parallel processors. These have now come of age, and we have thought it right to include amongst research papers two studies of state of the art relational databases running on *Parallel Hardware* - NCR/Teradata and Meiko. These show great promise for the future, particularly with regard to the scalability of the technology and the use of faster processors. Together with these is a research paper on the use of transputer networks.

The availability of parallel hardware leads nicely into the question of the use of Distributed Systems. Our second invited speaker *Dr Michael Brodie* from GTE Labs, USA, discusses the promises for these systems, where application programs and databases cooperate together over a network. But this leads on to the awkward problem of *Legacy Systems* which are crucial to an organisation, but very hard to migrate from. How are we going to change over and get the advantages of Advanced Systems?!

One of the big problems of early database systems was the so-called impedance mismatch between them and programming languages, both in the range of data types that could be stored, and in the handling of large sets. This has led to a range of implementations coupling various new programming languages to databases - Functional, Persistent and Logic Programming. It has also led to more advanced *Conceptual Data Models* which are implemented in these languages, as described by three papers.

One particular feature of advanced data models is the need, long foreseen by Nijssen, to capture as much of the semantics of the data, including constraints and active rules, in the database. *Logic Programming* systems have been very useful for this purpose, and our final section discuss systems that use it for active rules, program transformations and constraints.

I am particularly grateful to the program committee of 16 people who picked the selection of 12 papers from 36 submitted. Although there was a wide variety of topics, it is interesting that these themes emerged so strongly for presentation at the 10th BNCOD conference. I am also very grateful for the industrial members of the program committee, who guided us in the selection of industrial papers, using slightly different criteria from the academic papers. Thus we hope that people working in industrial software development, and engineering design will find much to interest them in this book.

Acknowledgements

Finally, may I say that these proceedings represent the strength of a vigorous database community in Britain, without whose support the annual conference could not take place. I am particularly grateful for advice and support from Alex Gray, as steering committee chairman, and from Elizabeth Oxborrow and Mike Jackson who ran earlier conferences. Nearer home, I am very grateful to my co-editor Rob Lucas, to my research students, who have helped organise the conference and to the departmental secretaries Irene Kavanagh and Katie Blanchard who coped with much of the day to day work and are the unsung heroes!

Most of the work in the UK has been supported over the years by the Science and Engineering Research Council, to whom we are all grateful, and it is to be hoped that they will see the fruits of this research in these proceedings as an encouragement to them to support the proposed special initiative in Advanced Databases and Large Knowledge Bases from 1992.

April 1992

Peter M D Gray
Conference Chairman

Conference Committees

Program Committee

P.M.D. Gray (University of Aberdeen) - Chair
J. Bocca (University of Birmingham)
T.J. Bourne (SIAM Limited)
W.A. Gray (University of Wales, Cardiff)
A .F. Grundy (University of Keele)
M.S. Jackson (Wolverhampton Polytechnic)
K.G. Jeffery (SERC)
R.G. Johnson (Birkbeck College, London University)
J.B. Kennedy (Napier, Edinburgh)
R.J. Lucas (Keylink Computers Limited)
J.K.M. Moody (University of Cambridge)
M. Norrie (University of Glasgow)
E.A. Oxborrow (University of Kent)
N.W. Paton (Heriot-Watt, Edinburgh)
G.C.H. Sharman (IBM, Hursley)
M.J.R. Shave (University of Liverpool)

Steering Committee

W.A. Gray (University of Wales) - Chair
P.M.D. Gray (University of Aberdeen)
A.F. Grundy (University of Keele)
M.S. Jackson (Wolverhampton Polytechnic)
E.A. Oxborrow (University of Kent)
M.H. Williams (Heriot Watt University)

Organising Committee

R.J. Lucas (Keylink Computers Limited)
G.J.L. Kemp (University of Aberdeen)
P.M.D. Gray (University of Aberdeen)
D. Nikodem (University of Aberdeen)
S.M. Embury (University of Aberdeen)
S.Leishman (University of Aberdeen)

Contents

Invited Papers

The Promise of Distributed Computing and the Challenges of Legacy Systems . . . 1
M.L. Brodie (GTE Labs, Boston, MA, USA)

Object-Oriented Requirements Capture and Analysis – The Orca Project . . . 29
D.J.L. Gradwell (Data Dictionary Systems Limited, Camberley, UK)

Object-Oriented Databases

A Model for Versioning of Classes in Object-Oriented Databases. 42
S.R. Monk, I. Sommerville (Lancaster University, UK)

A Storage Manager for the Hypernode Model 59
E. Tuv, A. Poulovassilis, M. Levene (University College, London, UK)

Views and Formal Implementation in Three-Level Schema Architecture
for Dynamic Objects 78
G. Saake, R. Jungclaus (Technical University Braunschweig, FRG)

Parallel Implementations and Industrial Systems

The Meiko Computing Surface: A Parallel and Scalable Open Systems
Platform for Oracle 96
A. Holman (Meiko Limited, Bristol, UK)

A Study of a Parallel Database Machine and its Performance –
The NCR/Teradata DBC/1012 115
J. Page (NCR/Teradata Limited, Chertsey, UK)

Control of a Large Massively Parallel Database Machine Using
SQL Catalogue Extensions, and a DSDL in Preference to an Operating System . . . 138
M. Unwalla, J. Kerridge (The University of Sheffield, UK)

Non-Relational Data Models

Integration of Modal Logic and the Functional Data Model 156
D.R. Sutton, P.J.H. King (Birkbeck College, University of London, UK)

The Raleigh Activity Model: Integrating Versions, Concurrency,
and Access Control 175
M.H. Kay, P.J. Rivett, T.J. Walters (International Computers Limited, Reading, UK)

A Graphical Data Modelling Program with Constraint Specification and Management . 192
R. Cooper, Z. Qin (University of Glasgow, UK)

Logic Programming and Databases

Association Merging in a Schema Meta-Integration System for a Heterogeneous
Object-Oriented Database Environment 209
M.A. Qutaishat, N.J. Fiddian, W.A. Gray (Univ. of Wales, College of Cardiff, UK)

Generating Active Rules from High-Level Specifications 227
O. Díaz (Univ. of Aberdeen, UK, and Univ. of País Vasco, San Sebastián, Spain),
S.M. Embury (University of Aberdeen, UK)

Employing Integrity Constraints for Query Modification and
Intensional Answer Generation in Multi-Database Systems 244
M.M. Fonkam, W.A. Gray (University of Wales, College of Cardiff, UK)

THE PROMISE OF DISTRIBUTED COMPUTING AND THE CHALLENGES OF LEGACY SYSTEMS

Michael L. Brodie
Intelligent Database Systems
GTE Laboratories Incorporated
brodie@gte.com

ABSTRACT

The imminent combination of computing and telecommunications is leading to a compelling vision of world-wide computing. The vision is described in terms of next generation computing architectures, called Enterprise Information Architectures, and next generation information systems, called Intelligent and Cooperative Information Systems. Basic research directions and challenges are described as generalizations of corresponding database concepts. No matter how compelling and potentially valuable the vision may be, it is of little use until the legacy problem is solved. The problem of legacy systems migration is described, in the context of distributed computing, and is illustrated with lessons learned from actual case studies. The basic research directions and challenges are recast in the light of the reality of legacy systems. Recommendations for realizing the vision and meeting the challenges are given including the search for the elusive Killer Application.

1. World-Wide Computing

My professional goal is to contribute to making the world a better place by providing solutions to significant, real problems. As a computer science researcher this means that I want to produce the highest quality research and technology that is ultimately applicable to real problems so that the results are consistent with my beliefs. In this regard, I have very high hopes and expectations for the potential benefits of world-wide computing. The vision is that in world-wide computing the necessary computing resources (e.g., programs, information bases, information systems) can interact to cooperatively (or collaboratively) to solve problems effectively and efficiently and to do productive work. This will all happen transparently to the location or nature of the participating systems.

In this section, I describe a world-wide computing vision in terms of cooperation amongst information systems augmented by a telecommunications vision that provides communication on a scale previously unthinkable by computer scientists.

1.1. The Vision

The vision of distributed computing is compelling. It says that soon the dominant computing paradigm will involve large numbers of heterogeneous, intelligent agents distributed over large computer/communication networks. Agents may be humans, humans interacting with computers, humans working with computer support, and computer systems performing tasks without human intervention. Work will be conducted on the network in many forms. Work task definition will be centralized (e.g., a complex engineering task) and decentralized. Tasks will be executed by agents acting autonomously, cooperatively, or collaboratively, depending on the resources required to complete the task (e.g., monitoring many systems of a patient or many stations in a factory). Agents will request and acquire resources (e.g., processing, knowledge, data) without knowing what resources are required, how to acquired them, or how they will be orchestrated to achieve the desired result. A goal of this vision is to be able to use, efficiently and transparently, all computing resources that are available on computers in large computer/communications networks.

1.1.1. Cooperative Work

Computers should support humans and organizations in their natural modes of thinking, playing, and working. Consider how complex activities are in human organizations, such as a hospital (Figure 1). Each human agent (e.g., doctor, technician, nurse, receptionist) provides capabilities to cooperatively achieve a goal (e.g., improve the health of a patient). For a doctor to complete an analysis of a patient, the doctor may need the opinion of another doctor, the results of a laboratory test, and personal information about the patient. In general, the analysis is broken into sub-activities and appropriate agents are found for each sub-activity. Each sub-activity is sent to the appropriate agents together with the required information in a form that the agent can use. Cooperating agents complete the sub-activities and return the results in a form that the doctor can use. The doctor then analyzes the results and combines them to complete the analysis, possibly by repeating sub-activities that were not successful or by invoking new sub-activities.

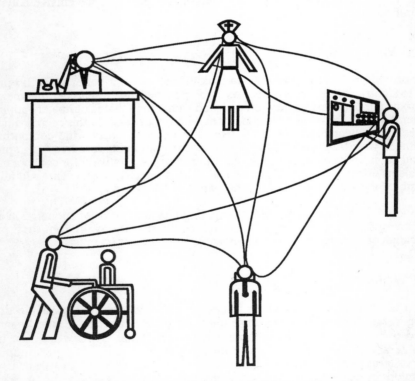

Figure 1. Cooperating Agents in Medical Care

Such cooperative work requires considerable intelligent interaction among the agents using knowledge of who does what, what information is required, the form in which it is required, scheduling requirements or coordinating of tasks, how to locate agents, how to request that sub-activities be done, etc. The cost and quality of products of most human organizations depends on the effectiveness of such cooperation. In hospitals, the quality and cost of health care depend on effectiveness and speed of cooperation. Aspects of the cooperation can be seen as effective parts of the work being done (e.g., doctor's interaction to solve life critical problems) while others may be seen as counter productive (e.g., converting patient chart information into multiple computer formats for automated analysis steps). The cost and complexity of interactions in a hospital argue for their optimization. What cooperation aspects are effective and should be encouraged and which should be diminished?

Intuitively, it seems that the distributed computing vision could meet many requirements of cooperative work. The cost of an activity could be reduced by a computing infrastructure that makes appropriate interactions transparent to the agents. Computers could contribute to a more productive (e.g., effective and efficient) cooperative by intelligently supporting cooperation. In the next section, we examine forms of intelligence and cooperation that computers might support. We limit our scope to the cooperative work that might be supported by cooperating information systems (ISs) and the resulting requirements on the computing infrastructure, or systems technology.

1.1.2. Intelligent and Cooperative Information Systems

Intelligent and Cooperative Information Systems (ICISs) are seen as the next generation ISs, 5-10 years in the future. ICISs are collections of ISs that exhibit forms of cooperation and intelligence. Cooperative refers to interoperability (the ability to interact effectively to achieve shared goals, e.g., a joint activity). Intelligent refers, in part, to the ability to do this efficiently (i.e., have the system find, acquire, and orchestrate resources in some optimal fashion) and transparently (with the least human effort). The goal is that any computing resource (e.g., data, information, knowledge, function) should be able to transparently and efficiently utilize any other. Although some features of such systems are agreed upon, no one knows the exact nature of these systems. This subsection illustrates and suggests some initial ideas for ICIS functionality.

Most organizations have developed many application-specific but independent ISs and other computing resources. They soon find that almost all ISs require access to other ISs, just as the people in their organization need to interact. Such organizations have vast investments in valuable resources that cannot be used without great cost. For example, valuable data is bound to applications and is not available to others. There is a growing need for vast numbers of disjoint information / computing resources to be used cooperatively, efficiently, transparently, and easily by human users (e.g., clerks, scientists, engineers, managers). Consider, for example, the different ISs that must interact to support the functions of a hospital (Figure 2). To produce a patient bill, the billing system must obtain information from many hospital ISs (e.g., nursing records, doctors bills, pharmacy, radiology, lab, ward, food services).

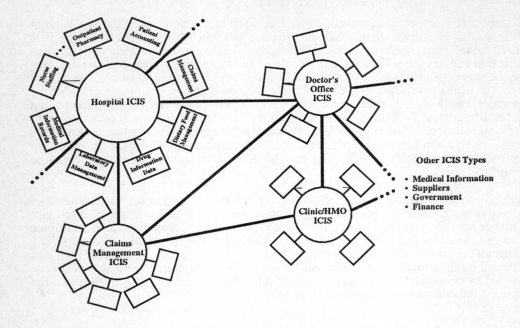

Figure 2. Health Care ICIS

Let's call such an effective combination of systems, a Health Care ICIS. The Health Care ICIS requires access between multiple, heterogeneous, distributed ISs that were independently designed to be used in isolation.

We consider two or more ISs that execute joint tasks to form a larger IS, called a Cooperative IS. We call an individual IS within a cooperative IS, a component IS. With various forms of transparency, a cooperative IS can act as, and be considered as, a single IS (e.g., the hospital billing system accesses to multiple ISs should be transparent to the user). A common goal for component ISs is to maintain autonomy while cooperating within the cooperative IS.

"Intelligent" features could be added to a cooperative IS. These features require of technology, or provide users with, more "intelligence" than conventional ISs. Intelligence has a potential role in user interaction, between the user and the component ISs to enhance the quality of interaction. Examples of such features include: presenting an integrated view of the multiple ISs; explanation; intensional queries; and presenting functionality through graphic, visual, linguistic support or other support (e.g., use of icons, templates, graph representations).

Intelligence also plays a role in enhancing IS functionality: Examples include:
• Enhanced decision making or reasoning capabilities (e.g., incorporate hospital rules into the Health Care ICIS);
• (Re) Active (e.g., when a new patient is registered, a transaction is triggered that checks the availability of rooms in wards and orders needed supplies);
• Non determinism (e.g., give me any one of the possible teams that has two doctors from cardiology, an anaesthetist, and a trio of nurses who are not already booked);

• Non-deductive forms of inference (e.g., induction such as learning rules or constraints from databases, reorganizing a schema based on current extensions of different classes, redistributing information based on access patterns; case-based reasoning, where information is structured according to "cases" and new situations are dealt with by finding similar ones in the information);
• Maintaining integrity constraints.
• Introspection: reasoning about meta-knowledge (e.g., a Health Care ICIS component reasoning about what it can and cannot do in the face of a request).

1.1.3. The Global Computer

In a separate universe far away, or so it seems, the vision for the next generation telecommunications technology is taking shape. It intends to permit any information to be communicated anywhere, at any time, in any form, to any agent (human or machine). The key technologies include pervasive, broad band, lightening fast, intelligent networks enabling universal information access to support information malls, multimedia communications, and business enterprise integration. This will require all-digital, broad band transport and switching; distributed intelligence and high-speed signaling; geographic independence for users and services; interoperability of diverse networks and equipment; transparency via common look and feel interfaces; etc. Sound familiar?

The telecommunications vision does not consider only agents in hospitals. A significant difference with the computing vision is the world-wide scale of telecommunications. Figure 3 illustrates agents interacting with agents across Europe, North America, and Africa. Current telecommunications advances involving cellular communications and satellites will soon permit point to point communication anywhere in the world, with or without old fashioned wires or new fangled fiber optics.

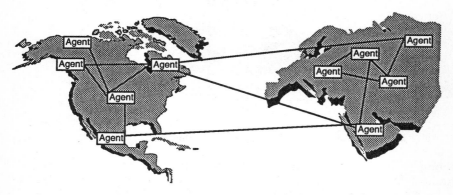

Figure 3. Agent Interaction In Telecommunications

There are striking similarities between the computing and telecommunications visions [WILL91]. The motivations are very similar, in terms of both applications (i.e., business) and technology. They both rely on similar technological advances. Indeed, the telecommunications vision, underlying Bellcore's Intelligent Network Architecture (INA) program, is stated simply as the addition of a distributed computing environment (DCE) or distributed processing environment (DPE) to the public network. The public network is the world-wide telephone system.

The vision of world-wide computing results from the combination of the computing and telecommunications visions. In this vision, the device (e.g., telephone, computer, FAX, television, answering machine) on your desk can be connected to the world-wide public telecommunications/computing network. It has transparent access to all allowable resources of the network. Your computer just became a global computer. You can transparently participate in ICISs world-wide, as illustrated in Figure 4. In computing terms, the scale is unimaginable, at least for me. There are currently approximately one device per citizen (i.e., $10^{**}8$) on the public network in United States. How many devices would there be in the global computer?

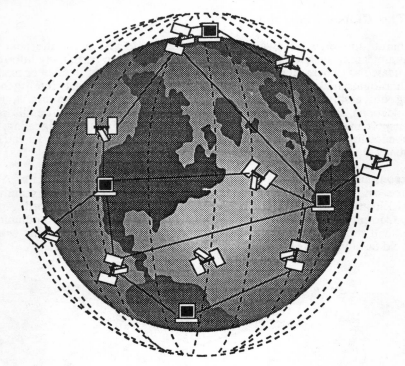

Figure 4. World-Wide Computing

The telecommunications vision critically depends on computing and *vice versa*. The implications of merging telecommunications and computing are profound. An obvious change will be a lack of distinction between computing and telecommunications technologies and businesses. The world-wide, public telephone system becomes a universally accessible DCE/DPE. In broad terms, these visions are widely agreed to. It is not news. It is taking a long time to realize them. New technology facilitates revolutions, it seldom brings them about. These visions are currently solutions looking for problems. For example, two major telecommunication / computing experiments in the United States have no compelling applications to drive it. The most advanced technology is being used to support computing and communicating hospital imagery and visualization of scientific data. These are not the *killer applications* that are in such great demand that they alone will force the realization of the visions, and which we return to in section 3.

The remainder of the paper addresses technical ideas and challenges in the realization of the distributed computing vision, possibly on the scale of world-wide computing. In addition to basic research challenges, there are the critical challenges of evolving the current technology base, including existing or legacy systems, towards the vision.

1.2. The Technology

The motivations for the telecommunication and distributed computing visions are quite similar. The primary motivation is for users to gain control of their technology/networks, for the users to control the distribution and deployment of their own data and application. In the past, hardware, and to some extent software, vendors had control (e.g., use any system or computer you like as long as it is Blue). A current major goal is vendor independence as expressed in the ill-defined phrase *Open Systems*. Another motivation is the dramatic cost reductions possible in moving computing from costly mainframes to workstations/mini computers. These strategic motivations relate to key technical motivations such as interoperability (i.e., ability to cooperate) and reuse of interchangeable components. The potential magic of these trends towards open, distributed computing/telecommunications is that they potentially support what appears to be more natural working/playing modes of humans and organizations (i.e., cooperative work). The magic is still potential due to the lack of killer applications. This subsection describes a pervasive vision of next generation computing architectures, the generalization to this environment of database concepts, and consequent research challenges. This sets the stage for the subsequent section which raises the question of legacy systems in the face of this vision.

1.2.1. Next Generation Computing Architecture and Object Space

The agent-oriented, cooperative work, described above, will be supported by a global object space, as illustrated in Figure 5. Co-operating agents (e.g., resources such as humans, computers, information bases) will interface to the global object space via a human or systems interface, depending on whether the agent is a human or a system. Each agent may request or provide resources to the global object space. The resource may be all or some of the capabilities of the agent. The interface layer will provide transparent access to the object space by mediating between the agent's languages, formats etc. and those of the object space. By the mid 1990's the notion of a global object space will become an architectural paradigm which will provide the basis of next generation computing environments. These environments will provide practical interoperability with limited efficiency, intelligence, and distribution.

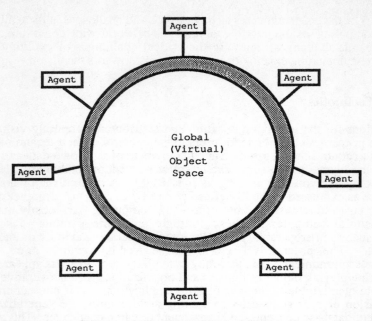

Figure 5. The Global Object Space

The object space can be considered to be a logical extension of a database. A database consists of data elements. Using the object-oriented approach, data and operations are encapsulated so that all computing resources (e.g., data, information, programs) can be seen as objects. Data management concepts can be extended to manage objects. Hence, the global object space provides a challenging opportunity for extending database concepts to global object management. Given the world-wide computing vision, the scale of the challenges is enormous. The opportunities for distributed computing are compelling.

The global object manager could potentially offer access to any subset of the union of the resources provided by the agents (e.g., user specific object spaces or object views). The object space may be largely virtual, since it is an implementation detail as to how the objects (i.e., agent-provided resources) are managed, stored, and accessed. A global object manager will support efficient and intelligent (e.g., transparent) interoperability between all objects. Hence, resources can be combined in unanticipated ways to meet new application requirements and opportunities. The object space will be based on the object-oriented approach and will be supported by a generic technology which will provide a tool kit for combining computing components in arbitrary ways. In this context, the notion of a single database management system (DBMS) as a separate component serving a wide range of applications will cease to exist. Instead, DBMSs become cooperating agents. Database interoperability will be supported by the global object space manager just as it supports interoperability between all agents.

Object space management technology is only one of many systems technologies necessary to support the vision. The remarkably successful database notion of extracting as much data management functionality from applications as possible and providing it in a generic DBMS (Figure 6) has been extrapolated to many computing services to arrive at an distributed computing architecture notion illustrated in Figure 6. The resulting architecture separates four systems functions:

- user interfaces
- applications (the minimum code necessary for the application semantics)
- shared distributed computing services (e.g., global object space management)
- a global object space

The distributed computing architecture is also called the Enterprise Information Architecture.

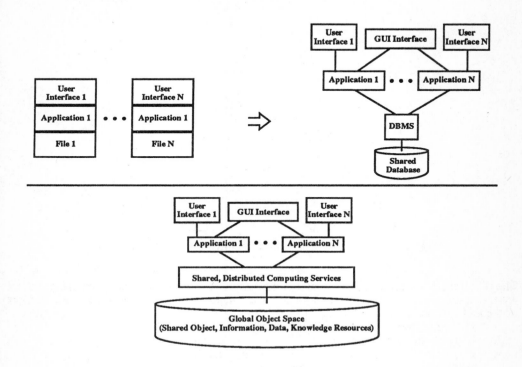

Figure 6. Distributed Computing Architecture

The most compelling idea of the distributed computing architecture is the concept of shared, distributed computing services. The principle is to provide as many computing services as possible as sharable servers in a distributed computing environment. The services are provided by systems or computing infrastructure technologies such as DBMS, OS, user interface management systems, and development environments. This is the home of the global object space manager. Collectively, the systems providing infrastructure support are being called **middleware.** Figure 7 illustrates details of the layers of the architecture:

- Human presentation interface
- Applications and System Applications Development Environments
- APIs
- Middleware (Distributed Computing Services)
- System Interfaces
- OS Network hardware.

and gives examples of the middleware.

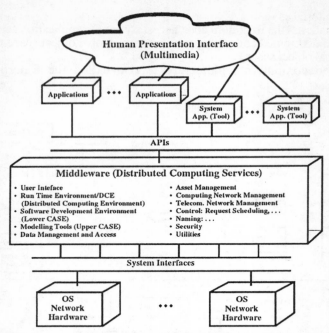

Figure 7. Enterprise Information Architecture with Middleware

The distributed computing architectures, middleware, and global object space management are much more than visions. The major software vendors have all announced their support of the architectural goals, including:

- open systems (i.e., standard interfaces or architectures)
- client-server computing
- distributed computing including distributed DBMSs
- advanced flexible user interfaces
- transparent multi-vendor interoperability
- transaction processing
- structured organization of corporate resources / components
- reliability and maintainability
- reduced communication costs
- single-point program maintenance and upgrading
- open access to low-cost workstation MIPS

Some vendors have announced and released middleware and related products, including:

- Enterprise Network Architecture (ENA) (Gartner Group terminology)
- DEC's Network Application Architecture
- IBM's: Information Warehouse Architecture
- IBM's System Application Architecture (SAA)
- IBM's Information Warehouse Architecture
- Advanced Networked Systems Architecture (ANSA) [ARM89]
- SOE: Systems/Standard Operating Environment (pervasive)
- DCE: Distributed Computing Environment (pervasive)
- DME: Distributed Management Environment (pervasive)

- OSI Network Management Forum
- Apple's Integration Architecture for the Enterprise: Data Access Language, MacWorkStation, MaccAPPC (LU 6.2)
- Tandem's Open Application Development Architecture and Open Enterprise Networking.
- Distributed Computing Environments (DCE) (see below)
- Bull's: Distributed Computing Model (DCM)

There is considerable activity towards achieving interoperability between arbitrary computing services via object-orientation and distributed computing technologies such as distributed databases. There are several research, product, and standards development projects exploring different aspects of global object management. The projects originate in disjoint technologies including databases (e.g., GTE's Distributed Object Management [MANO92a], Open Systems Liaison's Object Mapper, Stanford's Mediator-based SoD and KSYS, University of Florida's Federated Information Bases), programming languages (e.g., MIT's Argus), operating systems (e.g., Open Systems Foundation's OSF/1, APM Ltd's ANSA [ARM89]), communications (e.g., Open System Liaison's Software Bus), software engineering (e.g., Norway's Eureka Software Factory), and in new technologies that combine features of several technologies (e.g., Yale University's LINDA [CARR89]). The use of the object abstraction in integrating heterogeneous and autonomous components is also a characteristic of recent developments in personal computer application integration software, such as Hewlett-Packard's NewWave, Object Linking and Embedding (OLE) in Microsoft® Windows™, and inter-application communication (IAC) facilities in the latest Apple Macintosh® operating system.

Perhaps the most notable activity in global object management as a basis for interoperability, is that of the Object Management Group (OMG). OMG is a consortium of the major software and hardware vendors around the world. Within two years, it has proposed a guideline for a Common Object Request Broker (COBRA) [OMG91a] which provides the core functionality for interoperability to be provided by the global object manager, namely facilitating the exchange of messages between arbitrary objects in a distributed, heterogeneous computing environment.

Although object-orientation is in its infancy and is not deployed in practice to any significant degree, it plays a critical role in all of the visions described above. There is a pervasive industry commitment to object-orientation. This is demonstrated by the following strategies and products announced by major vendors.

- IBM's System View (OO is seen as critical to manage large scale systems)
- IBM-Apple agreement based in part on OO technology
- Apple uses OO in many of its current products
- International Standards (e.g., CCITT's TMN "Managed Objects")
- TINA's commitment to OO (a Telecommunications pre-standards body) [WILL91]
- Multi-vendor networks based on "Managed Objects"
- Microsoft's Object Linking and Embedding (OLE)
- IBM-Metaphor's Patriot Partner's Constellation Project
- DEC's Trellis OO Application Development Environment
- OODBMSs or DBMS support for OO: Ingres, Oracle, Objectivity/DB (DEC-Objectivity), Ontos (IBM-Ontos), and 13 other OODBMS products .
- Object Management Group (OMG): An industry consortium of most major players (IBM,. DEC, Sun, HP, etc.) to promote and develop object-oriented technology.

Another indication of the potential significance of and high expectations for object-orientation is the number of object-oriented standards efforts, including:

- X3H2-SQL (object-oriented support in SQL3)
- X3H4 Information Resource Dictionary Systems
- X3H6 CASE Integration Service
- X3H7 (Object Information Management) [FONG91]
- X3J4 "Object" COBOL
- X3J9 Pascal
- X3J16 C++
- X3T3-ODP (Open Distributed Processing)
- X3T1M1.5 (related to above)
- X3T5-OSI (Open Systems Interconnection)
- OSI/Network Management Forum
- JTC1 SC21/WG4 (Management of Information Services) CCITT's "Managed Objects"
- OSF's Distributed Management Environment
- TINA (a Telecommunications pre-standards body)
- Multi-vendor networks based on "Managed Objects"
- Object Management Group (OMG): An industry consortium of most major players (IBM,. DEC, Sun, HP, etc.) to promote and develop object-oriented technology.

Next generation computing architectures are well on their way from vision to reality. There is a pervasive agreement on many aspects of the vision including the architectural notion of middleware, the functionality of (global) object management, and critical role of object-orientation. There is less agreement on the need or means for integrating technologies so as to draw the greatest benefit from each technology, rather then re-inventing the wheel. These trends are led and largely determined by the computing industry and will, to a very large degree, determine computing environments for a long time to come. As described in the next section, basic research challenges must be met to realize the vision. To date, the research community has had little impact on formulating and realizing the vision. This is a major opportunity for the research community to do excellent research and make significant contributions.

1.2.2. From Database To Object Space Management

Global object space management can be seen as a logical extension of database management to the global object space. Database technology contributes such concepts on which to base object models as persistence, sharing, object management and migration, optimization, transactions, recovery, distribution, and heterogeneous database interoperability. However, the global object space poses additional challenges, not only based on the scale of the object space compared with that of a database. Global object management requirements are dramatically different based on the fact that heterogeneous objects are being managed. A critical, new requirement of global object management is support for general purpose interoperability. This subsection defines interoperability, outlines an approach to providing interoperability, and lists related basic research challenges.

1.2.3. Next Generation Database Research

ICISs were defined above in terms of the ability of two or more systems to interact to execute tasks jointly. This capability is the intuition underlying interoperability. However, there is no agreement on the functionality implied by the term "interoperability." Therefore, we provide here an initial definition and a discussion of the idea and of related objectives.

Initial Definition: Two (hardware or software) components X and Y can interoperate (are interoperable) if X can send requests for services (or messages) Ri to Y based on a mutual understanding of Ri by X and Y, and Y can return responses Si to X based on a mutual understanding of Si as (respectively) responses to Ri by X and Y.

This definition addresses the function of interoperability and not aspects of systems context in which it is provided. For example, two programs that call each other and that are written in the same language, under the same operating system, and on the same machine illustrate trivial interoperability. Specific systems challenges arise in providing interoperability by a DBMS to applications written using the DBMS. More challenges arise when providing it to applications written over heterogeneous, distributed DBMSs. Even more arise when providing it over arbitrary computer systems that may not support any DBMS functionality.

Interoperability does not require X or Y to provide both "client" and "server" functionality, to be distributed or heterogeneous, or to provide any forms of "transparency" with respect to each other unless such transparency is required to satisfy the above definition. However, given a particular systems context, interoperability may require some or all of these features. Alternatively, interoperability could be improved or its scope increased by advances in technology that increase the ease, efficiency, reliability, and security with which components interoperate. Some of these advances can be expressed in terms of various forms of transparency, that is the differences are hidden and a single view is provided. The following forms of transparency are generalized from those proposed for distributed databases.

- resource (e.g., seeing one system or resource provider versus needing to know the individual system(s) providing the service or information);
- language (i.e., using one language therefore not needing to know the language of the resource);
- distribution (i.e., not needing to know the location(s) of the resource(s) or how to transfer to and from them);
- logical/schema (i.e., having the appearance of one meta-information base describing such things as how features are modelled in individual resources);
- transaction (i.e., ability to run one, apparently local, transaction over multiple resources that appear as one resource);
- copy/replication (e.g., not needing to know that resources are replicated);
- performance (i.e., tasks execute efficiently independently of the location of invocation or of participating resources);
- data representation (i.e., not needing to know how information is stored);
- fragmentation (i.e., not needing to know that information is fragmented);
- location (i.e., programs access a single logical database, ignore the location of the actual data);
- transaction (i.e., transactions act the same (atomic, commit, abort) at one, two or more sites);
- advanced application development (i.e., supports the creation of "business rules" to be applied to all distributed processing);
- local autonomy for participant ICISs (i.e., individual components can access and rely on all resources; local operations are purely local, all components are treated equally);
- network/communication (i.e., communication protocols are transparent).
- hardware (i.e., execute components ignoring hardware platform);
- operating system (i.e., run components ignoring the OS)

These and other forms of transparency could be described from a system level perspective, e.g., consistency/integrity of copies of object/data/knowledge; augmenting systems with features to ensure system wide integrity (e.g., backup and recovery). Interoperability involves far more than transparency. It involves issues that arise when two languages or systems must interact including those involved with type systems, transaction systems, communication protocols, optimization, and systems architecture. These requirements pose basic research challenges to otherwise manageable database technology challenges.

Interoperability could be characterized as a form of "systems level intelligence" that enhances the cooperation between ICIS components. Consider the intelligence required to provide services, find resources, cooperate and carry out complex functions across component ISs without the user or component IS needing to know precisely what resources are available, how to acquire them, or how they will be orchestrated to achieve the desired result.

Let's consider an approach to providing global object management. This approach is that of GTE's Distributed Object Management project [MANO92a] and of the OMG. The scale and distribution of the object space leads to the distribution of global object management functionality into a collection of distributed object managers (DOMs). Figure 8 illustrates, in the Health Care ICIS, that medical agents, possibly assisted or simulated by ICIS components, are interconnected indirectly through DOMs.

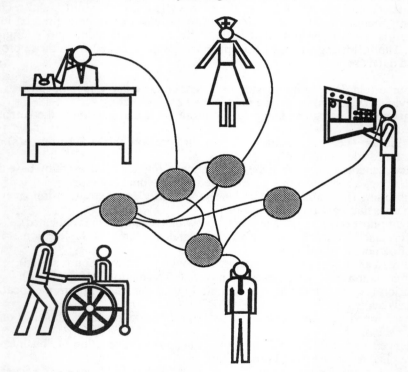

Figure 8. Health Care ICIS Interoperability Via DOMs

In the DOM approach, each resource has a client interface to the DOM, as illustrated in Figure 9. All DOMs have one common object model. Interfaces between resources and DOMs allow resources to be accessed as objects in the common object model. For clients, interfaces allow access to objects, and translate requests and results between the local type system and the common object model.

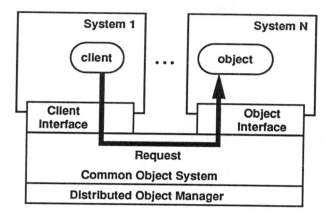

Figure 9. Role of A DOM

Consider as an example interaction a request by an object-oriented DBMS to copy text on what appears to it to be a document object (Figure 10). The request is routed by DOM of system 1 to the DOM of system 2. The interface to the non-object-oriented word processor allows its DOM to treat files as document objects. The system 2 DOM invokes the word processor, causes loading of the references text file, and invokes the requested operation via the interface.

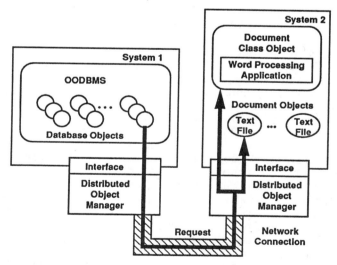

Figure 10. OODBMS Client Request of a Word Processor

Global object management involves all database research issues except that in the context of the global object space, the challenges are much greater. Database solutions may not extrapolate. The following is a list of global object management research challenges that appear significantly more difficult than the database counterpart.

- DOM object model: It must support all requirements of the multi-paradigm, distributed computing environment, not just object manipulation [MANO90]. It must provide a basis for mapping between arbitrary computing systems, not just DBMSs [OMG91b]. The proliferation of object model and object model standards, leads to a requirement for a least common denominator object model [MANO92b].
- Long-lived, distributed applications: An ICIS operation potentially involves operations over many distinct component ISs. Writing transactions corresponds to manipulating entire applications using operations like: start, abort, cancel; suspend, resume, backtrack; migrate computation; show computational state/history. This requires new abstractions for "programming in the large", new control mechanisms, new notions of correctness, and compensation. In short, new transaction models (e.g., open, nested, complex. multi-system operations) are needed. Unlike the conventional transaction model which is orthogonal to the relational data model, the DOM transaction model will have to be integrated with the DOM object model.
- Query optimization: Optimization of queries over the global object space involves optimizing operations over multiple database and non-database systems, vastly expanding the scope for optimization by potentially applying database optimization technology to arbitrary computing tasks.
- Naming in heterogeneous systems: Objects should be uniquely identifiable throughout their life regardless of their system of origin and current location.
- Semantic interoperability: The scale of the global object space makes the notion of a global schema completely infeasible. Indeed, it may be best to have no global anything, but name management, since at a minimum you must be able to reference objects. While DOMs will never solve the semantic integration problem, type systems seem to provide an excellent tools for mapping between systems.
- (Object)Views: We assume that complete semantic integration of all systems is infeasible. Hence, mapping between systems requires the ability to subset the respective systems so as to present the appropriate information (objects) to the other systems. This amounts to an object-view (analogous to a relational view). Views in relational databases still pose major challenges. In object-oriented systems, the problems are more difficult. [HEIL90] [SCHI89]
- Active Objects for active ICISs: Cooperative human interaction to achieve jointly agreed upon tasks requires response to conditions, actions, and events in the working environment. Analogously, cooperative information systems must also be able to respond to changing conditions, actions, and events. Techniques to facilitate these requirements include: rules (If C, do A), events (When E then If C then Do A), triggers, and alerters. These techniques make systems active in that they now react to changes. These techniques create complex temporal and conditional relationships between objects.
- Modelling: Conceptual modelling has been very unsuccessful with conventional databases. ICIS complexity and scale make the problems dramatically worse. Due to the early stage of development and experience, there are currently no effective, proven concepts, tools, or techniques for object-oriented systems design of the scale being considered here.
- Gateways: Interoperability involves the interfacing of computing systems. Hence, interfaces between systems are fundamental elements in corresponding

architectures (Figures 5, 7, 9 and 10). Such interfaces between heterogeneous DBMSs in distributed DBMS architectures are called gateways. They are complex, costly, and generally ad hoc (i.e., unique to the two systems being interfaced). A research goal is to develop generic and efficient gateway technology. How much knowledge should reside outside a component system in the gateway or DOM?

Requirements for global object management will come, in part, from the applications that they will support, such as ICISs. There are basic research questions concerning the nature of such applications. The following is a list of ICIS research issues:

• What forms of cooperation are required between components in an ICIS?
• What ideal architecture (=components & interfaces) is required to support ICISs?
• What are the modelling/programming paradigm requirements of an ICIS?
• What languages are required in the life-cycle of an ICIS?
• What does it mean for an ICIS or object to be (re)active?
• What forms of intelligent functionality are required for ICISs?
• What are the requirements for the repository or global directory service?
• What forms of interoperability will ICISs require?
• What are the transaction model requirements of an ICIS?
• What are the key optimization challenges in support of ICISs?
• How can core technology support the inevitable evolution of large-scale ICISs.

Due to the key role of object-orientation, it is important to realize the basic research challenges that exist in that domain. Currently there is no underlying theory comparable to the relational model for databases [BEER90]. There are inadequate means for dealing with the complexity and scale of object-oriented systems. There are inadequate concepts, techniques, and tools to model large (e.g., 200+) object systems. In terms of programming and execution, how can you describe and prove that the spreading invocation of operations will achieve some specific functionality? How do you optimally schedule the execution of such operations? Do objects schedule themselves or provide other systems functions such as concurrency control and security or is this done outside the object?

We may require new ways of thinking. The conventional idea of defining each specific relationship between an object and its related objects can't be right. Consider how fish "objects" interact in nature. Defining every relationship between 100 fish in a small tank may be doable, especially when you can see them all. Do fish really work like that? What happens in a boundless ocean with unlimited fish? They move beautifully in schools etc. probably without sending messages between every two fish.

2. The Challenge of Legacy Systems

Most large organizations are mired deeply in the "sins of the past", i.e. they are supporting very large (say 10^7 lines of code), geriatric (more than 10 years old), applications systems [STON91]. Such systems are typically in COBOL and typically use, at best, a tired technology DBMS (such as IMS) or no data base system at all. Such elderly systems will be termed **legacy** code, and they present a major headache to many organizations. Not only are they expensive to maintain, but also they are "brittle", and it is difficult to adapt them to changing business needs. Lastly, there is a widespread fear that these legacy systems will, one day, break beyond repair.

Legacy system problems are much more compelling and immediate than the vision of distributed computing. No matter how great the vision, it will be of little value if it cannot be integrated into the current information systems and technology base. In the IS world, demand for new systems and enhancements is outpacing available resources. Maintenance is consuming almost all resources, with less and less left for new development or major enhancements. A challenge here is to develop technology that permits enhancement and evolution of the current, massive investment in ISs.

Even if the distributed computing environment were in place, there are no known methods of migrating legacy systems to the new environment. Currently disjoint and heterogeneous information/computing resources must be made to cooperate efficiently and transparently. Without cooperation (e.g., via interoperability) and increased "intelligence" of these resources, the massive investment may be lost. For example, do you incorporate, into a organization's new distributed computing architecture, a mission critical, multi-million dollar, multi-million line COBOL system with all its faults and limitations, or simply replace it with a newly re-written system? There is technical and economic evidence that legacy systems cannot be re-written.

2.1. Legacy Systems Case Studies

This section illustrates the legacy systems problem via actual legacy system migration efforts, identifies solution directions and restates distributed computing research challenges in terms of legacy system challenges. The message of this section is that the visions described above do not explicitly address legacy systems. Researchers or industrial technologist should provide effective means to migrate from legacy systems and the installed technology base to newly offered technologies. The good news is that the potential cost reductions of the next generation computing and the avoidance of the sins of the past will pay for the vast migration costs.

2.1.1. Telephone Service Provisioning

Figure 11 illustrates eight very large and very real legacy information systems used in the provisioning of telephone service to telephone customers. When a customer calls to request telephone service, this combination of information systems supports what we will call the service order transaction. It consists of thirteen steps each supported by one or more legacy systems. Steps include validating the customer address, assigning a telephone number, allocating equipment for service, etc. As with most legacy systems, none were designed to cooperate with any other to achieve any task or goal.

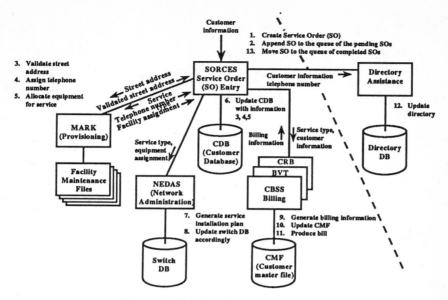

Figure 11. Service Order Transaction

Since telephone service provisioning is a fundamental business operation of the telephone company, the systems were made to interoperate (i.e., interact to execute tasks jointly) using existing technology. There is no transaction system to support the design, development, testing, and execution of the service order transaction, so it is done using available technology without the value of high level abstractions, locking mechanisms, transaction-oriented backup and recovery, performance tuning, etc. As you can imagine, such services might dramatically improve service order provisioning.

Major problems in constructing the service order transaction are due to the heterogeneity of the participating systems. They are almost all written in different languages and run on different computers under different operating systems. They all have different interfaces. In some cases, to interact with the system you must simulate a TTY terminal to simulate an on-line user. Each system has a different information base with naturally arising semantic inconsistencies between definitions and representations of similar concepts (e.g., customer, service order, street address).

The example is an excellent illustration of the need for interoperability and support technology. I estimate that the majority of legacy information systems actually interoperate or have requirements to interoperate in a similar manner.

A potential solution to some of these problems is called surround technology. Surround technology involves encapsulating each information system via a gateway. The gateway can be constructed to mediate between the encapsulated system and requesting systems, as proposed for DOMs. It can provide requesting systems with appropriate views and provide a basis for interoperability. Encapsulating the information system, the gateway provides a means of hiding any modifications to the legacy system (e.g., the evolutionary replacement of the legacy system by one or more information systems). The gateway concept is used in all legacy systems described in this section. Hence, research to facilitate the design, development, deployment, and modification of efficient gateways is critical to both legacy systems and future distributed computing architectures.

2.1.2. Cash Management System

Like all other legacy systems described in this section, the CITIBANK Cash Management System (CMS) was believed to be impossible to extend without massive risk and cost. Indeed, there have been several major failed attempts for CMS and the other legacy systems described here. This subsection summarizes a potentially successful attempt [STON91].

CMS supports check processing and other specialized services for large corporate customers. It allows a customer to maintain a so-called "zero balance" account, i.e. the bank will notify the customer of all the checks that are processed during a given day, and then allow the customer to cover the exact amount of these checks with a single deposit. Hence, the customer applies the minimum possible capital to cover his liabilities, and only on the exact day the capital is needed. A second service provided for large customers is the "reconciliation" of cleared checks. A customer can provide the bank with an electronic feed of all the checks that he writes each day. Then, the bank will match the issued checks against the ones that clear, and provide the customer with an electronic feed that indicates all checks which have cleared as well as those that are still pending.

In addition, CMS supports electronic funds transfers between customer accounts. When the initiator or recipient of the transfer is another bank, then funds must be electronically received from or transmitted to another bank. This requires connection to several electronic money transfer systems (e.g. Swift, Federal Reserve Bank).

Furthermore, the system supports so-called "lock box" operations. Here, mail is received from a post office box, opened, the checks deposited for the customer, and an accounting rendered. Such a service is appropriate for a customer who receives large numbers of checks in the mail, such as a large landlord or a utility.

Lastly, the system supports on-line inquiry and reporting of account status by customers as well as on-line transactions such as the previously discussed transfer of funds.

CMS encompasses 40 separate software modules that perform these and other functions, totaling around $8 * 10^6$ lines of code. Most of the code runs in a COBOL/CICS/VSAM environment; however, the connection to the Federal Reserve bank is implemented on a Tandem machine using TAL, and lock box operations are provided on a DEC VAX.

The majority of the system was written in 1981, and it has now grown to process between 1 and 2 million checks in a batch processing run each night and approximately 300,000 on-line transactions each day. The majority of the systems runs on an IBM 3090/400J with 83 spindles of DASD. CMS must continue to operate 24 hours a day, 7 days a week.

The following migration plan was proposed:

1) Peel the onion: Peel off successive layers of a complex system until only the "core" remained. Upper layers could be moved to a new environment in manageable sized "chunks". On-line reports and feeds are especially amenable to this treatment.

In CMS, we were left with a small "core" which had manageable complexity. It is our assertion that most complex systems can be peeled in this fashion. If CMS had been poorly architected, for example, if CITIcash had performed its own updates instead of calling CITIchecking, then the "core" would have been larger. In this case, we speculate that re-engineering of multiple kernels into a single kernel would have been the appropriate step. This was not required in CMS.

2) Decompose Function: When a complex system implements two or more functions that are logically separable, then the migration plan should untangle the multiple functions and migrate them independently. This is especially valuable when migration steps would otherwise be too large to perform.

3) Design the Target: The target system was designed as a Cash Management ICIS composed of less than ten component ICISs to run on a distributed computing architecture. The resulting design is the target of the migration strategy.

4) Migrate: Completely rewrite the selected components, one at a time, migrating the data and functionality thereby incrementally constructing the target system.

The key element of the migration plan is that it is an incremental rewrite of CMS and not incremental re-engineering. Although there has been much interest expressed in re-engineering legacy systems, our case study has indicated that virtually all code would be better re-specified using modern tools, especially fourth generation languages, report writers, and relational DBMS query languages. There may be legacy systems where re-engineering is a larger part of the migration plan; however, our experience did not indicate any significant use of this technique.

Several research areas emerged from this legacy system migration exercise. First, and foremost, a gateway was seen as critical to legacy system migration but its performance was seen as more critical than the other gateways used in other migrations described in this section. Another research area is support for database migration (e.g., from old to new) and application cutover. A third area was tools to analyze and extract systems specifications, database designs, and the logical structure of application code.

2.1.3. Facilities Management System

Many legacy systems have evolved from simple systems, by adding a small amount of functionality at a time, to become massive systems (e.g., millions of lines of COBOL). Fifteen to twenty years is ample time to embed every conceivable information systems blunder deep into the system. Such systems are seldom documented. This is typical of geriatric, legacy systems. MARK, a telephone facilities management system, is such a system. We focus here on only a few of the problems and a proposed solution. MARK is a mission critical system. The vast MARK database is a much more critical resource than MARK functionality. Many existing systems (i.e., 30-40 critical systems, over 1,200 lesser systems) depend on accesses to MARK. Many new information systems require access to the data. However, due to the inflexible data structures and the systems interface, the data can be considered inaccessible. As a result, between 40-60% of the data is duplicated in other systems. Oh, one additional thing, MARK must be in continuous operation, 24 hours a day, 7 days a week.

How do you migrate MARK from its current legacy system to a facilities management ICIS in a client/server distributed computing environment, following the distributed computing vision? The proposed migration strategy is as follows: First, construct a gateway to encapsulate MARK and any changes so the systems that depend on MARK are not affected. Second, design new databases that include necessary MARK data as well as meet newer requirements. Due to the lack of documentation, this will require treating MARK like a black box and studying its external behaviour. Populating the new databases is a challenge. Slowly migrate MARK functionality from MARK to the new databases using the gateway to direct requests to the appropriate system. Due to potential internal dependencies in MARK, it may be necessary to continue to maintain MARK in its full form even when functionality has been migrated to new systems. Eventually, throw MARK away.

Under cover of the gateway, any systems structure can be installed, including systems consistent with the distributed computing vision. However, the other legacy systems, over 1,200 in this case, must continue to be supported. Again, this emphasizes the importance of gateway research and technology. A major function of the gateway is to direct requests to the correct system. This provides an opportunity for an intelligent gateway to add view, query optimization, and transaction management support. Indeed, some level of these may be critical to the success of the migration. Interoperability research should consider such legacy systems migration requirements. Finally, in this legacy systems migration, as with all others in this section, object-oriented technology did not appear to provide a significant advantage and posed many problems.

2.1.4. The Corporate Customer Database

US West, a large American telephone company, has over 1000 information systems that deal with customer operations, none of which interoperate. Although each has its own customer "database", there are over 200 major customer databases. This is typical of most large telephone companies around the world. There are myriad legacy system problems in this nexus of customer operations support systems. Most of the systems are inflexible (e.g., data structures cannot be enhanced or modified) and very fragile. Bitter experience has often taught that large legacy systems cannot be re-written from scratch, the cold turkey approach. Stories of the failures of multi-million dollar, multi-year rewrites abound. Organizations feel that "You can't live with them and you can't live without them."

In recent years, many large organizations have investigated the idea of corporate information repositories. This suggests that all customer data be integrated logically and possibly physically into a corporate customer database. The conceptual modelling world has offered the global conceptual schema approach. The distributed database community has offered limited distributed database interoperability. To date, most such projects have failed. Each database has its own definition of "customer". The definition is used and depended upon by many applications. Even if the definition could be altered so that the data could be migrated to the new database, the old applications would likely fail. There may be good reasons for variations in customer definitions (e.g., regulatory, legal) that are inherently inconsistent. The scale of the customer database completely defeats all proposed global schema, integrated schema, and conceptual modelling solutions. The scale of the ICIS and world-wide computing puts the nail in the coffin. Even if we had the tools with which to conceptually map schemas, the scale of the problem is beyond the manpower possible to be deployed to the task.

These legacy systems examples help to focus the earlier identified interoperability research efforts. These experiences led to the hypothesis of no global anything and the need for more effective means for systems mapping tools such as type systems instead of conceptual models. Rather than pursue the infeasible and costly goal of complete integration, research should identify different forms of interoperability (e.g., powerful transaction and queries that achieve the required interactions). The example also emphasizes the importance of global naming schemes since it is a bad business practice not be able to find a customer's records, regardless of the system in which it is stored. Names are the minimum information that needs to be globally available. Global naming poses major problems since most legacy systems do not have logical or flexible naming schemes, if any, and systems that do are all inconsistent. Global naming schemes must address legacy systems or they will not be global.

2.2. Migration Challenges

Migrating from the current installed technology base involves the migration of two aspects. First, the existing systems technology and its architecture must be migrated into/replaced by the systems technology and architecture for distributed computing, as described in 1.2.1. Second, legacy systems must be migrated, as described in section 2.1. Both aspects of migration were studied in GTE. The resulting observations, summarized below, were compared with experiences in other large corporations and were found to be universal for large legacy systems. The universal recommendation for addressing these problems was incremental evolution.

2.2.1. Legacy Systems Migration Challenges

The more central (critical to the organization's functions) the IS is, the more severe the problems. Cold turkey re-writes do not work. There is no clean sheet of paper. You must deal with the existing systems, management, operations, technology, budget, environment, people, etc. Half of the problems (3, 5, and 7) concern embedding the new IS into the existing environment. These problems vastly complicate cold turkey replacement. The other problems (1, 2, 5) involve ensuring that the new IS captures all the functionality of the old IS. The following problems were identified as the most difficult and important.

1) That's All Of It, I Think
The old IS must continue to support its functions while the new IS is being built. The old IS can be enhanced faster than the corresponding requirements can be accommodated by the new IS.

2) Incomplete Specification Lead To Incomplete Functionality
The requirements for the old IS are never complete and are almost impossible to define. Many requirements have been met directly by coding solutions into the old IS without being documented. The old IS is the only real specification. (See also problem 5.) There is never a specification/documentation about the system that was implemented as opposed to requirements used to specify it. Many requirements couldn't be met hence approximations and work-arounds are used. These are seldom documented. The standard life cycle does not have as a deliverable "A complete specification or documentation of the system".

3) Ripple Effect Problem
An IS that is mission-critical naturally invites other ISs to connect to it. When you change to the mission-critical IS you must deal with all ISs that connect to it; or, how do we embed the new IS back into the operational environment? For example, you can't replace one old mission critical IS with one or more standard systems that cover the same functionality since they don't handle the requirements that the old IS provide and other current ISs currently depend on the old IS. The more central the IS is to the organization, the greater the ripple effect.

4) Rebuild the Organization
The old IS mirrors the infrastructure of the organization it supports. Changing the IS will require changes in the organization's infrastructure. This is a political and administrative issue.

5) The Outer Tar Baby: Dependencies To External Systems
Throughout the life of the old IS, vast numbers of small procedures or local systems have
been developed that depend on the old system (e.g., dump data from the old IS and use it
in a small system, utilities, report programs). Many, if not all of these have never been
documented or identified. First you must find them and then handle the requirement.
Example: A large organization found 1,200 undocumented utilities/small systems that use
one mission-critical IS.

6) We Want/Need It All
Users will not be satisfied with a new IS unless it offers them substantially more than the
old IS. Cost justification and other organizational incentives argue for more than the old IS
provided. It is easier to justify continual, expensive fixes than a costly re-write with
projected annual savings.

7) Jus' Load 'Er Up: Migration and Data Conversion
Once the new IS has been successfully implemented, you must migrate it into the
operational environment. This requires all of the data in the old IS to be converted into the
format of the new IS and that the new and/or old IS continue to support its functions. Once
the new IS is fully loaded it must be embedded into the existing operational environment.
(See problem 3.)

8) The Inner Tar Baby: Dependence & No Modularity
Like so many pre-database systems, the code and data of large, mission critical ISs are
intimately bound together. There is virtually no data independence. The system code and
data is not modular, hence it is difficult or impossible to identify a subset of data or
functions to extract or address independently from the rest of the system. Even though
current documentation can, and often does for expository reasons, describe the old IS in
logical groupings, the code is not so structured.

2.2.2. Legacy Systems Technology Migration Challenges

Legacy systems were designed to be supported by the existing, hence, legacy, systems
technology and architecture (e.g., simple flat file systems, ridged hierarchical DBMSs,
COBOL, TTY interfaces). The new systems technology (e.g., shared distributed
computing services described in section 1.2.1) and the distributed computing architecture,
which supports client server, may simply not support legacy systems, and *vice versa*. The
following problems were identified as the most significant problems with the current
systems technology base. Although the new technology base may not result in such
problems, there are no known means for migrating from the old to the new, except for cold
turkey (i.e., new systems on the new architecture, and good bye to the old). Evolutionary.
incremental means must be developed.

The following list summarizes the worst problems with current systems technology in
information systems environments.

1) Data Liberation
Users and systems can not easily access or store the necessary, often already existing
information as it is bound to applications in multiple systems.

2) Inability of Systems To Interoperate
Systems do not easily or adequately interoperate (e.g., batch *Vs* on-line /real-time; tasks
involve multiple systems that must interact).

3) Systems Designed to Be Inflexible

Poor design and development and older technologies and techniques have resulted in - systems that are difficult to maintain, evolve, and enhance, due to
• Inflexible systems design and development
• Inter-system dependencies
• Lack of modularity
• Lack of access to data
• Business rules and policy (the way business is done) are embedded in systems, is inaccessible, and not easily changed (e.g., difficult to change rules governing billing)

4) Inadequate Life Cycle

Current life cycles (which include Requirements Gathering, Specification, Design, Development, Testing, Implementation, Maintenance, Enhancement and Evolution), do not adequately address current problems and the requirements of long term plan (i.e., the design and development of systems that meet the goals - modular, maintainable, flexible, in a client-server environment). The inadequacies concern:
• Management and processes
• Speed
• Costs
• Can't handle the rate of change requests to existing and new systems
• Requirements gathering
• Specifications/Documentation
• incomplete documentation leads to
• Support environment (i.e., tools)
• lack of cross-functional, -process, -systems and -enterprise oriented views
• mainframe versus client-server orientation
• does not lead to flexible systems
• inadequate communication between the parties / steps
• lack of coordination of systems developments, evolution, enhancements
• inadequately addresses embedding new systems into the existing environment.
• Design does not adequately involve appropriate parties
• Design and development is not required to meet architectural and other guidelines
• Inadequate re-use of existing assets/resources (code, modules, systems)
• Poor coordination amongst systems modification and developments changes in systems negatively affect dependent systems
• Standards were avoided if appropriate arguments
• Existing development environment and methodologies do not support standards (e.g., diagramming, design, repository) hence, complicate the migration to a more standards compliant environment.

5) Diversity of information bases (including data definitions and related functions).

This is a data administration and standardization issue. For reasons such as: funding methods, a lack of knowledge of exiting systems and data, and inflexible systems (e.g., difficult technical issues in migration, conversion and cut over), there has been a proliferation of independent systems and information bases. In the past, standards were avoided. This has lead, in part, to the diversity.

6) Diversity of user interface and presentation formats, tools, and technology.

7) Inadequate System Responsiveness

Current systems performance does/will not meet real time needs.
Todays standards concern screen presentation times. They should focus on ensuring that the intended function or any related to it to meet business requirements be accomplished

within reasonable limits. This means that the right information is accessed and presented in a way appropriate to the viewer and the task.

8) Costs Invested In Existing Systems Technology Base
The massive investment in the existing systems technology make modification difficult to justify.

9) Proliferation of Independent Systems and Data

10) Inadequate Skills Match To Meet Current and Future Systems Technology Requirements

11) Lack Of Focus On Infrastructure In Systems Technology
Legacy systems projects acquired and used their own systems technology. Hence, systems technology was not considered as part of the infrastructure for systems. The new view of distributed, shared resources and the support of all systems via a system technology infrastructure is a new concept in the information systems world.

12) Inadequate Management Information, Measures, and Processes
Current metrics (e.g., reliability and up-time) are not adequate to meet current or future business requirements. There is a lack of management information to adequately manage.

As you can see from the above problem list, the legacy problem is far more than the migration of legacy information systems. Legacy systems depend on legacy systems technology, which depends on legacy concepts, tools, and techniques, which depend on legacy management, which all depends on legacy thinking, or homeostasis. Much of computer science is based on assumptions which are no longer true (e.g., Von Neuman machines, network communications as bottlenecks). The value of the legacy can be argued, but the problems, when you want to move on can be insurmountable.

3. Killer Applications For World-Wide Computing

The challenges we face in realizing world-wide computing and intelligent and cooperative information systems are far more than technical. The technical challenges are exciting, but they do not pose the greatest challenges. Legacy problems, ranging from technology to thinking, are also not the greatest challenges. The greatest challenge is to find ways in which computing can solve a major human problem or meet compelling human needs.

In telecommunication, computing, and the potential integration of the two, we have solutions in search of problems, on one hand, and a lack of solutions for existing hard problems on the other. These visions are not new. They are progressing very slowly. Again, the central problem is not the technology nor our legacy. These technologies do not yet meet a human need or solve a problem in a way that people would pay anything for. Originally, databases were hard to sell since they violated ways of doing business (e.g., shared data means loss of ownership and control). Distributed databases pose similar threats. Database are more acceptable as support for applications within divisions, when ownership is not lost. For managerial reasons, the original vision of corporate ownership of data is far from reality.

It takes a killer application to break the legacy. We have no creative, compelling applications for world-wide computing or ICISs. Lotus 1-2-3, almost on its own, started the PC/minicomputer revolution, which led to the movement of applications to the desktop and the economics (i.e., cheap workstation MIPS) that is leading to distributed computing and the demise of mainframes. Lotus 1-2-3, for less than $500, motivated managers to buy $5000 machines. If I were to offer you everything you currently have on your desktop plus a lot more, for a lot less cost, but on a mainframe, would you take it? I haven't met anyone who has said yes. Hence, the key point was not cost, nor the technology but rather what Lotus 1-2-3, the application, brought - personal autonomy, control, and power which led to personal innovation. It facilitated real work and met real needs in ways that people would pay for. That's what makes revolutions. For both next generation computing and telecommunications we have no such killer applications.

What do killer applications look like and how do you discover one? They should meet some real human, business, or societal need in ways that are compelling or even just acceptable to those with the need. Hence, to find it you must understand human or organizational needs. Computer scientists may not be as well suited to this as application domain experts. Computing and communications must be critical enabling elements. Computer scientists can help here. To find killer applications, hence to assist in realizing the visions, you should understand applications and interact with application experts, those people and organizations with the problems.

My current guess is that killer applications may not be individual applications but the result of multiple, possibly pre-existing applications, working in cooperation (e.g., not just spreadsheets, databases, text processors, schedulers, billing programs, etc. but some very useful combination of these). Correspondingly, future technical successes will come not from individual technologies but from the cooperation of multiple technologies.

To get over the legacy to find killer applications, we may have to use new ways of thinking, new perspectives. I will conclude with one currently popular method of trying to achieve progress in the information systems through taking new perspectives. It is called Process Re-Engineering.

Conventional information systems are designed to support specific functions in a business. For example in the service order transaction example, described in section 2.1.1, eight information systems each provide a specific function (e.g., one each for facilities provisioning, service order entry, customer information management, customer billing, bill auditing, network administration, directory information management). The problem with the service order transaction was that the systems were never built to cooperate. In terms of technology, there was no support for the transaction. This is a bottom up view of a business, focusing on specific functions.

In process re-engineering, the focus is exclusively on the critical business processes, the life blood of your organization. In the above example, it is telephone service provision. Hence, it is the service order transaction that is important rather than the supporting systems. With this orientation, concern is for the process to ensure that it goes smoothly from beginning to end, and for the role the business process plays in the organization. Processes place requirements on the supporting information systems technology. When business processes change, the information systems requirements must change. Function-specific systems may no longer be of use. Hence, information systems technology must be considerably more flexible than it is today. Process re-engineering encourages a new way of thinking of information systems. Perhaps a killer application is one that permits the combination of arbitrary information system components to meet the requirements of ever changing business processes.

It might be possible to imagine extrapolations of current information systems to intelligent and cooperative information systems in a variety of domains, such as health care. It might also be possible to imagine extrapolations of current telecommunications (e.g., plain old telephones, FAX, modems) to the communication of any information, in any form, at any time, to any location. But is beyond my power to imagine the potential of world-wide computing/communications and what contributions it might bring to make the world a better place.

References

[ARM89] *The ANSA Reference Manual*, Architecture Projects Management Limited, Poseidon House, Castle Park, Cambridge, U.K., 1989.

[BEER90] C. Beeri, "A Formal Approach to Object Oriented Databases", *Data & Knowledge Engineering*, 5 (1990) 353-382.

[CARR89] N. Carriero and D. Gelernter, "Linda in Context", *Comm. ACM*, 32, 4, April 1989.

[FONG91] E. Fong, et. al. (eds), "X3/SPARC/DBSSG/OODBTG Final Report", interim draft of 17 September 1991.

[HEIL90] S. Heiler and S. Zdonik, "Object Views: Extending the Vision", *Proc. 6th Intl. Conf. on Data Engineering*, Los Angeles, Feb. 1990.

[MANO90] F. Manola and A. P. Buchmann, "A Functional/Relational Object-Oriented Model for Distributed Object Management: Preliminary Description," TM-0331-11-90-165, GTE Laboratories Incorporated, December 31, 1990.

[MANO92a] F. Manola, M.L. Brodie, S. Heiler, M. Hornick, and D. Georgakopoulos, "Distributed Object Management", *Int'l Journal of Intelligent and Cooperative Information Systems* 1,1, April 1992

[MANO92b] F. Manola and S. Heiler. "An Approach to Interoperable Object Models", to appear, 1st Int'l Workshop On Distributed Object Management, August 1992.

[OMG91a] Object Management Group, "The Common Object Request Broker: Architecture and Specification", OMG Document Number 91.12.1, Draft 10 December 1991.

[OMG91b] Object Management Group Object Model Task Force, "The OMG Object Model", draft 0.9, OMG Document Number 91.9.1, September 3, 1991.

[SCHI89] J. J. Shilling and P. F. Sweeney, "Three Steps to Views: Extending the Object-Oriented Paradigm", in N. Meyrowitz, ed., *OOPSLA '89 Conference Proceedings*, ACM, Oct., 1989, *SIGPLAN Notices*, 24(10), Oct., 1989.

[STON91] M. Stonebraker, M.L. Brodie, J. Carbonell, J. Davis, P. Hawthorn, L. Markosian, S. Stolfo, and R. Wilensky, "Incremental Migration of Legacy Code", Unpublished paper, Fall 1991.

[WILL91] G. I. Williamson and M. Azmoodeh, "The Application of Information Modelling in the Telecommunications Management Network (TMN)", *Proc. Telecommunications Information Networking Architecture Workshop* (TINA91), March 1991.

OBJECT ORIENTED REQUIREMENTS CAPTURE AND ANALYSIS - THE ORCA PROJECT

D.J.L. Gradwell,
Data Dictionary Systems Limited,
16, Tekels Avenue,
Camberley,
Surrey,
GU15 2LB,
England.

Abstract

The Object Oriented Requirements Capture and Analysis method has been developed by the ORCA Project (Data Dictionary Systems Limited, Logica Cambridge Limited and the University of York). We believe that any well founded method must have a clear definition of the information to be collected during the use of the method. This paper describes the model of the information base (metamodel) for the ORCA method. It describes the concepts used by the method and the structures required to support their use.

ORCA provides techniques for the analysis of the purpose of a system and for arguing about whether subsystems meet the demands they place on each other. ORCA provides techniques for the modelling of intrinsic behaviour which are similar to other class modelling approaches. However, ORCA also provides techniques for modelling extrinsic behaviour, which we believe is a novel component of the ORCA method and a powerful aid to reuse.

The ORCA method has a number of notations to support both intrinsic and extrinsic modelling. These are not described in this paper, which concentrates on the concepts and their meta model.

1. Objectives of ORCA

The ORCA Project is a collaborative project involving the Data Dictionary Systems Limited, Logica Cambridge Limited and the University of York. The project is a three year project which started in mid-1990. It is part funded by the Department of Trade and Industry Information Engineering Directorate as part of the Information Engineering Advanced Technology Programme.

The objectives of the project are to develop an analysis method that:

- is strong in capturing requirements and in analysing similarities in those requirements so as to enable and promote reuse;
- is strong in modelling behaviour and determining similar behaviour;
- allows complex behaviour to be encapsulated;
- has a well understood and well specified information base;
- can build on the skills of current analysts and be taught to them;

2. Overview of the ORCA Method

ORCA is a method for the analysis of systems. By systems we mean systems in the broadest sense, including business systems. The ORCA analyst treats the human computer interface as one of many interfaces between subsystems.

ORCA views a system as having both a purpose and a behaviour. The behaviour is analysed both from an intrinsic and an extrinsic point of view.

Purpose is modelled using a context analysis technique. The purposive interactions between systems are analysed to see how one system relies on another to provide some behaviour. In turn, the other system guarantees, in some sense, to provide that behaviour. Problems arise when expectations do not meet the guarantee.

Extrinsic behaviour is modelled by the identification of systems and kinds (or types) of systems. We term types of systems 'Frameworks'. The interactions between Frameworks and their decomposition gives a model looking from the outside. This modelling of extrinsic behaviour is not reflected in classical object oriented techniques (Booch 1991, Coad & Yourdon 1990, Rumbaugh et al 1991) and is a novel component of the ORCA method. We believe that modelling extrinsic behaviour is an important aspect of planning the replacement of existing systems and of seeking appropriate component systems to reuse.

Intrinsic behaviour is modelled by the identification of objects, their classes and the ways in which they communicate.

Behaviour may be observed or desired. Observed behaviour describes the current system. Desired behaviour pertains to a future system.

3.   The ORCA Process Model

ORCA recognises that there are many process models for analysis, design and implementation. These range from the classic waterfall models to iterative models where each iteration only takes a few hours. Different situations and different skill levels will require the adoption of different process models.

ORCA provides techniques for modelling the purpose of a system, its extrinsic behaviour and its intrinsic behaviour. It will often make sense to proceed in this sequence. However, such work may be incremental, proceeding to implementation in a small area. At other times it will be appropriate to gain an overview of a wide area at a high level. ORCA purposive and extrinsic modelling is particularly appropriate for this type of analysis.

Thus the ORCA analyst (or his project leader) assesses the nature of his project and the techniques available. He then chooses an appropriate process model. Unlike other methods, ORCA does not prescribe a single process model for analysis.

4.   Notation for the meta-model diagrams

The ORCA class relationship diagramming notation is used in this paper to illustrate the structure of the information base for the ORCA method. At its simplest it is similar to entity relationship diagrams such as those used in SSADM Version 4. Thus a modelling concept is shown by a round cornered box and relationships by lines between the boxes. Relationships can be named at each end. Crows feet are used to show cardinality of the relationship. Dotted lines are used to show optionality.

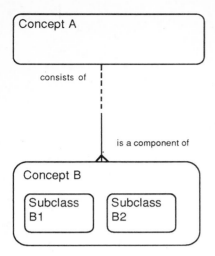

Figure 1:   Example simple class relationship diagram to illustrate notation

Figure 1 means that there are two modelling concepts, one called 'Concept A' and one called 'Concept B'. There is a relationship between them such that one occurrence of Concept A 'consists of' zero (the dotted part of the line), one or many (the crows foot) of Concept B. Concept B is always (the solid half of the line) 'a component of' exactly one (no crows foot) Concept A.   Subclasses are shown as boxes within boxes. Thus B! and B2 are subclasses of concept B.

In the full method the class relationship notation goes well beyond this. However, this is not needed to describe the meta models in this paper.

5.   Context Analysis: Modelling Purpose

In ORCA, Context Analysis is used to focus attention on understanding the business domain. ORCA defines a general purpose Context Analysis meta model that can be specialised either by adopting an existing set of techniques, such as critical success factors analysis or the Soft Systems Methodology, or as a basis for developing new techniques. The choice of a particular technique may depend upon a number of issues. For example, a safety critical system and a business information system may require different approaches.

ORCA takes a client-server view of systems. A system *guarantees* to provide certain services to another system. The second system *relies* on the first system. A correctly designed system is one where all the reliances of its subsystems are intended to be met by appropriate guarantees of service provision from the other subsystems. A system is pathological if it was not correctly designed (in that there is no subsystem guaranteeing to meet some reliance) or if any subsystem fails to meet its guarantees when operating, despite having been designed to do so.

Systems suffer under *constraints*. Constraints may be intrinsic or extrinsic. An intrinsic constraint is a result of the nature of that system. For example, a monochrome screen can not display a colour image. An extrinsic constraint is one that is imposed by one system on another. For example, the Inland Revenue and its associated Finance Acts require that tax payments be calculated according to a particular algorithm.

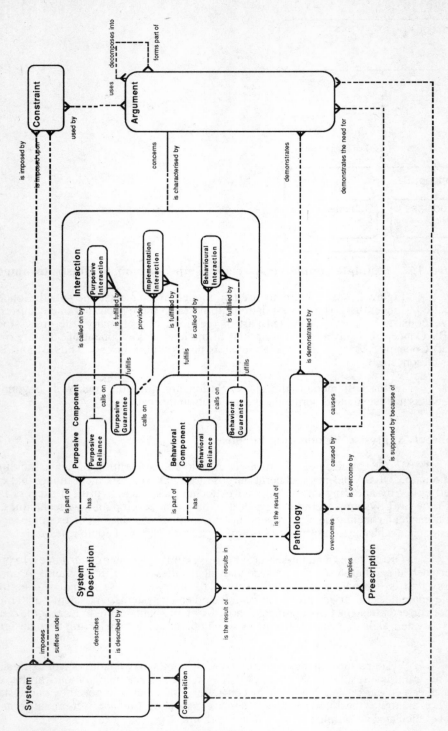

Figure 2:   **Context Analysis Meta Model**

A system can have one or more *system descriptions*. In the simple case there may be only one system description. However, others may arise in order to accommodate and record different points of view (similar in concept to Viewpoint analysis in the CORE methodology). In addition, there will be descriptions of the current system and the desired system and a number of stages on the progression from one to another.

Note that there is discussion continuing within the ORCA project concerning whether to model such aspects as multiple descriptions for one system explicitly in the meta model or whether it would be better to let the CASE tool or Information Resource Dictionary System handle version control, version comparison and configuration management implicitly. In figure 2 the difference between system and system description has been modelled explicitly. However, this difference has been ignored in later models as it would make the models much more complex. This is a general problem that will impact the design of meta models to support any method.

A system description has a number of components:

- *purposive components:* these might be business objectives, patient care objectives, political objectives or other statements about the purpose of the system. It may be possible to decompose high level objectives into smaller, more tractable components. Some objectives may be measurable. Such objectives are termed Critical Success Factors by some.

  An objective of a system may be to provide some service upon which another system can rely. For example, a power generation system may guarantee to provide electricity to a hospital intensive care ward. It will rely on the National Grid to supply its power most of the time and on a back-up generator subsystem to provide power when the National Grid fails.

- *behavioural components:* these components provide the capability of the system. Again, the reliances and guarantees can be discerned. At this stage of modelling ORCA is not concerned with the nature of the components, only the way they inter-relate. Later (see sections 6 & 7) they will be modelled in more detail.

- *arguments:* arguments can be made about how well guarantees meet reliances.

- *pathologies:* problems with the design of the system; and

- *prescriptions:* what to do to fix the system.

ORCA identifies three types of pathological condition (considering only two systems for simplicity of explanation):

- where the purposive guarantees which it is one system's purpose to provide do not fulfil the purposive reliances of the other system;

- where the purposive and behavioural descriptions of one or other of the systems fail to match. This could be either because the system's behavioural description is not a correct implementation of its purpose or the system's purposive description is not a correct characterisation of its behaviour;

- where the behavioural reliances and guarantees of the systems are incompatible. That is, the behaviour of one system, in terms of its behavioural guarantees fails to fulfil the behavioural reliances of the other system.

6. Modelling Intrinsic Behaviour

ORCA uses an object oriented extension of classical entity relationship modelling (Chen 1976) to model intrinsic behaviour. Thus a user of the Structure Systems Analysis and Design Method or of Information Engineering will be able to build on existing skills as he starts to use ORCA concepts.

At the instance level ORCA recognises the following concepts:

- *object:* an object is identifiable and has state and behaviour;

- *object reference:* that which allows an object to be identified and can be sent in a message;

- *message:* the content of a communication between objects;

- *relationship:* an association between objects;

- *value:* an element of a simple type. Typical examples are numeric values such as integers or reals. Unlike Smalltalk we do not treat values as objects. Objects are identifiable and remain distinct even if they have the same state.

Objects can be created or destroyed by other objects. This is regarded as a special case of message sending.

At the type level ORCA recognises the following concepts:

- *simple type:* a set of values;

- *class:* an abstraction of objects;

- *class type:* the type of an object reference that constrains that reference to be to an object of a given class or any subclass of it;

- *type:* which may be a simple type or a class type.

- *relationship type:* an abstraction of relationships;

- *feature of a class:* which may be either an attribute or an operation; A feature has a name, a signature (a structure of one or more named message parameters, each having a type and an indication as to whether the message parameter is sent or returned) and a semantics that determines how the object responds to messages that match the feature;

- *class identifier:* the set of attribute features that taken together serve to uniquely identify an instance of a class. A class may have more than one identifier.

- *pod:* a collection of classes;

- *inheritance:* A class A inherits from class B if it has the same relationship types, features and identifiers as class B and possibly others in addition. If class A inherits from class B then class A is a *subclass* of class B and class B is a *superclass* of class A. Inheritance relationships between classes form an acyclic graph. An object that is the member of a subclass is a member of all its superclasses.

An attribute is bound to either a value or an object reference. An attribute bound to an object reference represents a relationship. A relationship type has two 'Relationship Type Halves' whose (meta) attributes include the name and degree of the half. A particular class of relationship halves is the class that has 'part of' semantics.

Note that as currently specified, a class identifier can be made up of attribute features, which may themselves be either attribute features of a simple type (the relational view of the world) or attribute features of Class Type. Such features are related to a relationship type half. This makes it possible to say that an order is identified by its order and its part without knowing how order and part are themselves identified.

Thus far, we have not fully considered allowing Operation Features to be components of identifiers. Where an operation is a simple derivation of a new attribute from others this might be reasonable. How far one could go in this direction is not clear. Could an operation that returned a constantly changing value be said to be part of an identifier ?

Features of a class can be grouped by the analyst into *Facets* for ease of understanding. A feature can appear in more than one facet if that is helpful.

A *Message path* is defined from an object class to the feature of the object class for each potential route for messages. Except for broadcast messages, message path is only valid if there is a direct or indirect relationship specified between the pair of classes.

Constraints (invariants) can be specified over one or more classes. A special kind of constraint is an exclusive constraint that if an object is related to one object, it may not be related to others.

A particular kind of object, called a *collection structure* is useful in defining classes that collect objects of another class.

36

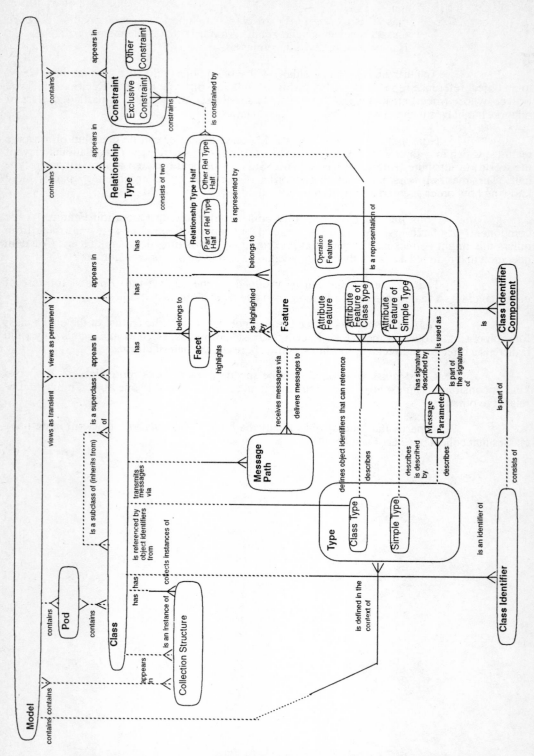

Figure 3: The meta model for modelling intrinsic behaviour in ORCA

7. Modelling Extrinsic Behaviour

ORCA models behaviour in terms of Frameworks. A Framework may describe some observed behaviour of an existing System or it may describe the desired behaviour of some future System. Several Systems may share the same behaviour and thus be described by the same Framework. Often it will be possible to describe a System by a single complex Framework and then decompose the complex Framework to show the detail. Sometimes however, a single complete model of a System may not be possible. In this case, a System may be described by several Frameworks each describing different aspects of the System.

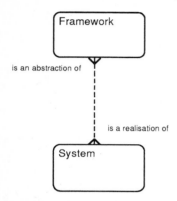

Figure 4:   Frameworks and Systems

Systems can be decomposed into subsystems and Frameworks decomposed into sub-Frameworks. The decomposition structures should match.

Sub-Frameworks can be decomposed into further sub-Frameworks until the analysis has proceeded far enough. Consider seeing a planet from afar. A dinosaur might look atomic with a limited range of observable behaviour. Much closer we might see that the dinosaur is made of cells each with its own very complex behaviour. Closer yet and we see molecules, closer again and atoms or sub-atomic particles come into view. This is the kind of degree of abstraction needed in the analysis of complex systems and which is provided by ORCA.

There are a number of different kinds of framework, which correspond to the ways in which they are (de)composed.

The simplest kind of ORCA framework is the *participation* framework. All other frameworks are built up of either more complex frameworks or participation frameworks. Note however that a participation framework is only atomic in the sense that it has not yet been analysed.

A participation framework is a framework that has one slot into which one *participant* fits. The participant suffers one *action*. The action can be to initiate or terminate the participant (birth or death), a mutation of state or an involvement with no mutation of state. We call the special case where a participant is involved in only a single action a *transient* action. In this case the transient participant(s) do not participate in earlier or subsequent behaviour. Their entire lifecycle appears to the analyst as a single event. The meta model is shown in figure 5. Note that a participant can fill many slots. Each action takes the participant from one of several possible states before the action to one of several possible states after the action.

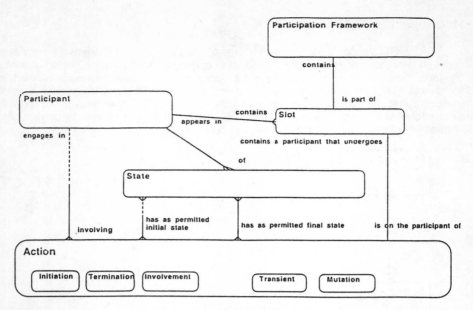

Figure 5: Meta model for a participation framework

In ORCA we deliberately distinguish between the concept of a participant and the concept of a class. A particular class may describe objects which are citizens described by a participant. However, we do not need to look inside the box to see this. While modelling the extrinsic view of a system, it is enough to see the external behaviour. Later on we can look at the inner workings and see perhaps a single class or possibly a complex framework that can be decomposed many times before classes can be discerned.

This late binding of the extrinsic model to the intrinsic model is a powerful aspect of ORCA that enable us to think about substituting one set of intrinsic behaviour for another. It is thus a key feature of the planning of new systems and the search for reuse.

A *Participant* denotes a role to be filled within the Framework. All the participants of a slot will have the same behaviour. When a system is realised, each participant will be an object of a single class, or a group of objects having some particular behaviour. We term such an object or group of objects a *Citizen*.

There are a number of more complex frameworks. A *communication* framework defines the possibility of communication between two simpler frameworks. Such a communication can be a single message or a complex, prolonged exchange of messages. During high level modelling we are not interested in the detail of the messages exchanged, only in the fact that there is communication. Later we may wish to study the sequence of messages sent and received.

A *choice* framework describes behaviour which conforms to the behaviour of any one of its components.

A *succession* framework describes behaviours that occur one after the other. Where these behaviours are the same we have the special case of repetition (iteration).

An *Ordering* framework describes dependencies between frameworks. In ORCA we can express partial ordering by supporting the definition of sets of dependencies as part of the framework definition. It makes no sense for a behaviour to depend upon itself, so the partial orderings must form an acyclic graph.

Sometimes we wish to replace a simple framework by a more detailed model. For example, we may look more deeply at the internal structure of a participation framework and discern other substructure. ORCA provides a *substitution* framework to support this process.

Sometimes a looser type of framework is needed. ORCA defines an *association* framework that defines a list of frameworks that together have some coherent overall behaviour.

Finally, having created a number of frameworks, we may need to combine them identifying common sub-frameworks. This kind of framework is termed a *composition* framework.

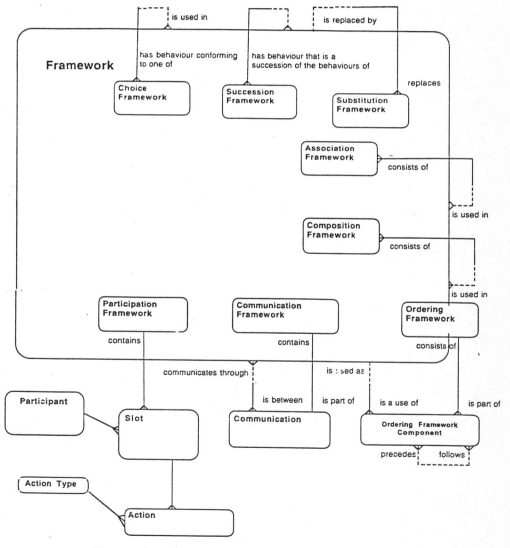

Figure 6: **The complete meta model for frameworks**

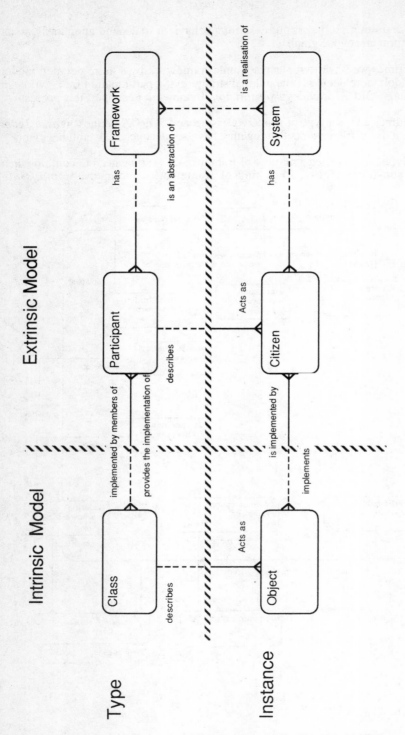

Figure 7: Key relationships between type and instance and intrinsic and extrinsic models

8. Instantiation

A framework is instantiated as a system or subsystem. A slot in a framework is filled by a participant. As described earlier, a participant can be instantiated by a single object playing a role in a system or by a group of objects playing that role. We call these players *citizens*. This separation allows us to model systems where alternate objects can take the same role. For example, an airline would allocate a particular aircraft to a particular operational flight, but a different aircraft might replace the first if the first proved faulty. The objects might not all be of the same class. In the airline example, the vehicle participant in the 'get passengers from London to Manchester' system would usually be of class aircraft. However, on a foggy day it would be of class train or coach. Thus ORCA is able to cope with situations that other methods might find difficult.

9. Linking the extrinsic and intrinsic models

The separation of the concepts of object and citizen introduces the possibility of a rather looser connection between the intrinsic model and the extrinsic model than is found in other methods. Indeed, many other methods make no distinction at all.

Figure 7 shows the relationships between the ORCA concepts at the type and instance levels. (See ISO 1990 for a definition of the concept of levels). A framework is instantiated as a system. A participant is instantiated as a citizen and a class as an object. The citizen is a role of one or more objects in the system. A participant is a the role of one or more classes in a framework.

References

[Booch 1991]

Grady Booch. *Object Oriented Design with Applications*. Benjamin/Cummings 1991.

[Chen 1976]

Peter P.-S. Chen. *The Entity-Relationship Model - towards a unified view of data*. ACM TODS, 1 (1), March 1976.

[Coad & Yourdon 1990]

Peter Coad and Edward Yourdon. *Object Oriented Analysis*. Yourdon Press Computing Series. Prentice Hall 1990.

[ISO 1990]

Gradwell David JL (Editor) *ISO/IEC 10027 Information Resource Dictionary System (IRDS) framework* International Standards Organisation 1990.

[Rumbaugh et al 1991]

James Rumbaugh, Michael Blaha, William Premerlani, Frederick Eddy & William Lorensen. *Object-Oriented Modelling and Design*. Prentice Hall 1991.

A MODEL FOR VERSIONING OF CLASSES IN OBJECT-ORIENTED DATABASES

S. R. Monk and I. Sommerville
Computing Department
S.E.C.A.M.S.
Lancaster University
Lancaster
LA1 4YR
UK

Abstract

This paper describes work carried out on a model for the versioning of class definitions in an Object-oriented database. By defining update and backdate functions on attributes of the previous and current version of a class definintion, instances of any version of the class can be converted to instances of any other version. This allows programs written to access an old version of the schema to still use data created to a changed schema.

1.   INTRODUCTION

In commercial database systems, schema changes are uncommon. The database schema is defined by a database administrator when the database is established and usually involves a fixed, relatively small number of entity types and relationships. When this is changed, the data managed by the database is updated to reflect the changes. Neither the schema nor the data in the database is automatically versioned when changes are made.

Most commercial database systems which are currently available have been tailored to the management of a large number of instances of a small number of types. However, hardware and software CAD systems require a database which efficiently manages a small number of instances of a large number of types [4, 5]. Furthermore, the schema for these systems often cannot be absolutely defined before the system is introduced as new system applications discover new schema requirements. Hence, changes to the schema are relatively common. As object-oriented databases support user type definition, the management of fine-grain objects and the unification of schema and data management, they are particularly suitable for the support of CAD application systems.

In an object-oriented database, a change to the schema, is accomplished by changing a class definition or by creating or moving a class definition within the class lattice. However, there may be applications which are tightly bound to one version of a schema and it is important that these applications continue to work correctly after a schema change has been implemented. Thus, they must be allowed access to previous versions of the database schema and also access to the data which have been created using that previous schema. The database must therefore manage several versions of its own schema.

• This work has been jointly funded by the Science and Engineering Research Council, UK and Zyqad Ltd. Nottinham, UK.

Schema versioning and schema modification are not the same thing. Kim [8] makes the distinction that schema modification is applied to a single logical schema, and involves changing say a class definition, without making a new version of the class, but at the same time updating - either immediately or as necessary - all instances of that class. Schema versioning involves the creation of a new version of a class. The assumption is made that every change to the schema results in a new version of one or more classes.

Establishing a new schema version for an object-oriented database involves making some change to the class lattice. Banerjee sets out a taxonomy for schema changes [1] which is summarised in [8]. The changes that can be made to the schema of an object-oriented database are shown in the hierarchies of Figures 1 and 2. In this hierarchy addition and removal are given as one entry in the hierarchy, as they are inverse operations, and can therefore be illustrated by one example in the proposed system for versioning classes. Specialisation and generalisation are combined for the same reason.

Our system currently supports six of these types of change and later examples (referenced in the diagram) illustrate the approach which we have adopted.

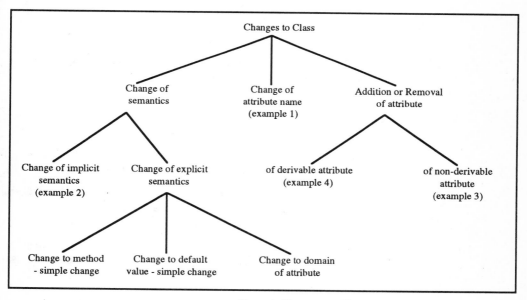

Figure 1 Changes to a Class.

The node of the tree 'change of implicit semantics' does not appear in Banerjee's hierarchy. This change only becomes possible when a class versioning is supported. An implicit change to the semantics of the class means that the although the class may have the same attributes after versioning as it did before, the meaning of the attributes has changed. When converting instances from one version of the class to the next, the values of those attributes must be changed according to the change in attribute semantics.

Explicit changes to the semantics deal with information about the behaviour of the class that is represented explicitly in the class definition, embedded in methods etc.

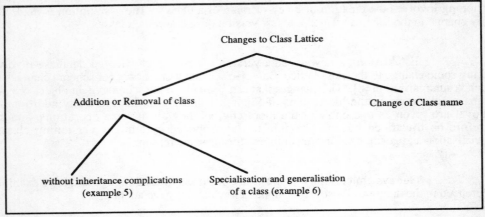

Figure 2   Changes to Class Lattice.

Creating a new version of an instance in a database involves modifying one or more attributes of that instance. A simple example of data versioning is shown below.

CLOSQL_documentation_V1   CLOSQL_documentation_V2

     User manual: Text.V1   User manual: Text.V2

     modified_on   3-3-90   modified_on: 4-4-90

The values of the 'User manual' and the 'modified_on' attributes have been updated for 'CLOSQL_documentation', creating a new version of the object.

Creating a new version of meta-data involves either a change to the attribute type or a change to the methods associated with the class definition. Simple examples of class versioning are shown below. For a detailed discussion on versions, see [6].

Person_V1   Person_V2   Extra Semantics :

     name   full_name   For every instance of Person,

                                             name = full_name

In this case, the name of an attribute has been changed, however, there is no reason why a more complex change should not be made, as in the example below.

Person_V1	Person_V2	Extra Semantics :
age	DOB	For every instance of Person,
		DOB = Todays_date - age

Here, a change has been made to how the concept of age is represented in the class.

We believe it is essential that data created under either schema version should be accessible using either schema version. That is, it should be possible to translate data both forwards and backwards to older and newer schemas. providing such a facility involves adding extra information to the meta-data when the schema is modified.

The work described here has been carried out in the context of an intelligent CAD system for chemical engineering applications which is currently under development using Lisp. Our part of that project has been to investigate the provision of a persistent store for CLOS [7, 16] and to investigate schema versioning in that store. The remainder of this paper is organised as follows. Section 2 describes related work in the field of schema versioning, especially the ENCORE system, Section 3 goes on to explain the class versioning system proposed. Section 4 concludes by outlining the implementational work carried out, and future research directions.

2. RELATED WORK

The problems of schema modification, and schema versioning especially, have been given very little attention by the developers of object-oriented database management systems (OODBMS). The ORION [9, 10] and GemStone [3, 11, 13] systems both support schema modification schemes. Neither address the issue of schema versioning. The only well published system that attempts to support schema versioning is the ENCORE system.

2.1 The ENCORE System

The ENCORE system [2, 14, 15] is a prototype OODBMS that addresses the problem of schema versioning. Classes can be versioned, and the set of versions of one class is called the 'version set' of the class. In every version set there is one version that is termed the current version, and is always the version most recently created.

In addition to a version set for each class, there is also a 'version set interface' for the class. This is a virtual class definition, that contains the union of all attributes of the versions of that class. When the class has only one version, the version and the version set interface are identical. As new versions of the class are created, the version set interface is extended to add extra attributes.

It is the version set interface that is visible to the user, presenting a single view of the version set of the class. Since attributes are never removed from the version set interface, any program written to communicate with the version set interface, will always find a reference to the attribute it requires, even if that attribute does not exist for instances of some versions of the class. For this reason a handler is defined for every attribute of a class version that appears in the version set interface, but not in that version of the class definition. These handlers can return values, so for example default values can be returned for an attribute that does not exist in some other version of the class, but is required in the version of the class expected by the query.

Figure 3 shows how ENCORE would represent three versions of the class 'Person'.

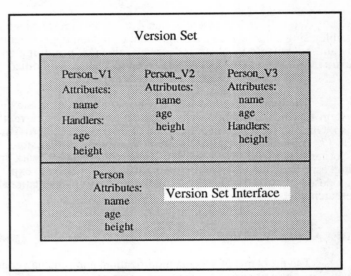

Figure 3 Version Set Interface in ENCORE

In Figure 3, a handler could be defined for age that returns 0 as a default value, when an attempt is made to access the age attribute for instances of the class Person_V1.

The ENCORE system is efficient in situations where there is a need to access instances from different versions, since the version set interface provides a single interface to all versions. In ENCORE, attributes of the same name but referenced in different versions of a class are assumed to represent the same information in both versions. This means that is not possible to represent a change in the semantics of the attribute between versions, such as the changing of units of height from cm to inches.

3. CLASS VERSIONING USING UPDATE/BACKDATE FUNCTIONS

Our approach to class versioning requires the database administrator, on creating a new version of a class, to specify how to convert instances of the previous version to the new version, and vice-versa. The conversion process is specified for each attribute in 'update' and 'backdate' functions. The update function specifies what is to happen to the attribute when it is converted into the next version, and the backdate function the converse.

Since a class version will usually have more than one attribute and hence more than one update and/or backdate function, the set of update and backdate functions for a class are grouped into an 'update method' and 'backdate method' for the class version. Figure 4 shows the arrangement of versions of a class.

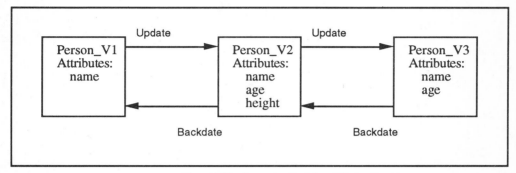

Figure 4 Versions using Backdate / Update Functions.

When a new version N of a class is defined, the backdate function for that class is defined and at the same time the update method for version N-1 is defined.

Only linear versioning is currently supported. That is, a new version can only be generated from the latest version. This appears to be all that is required in the application domain we are currently investigating but we recognise that other domains may require a tree rather than a sequence of schema versions to be supported.

The following sections include examples that were taken as realistic examples of the kinds of change that are likely to be made to the schema of a database that holds information representing chemical process plant. The examples of changes given were elicited from the developers of a project for the automatic laying out of chemical plants [12]. These changes are made in the context of the proposed update/backdate model of schema versioning. The changes that are made to the schema are expressed in diagrammatic form, and the update and backdate methods as pseudocode.

Queries are made to a class, the version of which may or may not be specified. If the version is not specified, then the latest version of the class is assumed. Instances of all versions of the class must be made available to the user in the form of the version specified or implied in the query.

If the desired version for the query is N, then instances of version N+1 can be converted into instances of version N by invoking the backdate method for N+1. Instances of versions greater than N+1 are converted to instances of version N by successively applying the backdate method. This differs from ENCORE where the code for conversion is all relative to the version set interface rather than between successive versions of the class, as shown in Figure 6.

48

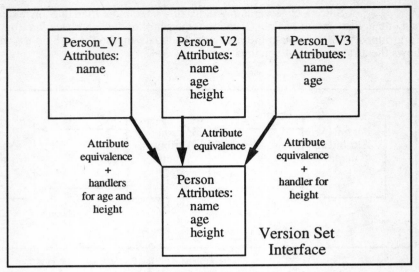

Figure 6 Handlers in ENCORE

Figures 1 and 2 illustrate the types of change which may be applied to the schema. The examples described below show how these types of change may be supported using update/backdate methods.

3.1. Notation

The schema changes are shown as before and after diagrams of the schema. The before version is labelled V_n and the after version V_{n+1}. A dot notation is used with V_n and V_{n+1}, so Pump(V_n).flowrate, means the value of the flowrate attribute of any instance of version n of the class Pump.

The notation for schema diagrams is that Classes are boxed nodes, and the directed arcs between them represent attributes, the type of the attribute being the class to which the arc is directed. For example, Figure 5 shows the Class Pump, with a single attribute flowrate whose type is the class Number.

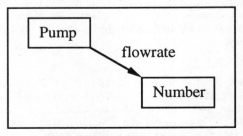

Figure 5 Schema diagram notation.

Class / sub-class relationships are denoted by a very thick arrow. The arrow is directed to the subclass.

The absence of new data is indicated by the pseudo-code function 'exception'.

3.2. Changes to Attributes

Example 1 shows how a new version of a class can be created in order to rename an attribute. The update and backdate functions simply translate references from one name to another.

Example 1- Change of Attribute Name

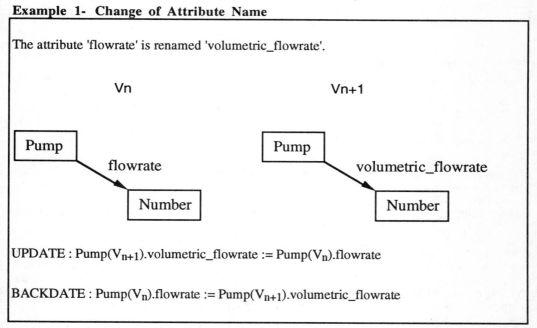

The attribute 'flowrate' is renamed 'volumetric_flowrate'.

Vn

Vn+1

Pump

flowrate

Number

Pump

volumetric_flowrate

Number

UPDATE : Pump(V$_{n+1}$).volumetric_flowrate := Pump(V$_n$).flowrate

BACKDATE : Pump(V$_n$).flowrate := Pump(V$_{n+1}$).volumetric_flowrate

Example 2 shows how an attribute may keep the same name after a new version of its class is created, but have different semantics. In this example, the units of 'flowrate' are changed from L/second to ml/second.

Example 2 -   **Change of Implicit Semantics**

In this case, change of units of a physical property by a factor of 1000.

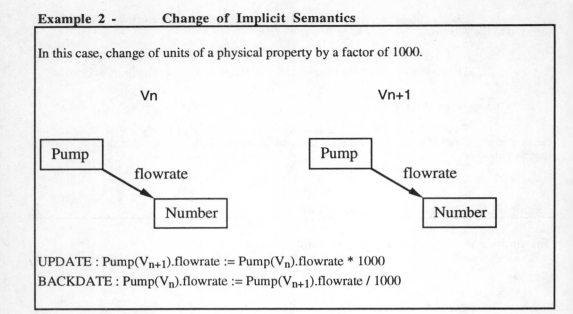

UPDATE : $Pump(V_{n+1}).flowrate := Pump(V_n).flowrate * 1000$

BACKDATE : $Pump(V_n).flowrate := Pump(V_{n+1}).flowrate / 1000$

3.3   Loss of Information

Where attributes are added or removed during the versioning of a class, there is a change in the information that the database is expected to contain. So, in example 3, when converting an instance of version N+1 of Pump to an instance of version N of Pump, the value that was associated with the attribute 'power' would normally be lost.   However our system automatically stores such lost values, restoring them when the instance is re-converted.

The converse situation could arise when a program that accesses the database and was written for instances of version N+1 of Pump tries to access an instance of version N that has no 'power' attribute. In this case, the problem is not one of loss of information, but of information that was never supplied to the system in the first place, but is now required. Under such circumstances, a number of options are available to the user.

- Make the application program responsible for trapping such information gaps.
- Define an update function that attempts to derive a default value for the attribute, as is done in example 4.
- Define an update function that prompts the user to supply the missing value.

Example 3 - **Addition of Non Derivable Attribute**

A new attribute 'Power' is added to the class definition.

Vn   Vn+1

Pump   Pump

power

Number

UPDATE : Pump(V_{n+1}).power := exception("No value for power attribute")
BACKDATE : nil

Example 4 -   **Addition of Derivable Attribute**

A new attribute 'Power' is added, whose value can be derived from the other attributes.

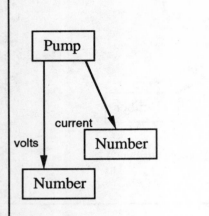

Vn

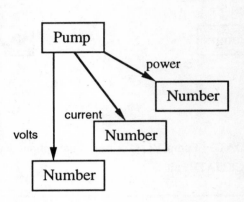

Vn+1

UPDATE :

$Pump(V_{n+1}).volts := Pump(V_n).volts$

$Pump(V_{n+1}).current := Pump(V_n).current$

$Pump(V_{n+1}).power := Pump(V_n).current * Pump(V_n).volts$

BACKDATE :

$Pump(V_n).volts := Pump(V_{n+1}).volts$

$Pump(V_n).current := Pump(V_{n+1}).current$

3.4   Class Versioning and Inheritance

Versioning of classes must take into account the inheritance lattice of the classes that are being versioned. There are obvious similarities between the versioning of classes and schema modification by creating a sub-class at run-time.

•   A sub-class modifies a class definition (by the addition of attributes), as can a class version.

•   The original class and its sub-class co-exist in the same way as versions of a class.

However there are a number of important differences between the two processes.

•   The set of modifications that a subclass can make to a class is limited to the addition or modification of attributes. Attributes cannot be removed for instance.

•   There is no provision for the conversion of instances of a class to instances of the sub-class, as there is for converting instances of one version of a class to instances of another version.

•   Motivation - a system would not be designed with versions of a class in place from the beginning, in the same way as an inheritance lattice would be designed into a new system. The class lattice provides a convenient structure for the data, whereas class versions are intended to provide fixes to a database structure that has become inappropriate.

If a class that has sub-classes is versioned, then it can be argued that each of the subclasses should be versioned as well, as shown in Figure 7.

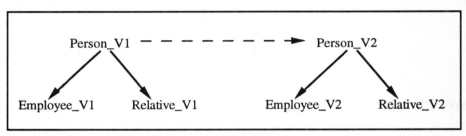

Figure 7   Versioning of Sub-classes.

Two versions of the classes 'Employee' and 'Relative' are necessary to be able to create instances of 'Employee' that inherit the attributes of 'Person_V2'. This could be termed deep versioning. The alternative, shallow versioning, would be to only version the class 'Person' and not its sub-classes. Deep versioning is a sensible default, however occasionally it may be that the reason that 'Person' was versioned was that it was no longer appropriate for it to comprise two sub-classes. In our system it is assumed that sub-classes are not automatically versioned along with their parent class, but that code may be included in update functions to accomplish this should it be appropriate. This is at variance with the ENCORE system which versions the subclasses automatically.

The following two examples show how the update/backdate methodology can be used to change the structure of the class lattice.

Example 5 -   **Addition of Class Without Inheritance Complications**

In this case, the way connections between instances of Equipment are made is changed to add an intermediary class, 'Stream' representing the connection explicitly and allowing the connection to have attributes.

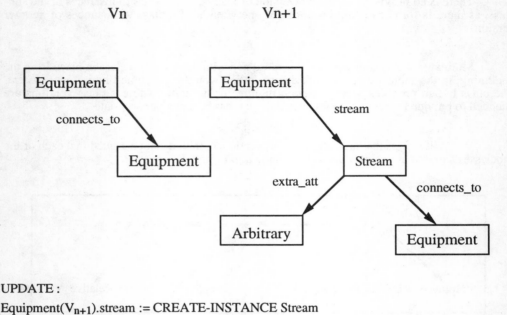

UPDATE :

Equipment(V_{n+1}).stream := CREATE-INSTANCE Stream

Equipment(V_{n+1}).stream.connects_to := Equipment(V_n).connects_to

Equipment(V_{n+1}).stream.extra_att := exception("Value not known for extra_att attribute")

BACKDATE:

Equipment(V_n).connects_to := Equipment(V_{n+1}).stream.connects_to

KILL Equipment(V_{n+1}).stream

NB. KILL expresses the notion of deleting an instance, and CREATE-INSTANCE of creating a new instance of given class.

Example 6 -   **Specialisation of a Class**

In this case, Pump is specialised to Centrifugal_Pump, so pumps instantiated as V_n, need to be moved to Centrifugal_Pump (if appropriate) with queries on the class Centrifugal_Pump.

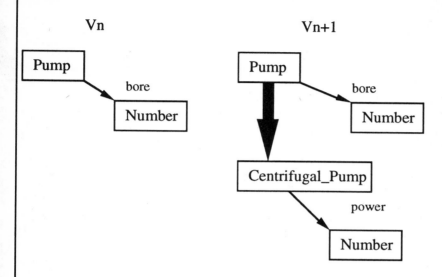

UPDATE :

IF exception("Should this instance be of class Centrifugal_Pump NOT Pump ?")
THEN

       new_cent_pump := CREATE-INSTANCE Centrifugal_Pump

       new_cent_pump.power := exception("Value not known for attribute power")

       new_cent_pump.bore := Pump(V_n).bore

       KILL pump(V_n)
END IF

BACKDATE :

new_Pump := CREATE-INSTANCE Pump

new_Pump.bore := Centrifugal_Pump(V_{n+1}).bore

KILL Centrifugal_Pump(V_{n+1})

4. CONCLUSIONS

In this paper, two approaches to schema versioning have been described. The version set interface approach taken by the ENCORE system and the update/backdate methods used by our system. ENCORE relates all the versions of a class to one version set interface, whereas the update/backdate system relates each version to the subsequent and previous versions. Differences and features of the two systems are listed below.

1. The update/backdate system allows changes to the semantics of attributes, such as in example 2, which is not possible using the version set interface approach. The version set interface relies on the information being stored in an attribute of a particular name being the same for all versions of the class.

2. ENCORE only allows the definition of default values for attributes added by a new version of the class, whereas our system provides additional storage for new attributes.

3. Another advantage of the update/backdate approach lies in the dynamic creation of new classes and instances during a query that accesses across versions. Example 5 shows how this facility can be used.

4. Both systems can handle reading and writing to attributes of instances accessed across versions of the class. ENCORE does this by allowing the definition of two handlers for each attribute, one for reading and one for writing. Our system simply leaves the new version of the instance in the database to be written to as desired.

5. For both systems, instances are only stored once, there is no need to maintain multiple versions of instances. However in our system, some extra storage is required to keep 'lost values'.

The work described here on update and backdate functions has been implemented in a prototype object environment called CLOSQL. CLOSQL is written in CLOS [7, 16]. A graphical user interface has been prototyped for the system, that provides a graphical representation for class versions. The graphical interface is implemented on top of a query language that is implemented in a functional manner, and uses the familiar SQL keywords SELECT and FROM. The query language supports creation and versioning of classes, queries on all members of a class (with filtering on a predicate), as well as the invoking of methods with arguments.

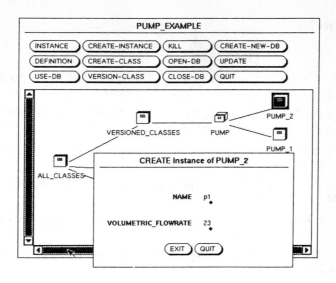

Figure 8 Screen from CLOSQL.

There are a number of areas in which the update/backdate model of class versioning could be extended.

1.   *Optimising version changes* The continual converting of instances form one version to another may impose an unacceptably large overhead. It may be that, from time to time, the whole database could be brought up to date, and all old versions of data converted to the current version. This would not sacrifice the ability of programs written to the old schema to access data written to the new, because the backdate methods would still exist to recreate the old data as necesary.

2.   *Non-linear versioning* If the concepts of current and latest version are separated, as Katz [6] suggests, then networks of versions become a possibility. This could allow a user to develop different schemas in parallel. One use of this may be to allow different users to view the same data through different schemas. For example, a database that represented the design of a chemical plant could be viewed through one schema by the electrical engineer, that only made the electrical attributes of equipment visible. The civil engineer could have his or her own schema that just revealed the structural requirements of the equipment. The concept of update/backdate methods has been applied to this problem in a prototype system for representing views.

Class versioning seems to be a fertile and much underdeveloped area of database research. The work carried out here has tried to produce a model for class versioning which is as flexible as possible in the changes that can be made to the schema, without impairing the operation of programs designed to operate on the database, or imposing an unnecessarily large overhead on the system.

5. REFERENCES

[1] J. Banerjee, W. Kim, H. Kim and H. Korth, "Semantics and Implications of Schema Evolution in Object-Oriented Databases.", ACM SIGMOD, pp. 1987

[2] T. Bloom and S. Zdonik, "Issues in the Design of Object-Oriented Database Programming Languages", OOPSLA'87, pp. 441-451, 1987

[3] P. Butterworth, A. Otis and J. Stein, "The Gemstone Object Database Management System", Communications of the ACM, 34(10), pp. 64-77, 1991

[4] C. M. Eastman, "Database Facilities for Engineering Design", Procedings of the IEEE, 69(10), pp. 1249-1263, 1981

[5] R. Katz and T. Lehman, "Database Support for Versions and Alternatives of Large Design Files", IEEE Transactions on Software Engineering, 10(2), pp. 191-200, 1984

[6] R. H. Katz, "Toward a Unified Framework for Version Modeling in Engineering Databases", ACM Computing Surveys, 22(4), pp. 375-408, 1990

[7] S. E. Keene, "Object-Oriented Programming in Common Lisp - A Programmers Guide to CLOS.", Addison-Wesley, 1989

[8] W. Kim, "Introduction to Object-Oriented Databases", The MIT Press, 1990

[9] W. Kim, N. Ballou, J. Garza and D. Woelk, "A Distributed Object-oriented Database System Supporting Shared and Private Databases", ACM Transactions on Information Systems, 9(1), pp. 31-51, 1991

[10] W. Kim, J. F. Garza, N. Ballou and D. Woelk, "Architecture of the ORION Next-Generation Database System", IEEE Transactions on Knowledge and Data Engineering, 2(1), pp. 109-124, 1990

[11] D. Maier, J. Stein, A. Otis and A. Purdy, "Development of an Object-Oriented DBMS", OOPSLA'86, pp. 472-482, 1986

[12] A. McBrien, J. Madden and N. Shadbolt, "Intelligence methods in process plant layout", 2nd Int Conf IEA/AIE-89, pp. 1989

[13] D. J. Penney and J. Stein, "Class Modification in the GemStone Object-Oriented DBMS", OOPSLA'87, pp. 111-117, 1987

[14] A. H. Skarra and S. B. Zdonik, "The Management of Changing Types in an Object-Oriented Database.", OOPSLA'86, pp. 483-495, 1986

[15] H. Skarra, B. Zdonik and P. Reiss, "Observer: An Object Server for an Object-Oriented Database System", CS-99-08, Brown University,Dept of Computer Science, Providence, Rhode Island 02912, 1987

[16] G. L. Steele, "Common LISP - The Language", DIGITAL Press, 1990

A STORAGE MANAGER FOR THE HYPERNODE MODEL

E. Tuv[1] , A. Poulovassilis[2] and M. Levene[3]

[1,3] Department of Computer Science,
University College London,
Gower St., London WC1E 6BT
e-mail : {e.tuv, m.levene}@uk.ac.cs.ucl

[2] Department of Computing,
King's College London,
Strand, London WC2R 2LS
e-mail : a.poulovassilis@uk.ac.kcl.cc.oak

Abstract

We describe the implementation of a Storage Manager (SM) for the Hypern-ode model, a new data model whose aim is to integrate object-oriented and deductive databases. The single data structure of this model is the hypernode, a directed graph whose nodes may themselves be directed graphs. The components of the SM manipulate these graphs in a persistent store. The main effort of the first prototype of the SM has been to develop a modular and extensible system which can be used as a reliable and stable core for future versions. In particular, the SM caters for object-identity and referential sharing between hypernodes, large and dynamic hypernodes, clustering strategies on secondary storage, and retrieval operations which utilise indexing techniques. The main contribution of the SM is the single graph data structure which permeates throughout all the levels of the implementation; in this way efficiency can be achieved within all the components of the SM as a result of optimising this data structure, and also interfacing between the components of the SM is simple and uniform.

1   Introduction

Recent database research has focussed on deductive and object-oriented databases [ULL88, GAR89]. These are largely complementary : the former supports both stored and derived relations and the latter supports data abstraction mechanisms such as classification, identification, encapsulation and inheritance. Hence, recent database research has aimed at integrating the two paradigms. This integration has generally taken the route of extending logic-based deductive database languages with features such as object identity, sets, functions, methods and inheritance [ULL91]. Taking a different approach, we have developed a graph-based model called the *Hypernode Model* [LEV90, POU90]

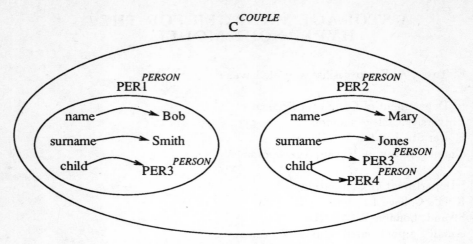

Figure 1. An example hypernode.

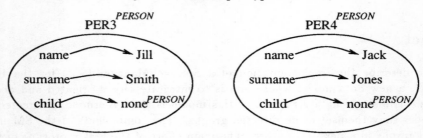

Figure 2. Further hypernodes.

to support such an integration. In contrast to other graph-based data models [CON90, GYS90, LEV91, TOM89], we use *nested*, possibly recursively defined, directed graphs termed *hypernodes*.

A hypernode is a pair, (N,E), of nodes and directed edges such that the nodes of N are either primitive values or themselves hypernodes. Hypernodes have unique value-independent labels which serve as object identifiers. We illustrate a hypernode in Figure 1. It represents a couple, C, consisting of two people, PER1 and PER2, whose children are nested within further hypernodes. In Figure 2 we show the children of person PER2, which would become visible if we "exposed" the hypernodes labelled PER3 and PER4.

The labels C and PER1-PER4 in these figures are superscripted with the tags COUPLE and PERSON, respectively. These tags indicate the *types* of their associated hypernodes and are omitted whenever they are understood from context. Types give us a means of defining database schemas and of enforcing constraints on the structure and content of hypernodes (see [POU90] for a detailed description of types). In fact, types are just hypernodes and so can be queried and updated using the same formalism as for data. We also note the use of the node $none^{PERSON}$ in Figure 2 - it is null value of type PERSON denoting "does not exist".

The hypernode model comes equipped with a computationally powerful declarative language called Hyperlog. Thus, the model and language share features with both

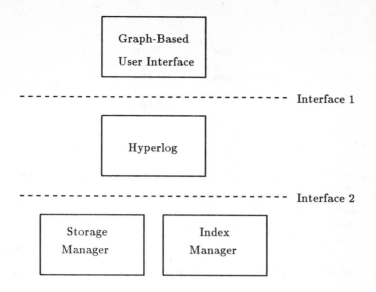

Figure 3. The Hypernode Database System Architecture.

deductive and object-oriented databases. In common with other deductive database languages, Hyperlog is rule-based and supports derivation rules and database updates. In common with object-oriented databases the hypernode model supports complex objects and the data abstraction concepts of classification (via types), identification (via unique labels) and encapsulation of data (via the nesting of graphs). In [LEV91] we showed how structural inheritance is also supported naturally by nested graph structures.

Several advantages to database management accrue from our use of nested graphs. At the physical level the implementation of a single persistent data structure (the graph) allows special-purpose storage and indexing techniques to be developed and optimised. At the conceptual level hypernodes provide a formally-defined yet simple data structuring tool, capable of representing complex database schemas and objects. Finally, at the external level, graph-based formalisms generally enhance the usability of complex systems [HARE88]. Furthermore, the *nesting* of hypernodes provides greater flexibility in the design and browsing of densely connected database graphs. Thus, the hypernode model is promising for application domains such as CAD, CASE and *Hypertext* [NIE89].

We are currently implementing a prototype DBMS for the hypernode model which we intend to evaluate via a hypertext application. The three-level architecture of our DBMS is illustrated in Figure 3 (cf. System R [AST76]).

At the lowest level, the Storage Manager stores hypernodes and types as labelled graphs, $G = (N,E)$, and the Index Manager supports efficiently two operations :

(i) *Value-to-hypernode.* Given a primitive node, n, return the set of labels $\{G_1, \ldots, G_r\}$ such that for each graph $G_i = (N_i, E_i), n \in N_i$, and

(ii) *Label-to-Hypernode.* Given a label, G, return the set of labels $\{G_1, \ldots, G_r\}$ such that for each graph $G_i = (N_i, E_i), G \in N_i$.

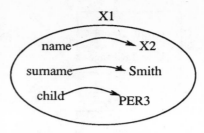

Figure 4. A query hypernode.

These operations are invoked by the Hyperlog evaluator during its execution of Hyperlog programs. An example of a simple query hypernode is illustrated in Figure 4. This query returns the set of all PERSONS who satisfy the following two conditions : (i) they all have the surname *Smith* and (ii) they all have the child referenced by the label *PER3*. This query makes use of both the above operations. It first retrieves all labels which satisfy the first condition using operation (i), then it retrieves all labels which satisfy the second condition using operation (ii). The intersection of these two sets of labels and the set of PERSONS is the required result.

The main aim of this first prototype DBMS is to demonstrate the feasibility of the hypernode model and Hyperlog in a single-user environment. Transaction management, concurrency control and recovery will be incorporated during a second phase, and at the first instance we envisage that conventional techniques will be employed [GRA78]. For simplicity, in the rest of the paper a transaction will be considered as a single execution of a Hyperlog program.

In parallel to the research and development of data models for complex objects, such as object-oriented data models and the nested relational data model [SCH90], a large research effort has been invested into the development and research of storage management systems to support these models. A short survey of these storage management systems can be found in [KHO90]. These storage managers provide support for object identity, referential sharing, and large and complex objects, which are also requirements of the hypernode model. Our storage manager is unique in that the single graph data structure permeates through all levels of the system. Furthermore, this implementation strategy yields a more efficient storage manager than would have resulted from implementing our hypernode data structure on top of an existing kernel. We have chosen not to use an existing system since we require a flexible modular system that allows us to modify the policy of any given component without affecting the rest of the system.

In this paper we are specifically concerned with the design and implementation of the, Storage Manager (SM) and, to a lesser extent, Index Manager (IM) components of the above architecture. The SM is a set of modules carrying out the manipulation of graphs in a persistent store. It also provides support for different placement strategies [VAL86] for graphs. The SM is built on top of a kernel system which provides the low-level storage management of variable-length untyped streams of bytes. This kernel ensures portability, allowing the SM to be installed in different environments. Our current SM is being developed under UNIX[1], where the kernel has to overcome the well-known problem

---

[1] Unix is a trademark of AT&T Bell Laboratories

of the UNIX file system whereby large files may be physically fragmented on the disk.

The outline of the rest of the paper is as follows. In Section 2 we discuss the requirements for the SM, and the particular problems they pose, with respect to the hypernode model and its intended application domains. In Section 3 we describe our implementation of the SM: we discuss the motivation behind its design, give an overview of the overall architecture, and describe the functionality and implementation of each of the modules. In Section 4 we discuss indexing and clustering issues. Finally, in Section 5 we give our concluding remarks and discuss ongoing and further research issues.

2 Requirements for the Storage Manager

The hypernode model presents particular requirements which must be met by the Storage Manager. In this section we enumerate these requirements and the problems they pose. In the sections that follow we demonstrate how these problems are solved in our implementation.

Object Identity and Referential Sharing. A hypernode can be referenced by any number of hypernodes via its unique label. Thus, when a hypernode is deleted, there may remain other hypernodes which still reference it . This may cause problems with *referential dangling* if the referenced location is subsequently overwritten with other data at the storage level, or if a reference to deleted data exists. For example, in Figures 1 and 2, while updating PER1 one can delete the hypernode labelled PER3 and in addition remove its label. In this case a reference to PER3 remains in PER2 and causes referential dangling.

Large or Complex Hypernodes. Hypernodes may be large or complex as a result of a number of characteristics, any combination of which is possible :

(i) A large node set : for example a hypernode representing a program which consists of a large number of modules, or a document with a large number of paragraphs.

(ii) Large primitive nodes : for example a primitive node which is a large item of text in a hypertext database, or a bitmap representing a detailed image.

(iii) A dense edge set : the number of edges between the nodes of a hypernode can be $O(n^2)$, where n is the number of nodes, for example in the transitive closure of an accessibility graph in a hypertext database (created to increase browsing efficiency), or in the design of a VLSI chip with many inter-connections between its components.

Dynamic Hypernodes. Hypernodes may be highly dynamic i.e. nodes and edges may be added and deleted arbitrarily and frequently, for example in a hypertext system where a user's view of the database, which is represented as a graph, can be changed dynamically. Thus the storage techniques employed for hypernodes should support such updates efficiently.

Clustering. Conventional storage strategies like vertical and horizontal partitioning are not sufficient for the hypernode model since hypernodes do not relate to each other solely via static properties such as their type or node values but also via their linkage (e.g. the pattern of referencing between hypernodes) cf. [VAL86]. For example, a set of hypernodes which is accessed by a specified root hypernode should be clustered together with this root hypernode. Examples of some options for clustering can be found in [HOR87]. Moreover the dynamic nature of a hypernode database, and especially the dynamic linkage between hypernodes, implies that *dynamic* clustering schemes are required, as in CACTIS [HUD89] for example, and also reclustering schemes.

Retrieval. In conventional index strategies for relational databases [AST76] *keys* are defined and maintained over the scope of a single relation. On the other hand, the hypernode model and its intended application domains require retrieval of any node in the scope of the whole database, for example as in ANDA [DES88] for the nested relational model.

Extensibility. The SM implementation must be extensible in the sense that new types of hypernodes can be added without making any code changes. Furthermore, although the current prototype is intended for a single-user single-site environment, it should serve as the core for a future multi-user, distributed environment, and for new policies such as new buffering and clustering policies.

3 Implementation of the Storage Manager

In the implementation of the SM we attempted to address the requirements outlined in Section 2 above. Here we describe the architecture of the SM and the implementation of each one of its components. In 3.1 we give the overall architecture of the SM. In 3.2 we focus on the support which is provided by the kernel of the SM. In 3.3 we give a description of the physical representation of hypernodes, both in secondary storage and in memory. The characteristics and uses of labels of hypernodes are described in 3.4. Finally, the buffering of hypernodes in memory is discussed in 3.5.

3.1 Overall Architecture

The primary goal in the development of the prototype SM was to build a stable core system which could subsequently be extended, modified and tested in almost all of its functionalities and modules. For that reason we decided to build a *modular* and *extensible* system. Like EXODUS [CAR86] and DASDBS [SCH90] we adopted the approach of building this system over a *Kernel* that provides a low-level implementation of a persistent store for objects, which are just uninterpreted streams of bytes. The architecture of the SM is illustrated in Figure 5.

Each file in our DBMS is termed an *object store* and each object store is identified by a unique identifier, the *object store id*. The logical address of any object is the composition of the object store id with an offset within that object store. The functionality of an object store is thus similar to the *files* of the EXODUS system [CAR86] and the *bags*

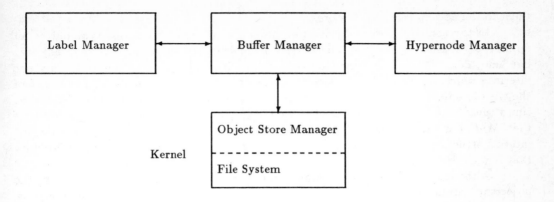

Figure 4 : A high level block diagram of the SM

of CMS [ATK83]. However, our object stores differ from these data structures in their internal organisation.

The *Kernel* module provides secondary storage management, and attempts to cluster the objects it manages in contiguous locations in secondary storage. In order to allow extensibility, the Kernel has minimal semantics embedded into it. Thus, it has no knowledge of hypernodes, types, and labels, and recognises only untyped streams of bytes. The Kernel frees the higher levels of the SM from interacting with the operating system and the hardware media. The Kernel also overcomes some of the problems inherent in file systems which are provided by conventional operating systems. In UNIX, for example, a large file may be fragmented into several pieces located in different areas on disk. In contrast, the Kernel's file system allocates contiguous pages on the secondary storage medium for each object store.

On top of the Kernel is the *Buffer Manager* module. This module maintains objects in memory in their in-memory format and is responsible for transferring hypernodes between secondary storage and memory on demand. In order to locate the physical address of a hypernode and to retrieve the hypernode from the Kernel, the Buffer Manager uses the services of the *Label Manager* to map the label to the physical address of the hypernode. It then uses the *Hypernode Manager* to translate the hypernode from its secondary storage format into its in-memory format. We discuss these components and the interaction between them in more detail in sections 3.2 to 3.5 below.

3.2   The Kernel

The Kernel module comprises two sub-modules, the *File System* and the *Object Store Manager*. The interface to the Kernel is via messages that are sent to the latter which reads, writes and retrieves *objects*, regarding them as uninterpreted streams of bytes. The Object Store Manager allocates and deallocates objects within object stores and controls space utilisation at the object store level, while the File System allocates and deallocates object store *pages* on request from the Object Store Manager. The Object Store Manager also handles requests from the Buffer Manager (see 3.5) and dispatches them to the appropriate object store.

In the context of the Object Store Manager, an object is of one type only : an uninterpreted stream of bytes. The Object Store Manager supports objects of any size but hides details regarding their storage from its clients, providing them with only one interface which is independent of the size of its objects. Thus, from the point of view of the clients, objects are stored contiguously on the secondary storage medium, even if at times this is not necessarily so. Unlike the Object Store Manager, the higher levels of the SM *do* have knowledge of the internal structure of objects and *can* operate on this internal structure. This fact is one of the key ingredients to the support of extensibility that is provided by the kernel.

Although the Object Store Manager has no knowledge of the semantics of the objects it maintains, it can accept *hints* from its clients regarding the placement of objects. For example, a client can provide a preferred address (location) for an object, in order to allow physical clustering of logically related objects cf. CMS [ATK83] and EXODUS [CAR86]. The client can also specify an expected maximum size for the object, in order to pre-empt movement of the object as it grows. Objects can be moved within and between object stores when necessary. The File System ensures that the pages of an object store are in fact stored contiguously in secondary storage.

3.3 The Hypernode physical data structure and its interface

In this sub-section we describe the physical representation of a single hypernode in secondary storage and in the buffering area. In our design of this physical data structure we were motivated by a number of principles :

(i) Clients must interact with hypernodes via a pre-defined interface of primitive operations (see 3.3.2). In addition, this interface must be uniform for all hypernodes irrespective of their size and complexity.

(ii) Several of the hypernode operations query or retrieve only a portion of a hypernode (for example, *get node, is a node in a hypernode*), so the physical data structure should allow access to these components only and should not retrieve into memory the hypernode as a whole. This is crucial for hypernodes with a large number nodes or with large sized primitive nodes.

(iii) The cost of retrieval and update operations on sub-parts of large hypernodes should be as independent as possible of the overall size of the hypernode. For example, a modification to a hypernode with a small number of large-sized of primitive nodes should be as efficient as a modification to a hypernode with the same number of small-sized primitive nodes.

(iv) The actual data of a hypernode should be maintained contiguously on disk, so that the retrieval of a hypernode requires a minimal number of disk accesses. Thus, we have tried to keep the data structure as *linear* (i.e in a contiguous array of characters) as possible and to avoid pointer chasing on the secondary storage. A large hypernode may have to be divided into a set of linear spaces which are clustered together by the kernel.

(v) It has been shown, for example in [SCH90], that copying and translation of complex objects between their in-memory format and their secondary storage format can be a bottleneck in a storage system, so seamlessness between the on-disk and in-memory format of hypernodes is required. In particular, we have designed a data structure which requires only a minimal translation between disk and memory without degrading the performance of either the on-disk or in-memory operations on it. We have described the on-disk strategy in point (iv) above. In contrast, the in-memory storage and manipulation of hypernodes is made more efficient by utilising pointer chasing via dynamic data structures such as linked lists.

(vi) Instances of hypernodes of the same type can share common information and this should not be replicated in each instance of that type but instead should be stored at the type level. Thus, with each type in our system we associate a *template* hypernode which consists of the nodes shared by all instances of that type (cf. static class members in C++ [STR86]).

In the SM we support only one data structure, namely the hypernode, which is sufficient to emulate other data structures such as lists, tuples and sets. Other storage managers have to support several different data structures : for example FAD [BAN87] supports tuples and sets and O_2 [VEL89] supports tuples, sets and lists. Moreover, most of the existing systems that do utilise one data structure only, such as AIM-P [KUS87] and DASDBS [SCH90] (i.e the nested relation), are limited to hierarchical structures and do not support a general directed graph.

3.3.1 The Hypernode physical data structure

Figure 6 illustrates the general hypernode data structure. As is shown in this figure, the data structure consists of three main parts : the header part, the nodes part and the edges part. The main idea behind the design of the hypernode data structure is our desire to keep the layout of the data in a contiguous *array* of characters. In this structure, *pointers* are either offsets into that array or an address of another object in the same object store. When one of the parts of the hypernode becomes *too large* (e.g it outgrows a page size) then it is separated from the original array and is maintained as a separate object in the same object store. It is written by the kernel to a location which is as near as possible to its original location. In this case the pointer to that part is modified to the address of the separated object. By separating large parts of the hypernode from its other parts we ensure that the length of any single subpart will not affect the overall behaviour of operations on the hypernode. For example, a small hypernode with one large node is maintained in two separate areas; the large node resides in the first one, while the remaining parts of the hypernode reside in the second.

Header part. The header part is of fixed length and contains general information about the hypernode such as its number of nodes, the number of nodes in the template hypernode, and pointers to the different parts of the hypernode.

Nodes part. This consists of two sub-parts, a list of *node headers* and an associated *data part.* Each node header contains information pertaining to one node in the hypern-

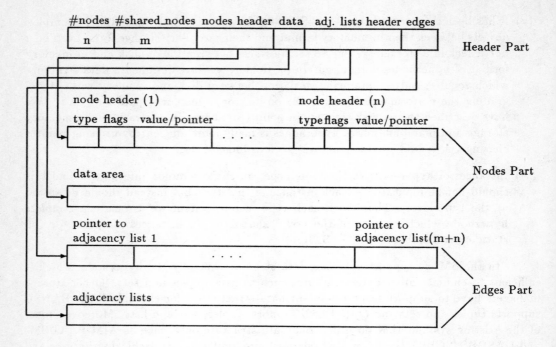

Figure 6 : Hypernode data structure

ode, such as the type of the node (a primitive type or a label), a flag to indicate whether that node has been deleted, and either the value of the node (for integers and labels), or a pointer to the node value i.e. either the offset in the data area part or the address of a separated object.

Each node within a hypernode has an associated locally unique identifier termed the *Node Id*. This is the entry number of the node in the node header list. The value associated with the Node Id may be changed during the lifetime of a hypernode as a result of the deletion of some other nodes and the compression process which reclaims unused data in the data area part and in the node header list. Node Ids are hidden from end-users who can only access nodes by their values. However, for optimisation reasons, Node Ids are available to several modules of the SM so that nodes can be manipulated without knowledge of their actual values. Node Ids are non-zero integers (zero is reserved for error handling). A negative Node Id is a reference to the shared node list within the template hypernode. For example, Figures 7a, 7b and 8 illustrate the template hypernode associated with the PERSON type and an instance of that type, PER2. In these figures the node types S and L, correspond to stream of bytes and label respectively.

The second sub-part of the nodes part is an array of characters containing the values of primitive nodes. From time to time this array may have to be compressed, for example after many deletions which have occurred to a particular hypernode.

Edges part. For each node in the hypernode and in its associated template hypernode we maintain an adjacency list. A list of pointers, one corresponding to each node, point to these adjacency lists which are stored as a contiguous array of Node Ids. The

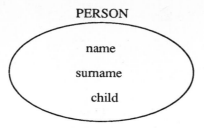

Figure 7a. The PERSON type template.

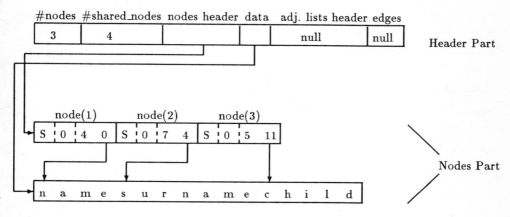

Figure 7b. The physical representation of PERSON.

same idea of offsets being converted into references to separate objects is used for storing this contiguous array as it grows.

Edges between a template hypernode and its instances are not common to all that type's instances. Thus, each hypernode also maintains all the edges between its internal nodes and its template nodes (thus, in Figure 6 the number of adjacency list pointers is m+n).

3.3.2 Operations on hypernodes

The operations on hypernodes fall into four categories :
1. *Update operations.*

(i) *Add a node to a hypernode.* This operation accepts a node value as input and appends it to the node header list and also to the data area if required. If the new node is a large primitive node then it is separated from the data area of the hypernode and a reference to it is appended to the node header list. The return value of the operation is a Node Id. If the input node value exists in the hypernode then the input is ignored and the return value is its Node Id. If the operation fails then the Node Id value returned is zero.

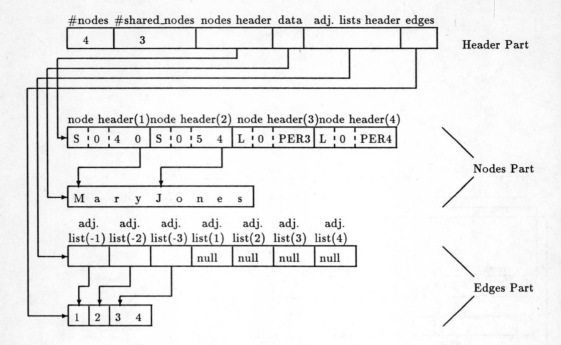

Figure 8. The physical representation of PER2.

(ii) *Add an edge to a hypernode.* The edge can be supplied as a pair of node values or Node Ids. The edge is inserted into the appropriate location in the list of edges. The two nodes must exist in the hypernode otherwise an error code is returned by the operation.

(iii) *Remove a linked node.* The input node may be a value or a Node Id. If the node is found it is tagged as deleted and its space may be reclaimed later. The edges to the node are also checked and removed. If the node is not found an error code is returned by the operation.

(iv) *Remove an isolated node.* The input to this operation must be an isolated node. If the node has edges to it or from it, an error code is returned by the operation.

(v) *Remove an edge.* The input to this operation is an edge. If the edge is found it is removed from the list of edges.

2. *Traversal operations.*

(i) *Get all references from a node.* This operation is used to get a set of Node Ids where each one of them is referenced by a specified node. If the set is empty then the return value is NULL.

(ii) *Get all references to a node.* This operation is similar to the above operation except that it looks for the nodes that reference a specified node.

3. *Membership operations.*

  (i) *Is a node in a hypernode.* This operation is used to check whether a specified node is contained in a specified hypernode.

  (ii) *Is an edge in a hypernode.* This operation checks whether a specified edge is contained in a specified hypernode.

4. *Retrieval operations.*

  (i) *Get node.* This operation is used to obtain a node value given a Node Id. If the node value is not a label or a fixed length primitive, such as an integer, its length must be obtained first. In this case a pointer to the address of its value is returned by the operation.

3.4   Labels and Label Tables

One of the most important concepts of the hypernode model is the fact that each hypernode is equipped with a system-wide unique identifier, its *label*. Thus labels provide hypernodes with *object identity* [KHO86]. The label is a built-in value associated with a hypernode at its time of creation and is the mechanism whereby hypernodes can reference each other. In general, one label can be referenced by more than one hypernode. This referential sharing raises the problem of *referential dangling* which occurs whenever a reference to a hypernode exists but the hypernode itself has been deleted and its label has possibly been reused for the creation of a new hypernode.

There are several ways of implementing this unique identity of hypernodes (see [KHO86]). In our system we have adopted an approach similar to that of ORION [KIM88] whereby each label consists of two components, the type of the hypernode and an instance identifier. We maintain labels in one or more tables termed *label tables*. One label table is maintained for each hypernode type defined in the database. In addition, a system-reserved label table is used as a metalevel table for all types. Each entry in a label table contains information pertaining to one label. This information is used to control access to, and manipulation of, the hypernode associated with the label. Interaction with the label tables is controlled by the *Label Tables Manager*.

The primary usage of the label tables is to provide a mapping from labels to the physical addresses of hypernodes. A further important function of the label tables is the creation of new labels. A new label is requested automatically when a new hypernode is created, and the table of the appropriate type supplies this new label. Each label table maintains information on used labels and employs a very simple hashing scheme to accelerate access to specific entries.

The provision for a separate label table for each type, as opposed to one global table, is useful for several reasons : scanning hypernodes of the same type is made simple, changes to the type structure of hypernodes are easier to maintain (for example, the deletion of a type), access to a hypernode's label entry is direct, and space utilisation of each table is maximal (i.e unused space in the table is minimal).

There are two operations supported by the SM which can cause referential dangling : one is the *delete* operation of a hypernode and the other is the *wipe* operation of a hypernode. When a hypernode is deleted its internal space is reclaimed and its label is mapped to a special null address. In contrast, the wipe operation is more intricate since it removes both the hypernode and its label, which can subsequently be re-used. In the implementation of wipe, references to the hypernode must be located and modified to reference a special null label. Each label table has an entry where the instance part of the label is this null label and the address is the null address; in Figure 2, $none^{PERSON}$ is an example of the null label of type PERSON. All the references to a specified hypernode can be located in one disk access since the Index Manager (see Section 4) maintains such an index for all the labels in the database.

In the current implementation of the DBMS hypernodes persist between transactions as result of explicit requests to the SM. Not all hypernodes are required to persist between transactions so, since the outcome of not reusing labels of non-persistent hypernodes would be overly large label tables, the wipe command is used when removing transient hypernodes.

The disadvantage of our implementation of labels is the indirection mechanism used to access any hypernode : we need two accesses, one to obtain the address from the label and another to access the hypernode itself. However, in practice, buffering of hypernodes in memory reduces the actual number of disk accesses (we discuss our buffering mechanism in more detail in 3.5). The advantage of our implementation is that whenever a hypernode is accessed its type is also available, and so any specific information associated with that type can be retrieved automatically. An example of such information is the template hypernode which acts as a common structure for all instances of that type and so is not stored within instances (see Figures 7b and 8 where the nodes of the PERSON template hypernode are referenced by PER2 and are not physically stored in PER2)

Finally, since our system is typed we are concerned with *migration* of hypernodes from one type to another. This operation can be implemented at the same cost as the wipe operation since all the references to the hypernode have to be found and modified.

3.5   The Buffer Manager

DBMSs that use the buffering services of the operating system suffer from several disadvantages [STO81]: the operating system has no knowledge of the implementation it serves so the buffer management it provides is not always suited to the requirements of the DBMS; the page-based buffer management used by virtual memory systems is inefficient in the environment of a complex object DBMS since the size of an object is not necessarily bounded by the page size; a further problem with page-based buffering is that objects in their in-memory format are likely to be different from objects in their on-disk format and translation between the two formats is cpu-intensive[SCH90].

Our solution to the above problems is similar to that of ORION[KIM90] and LOOM[KAE81]. Our buffer is divided into three areas : the first area is used by the page pool in order to fetch pages from the disk, the second area is used for buffering hypernodes, and the third area is an *access table* controlling access to individual hypernodes. Each entry of the access table is associated with one hypernode of which some portion is present in the buffering area. The number of entries in the access table may be very large and so the Buffer Manager uses hashing to accelerate access to entries.

The information stored in each entry of the access table is used to control access to hypernodes and comprises the address of the hypernode in secondary storage (if it is a new hypernode then this value will be the null address), a *dirty* flag which indicates whether the hypernode has been modified (in which case it has to be updated in the persistent store), the address of the hypernode in the buffer, and obviously the label of the hypernode in order to identify the correct entry in the label table lookup process. In the current version of our DBMS we do not cater for concurrency control and security, but it would be quite natural to add such information to the access table since the smallest unit of security and concurrency control will be a single hypernode and hypernodes are always accessed through this table.

When Hyperlog requests a hypernode it passes its label to the Buffer Manager which tries to locate the label in the buffering area. If found, the hypernode can be retrieved; otherwise a *hypernode fault* (cf. object fault [KIM88]) occurs and the hypernode is retrieved from the disk by the Buffer Manager which uses, for this purpose, the label tables and the Kernel. If there is not enough memory in the buffer area then the Buffer Manager employs a replacement policy to obtain enough room (currently we use a LRU mechanism). Furthermore, hypernodes are written to disk by an explicit command. Hypernodes that are written to disk may still remain in the buffer in case they are required by other transactions.

4   Clustering and Indexing

In this section we address two further physical-level aspects of the hypernode DBMS which are outside the scope of the storage manager, namely clustering and indexing.

4.1   Clustering

The smallest unit of clustering is the hypernode itself since it represents a conceptual clustering of attributes and related hypernodes (via their labels). However, different placement policies can be obtained as in ObServer [HOR87] and in addition a hypernode may be stored separately from its referenced hypernodes.

Hypernodes are clustered together physically on the disk in units of object stores which are provided by the Kernel. In the current version a default clustering mechanism is defined in the database at creation time and can be modified on-line at any stage. Two different policies are supported : one is to store each hypernode in an object store according to its type, and the other one is to store all new hypernodes in a default object store. This default object store can be changed dynamically. Moreover each hypernode may be written to a different object store from the default, and at location as near as possible to a specified location, typically the physical address of another hypernode.

4.2   Indexing

In relational databases primary indexes can be built on a selected key attribute or on a number of such attributes, and additional secondary indexes can be built on request

[AST76]. In contrast, in the hypernode DBMS we need to provide general-purpose secondary index support for the retrieval of hypernodes given a partial specification of their node and edge sets. Two basic operations are supported by the Index Manager which are sufficient to implement such retrieval requests, namely *Value-to-hypernode* and *Label-to-hypernode*, discussed in the introduction.

A separate data structure is used to implement each of these operations due to the simple fact that with primitive nodes a pre-defined order is available while there is no such natural ordering over labels. Thus, for operation value-to-hypernode we use a simple *prefix B-tree* [BAY77] while for operation label-to-hypernode we use the same hashing technique as for the label tables. Both the leaves of the B-tree and the hash value of a label reference to a list of labels which is ordered by type. Template nodes, which we recall are not stored within instance hypernodes, appear only once within these indexes and return labels of template hypernodes. These labels are recognised as such by the higher modules of the architecture and are replaced by instance labels as required.

The default scope of our indexes is the entire hypernode database. However, this default can be overridden in the database schema. Moreover, the indexes are extensible in the sense that further special-purpose access methods can be implemented for specific types in higher levels of the system. For example, we are investigating the implementation of full text retrieval indexes for our hypertext application. Finally, in the current DBMS we support two primitive types, integer and byte stream, where the ordering defined over streams is a native character comparison. Although for new primitive types new index techniques are required, we can use the current index over byte streams for a range of new types such as text in a hypertext system.

5   Concluding remarks

The major effort in the implementation of this first prototype version of the SM was in creating a stable and reliable system which can be used as a core for future research and development. We have shown that the SM caters for all of the requirements we identified in Section 2. In particular, labels provide us with object identity and referential sharing. With respect to complex, dynamic hypernodes our internal representation of a hypernode is efficient for both in-memory and secondary storage manipulation irrespective to its size and complexity. Clustering is supported by segmentation of secondary storage into units of object stores and retrieval is supported over the whole scope of the database. The modularity of the system and the minimal semantics embedded into the kernel are key ingredients for the extensibility of the SM. The SM has been implemented in C++ under UNIX. The object-oriented features of C++ have proven to be useful in supporting the modularity of the SM.

The major contribution of the SM is the single graph data structure which permeates throughout all the levels of the implementation. This is unlike other system managers which cater for several different data structures, such as sets, lists and tuples. There are several advantages to our approach : efficiency can be achieved within all the components of the SM as a result of optimising this data structure, interfacing between the components of the SM is simple and uniform, and a compact interface is provided to Hyperlog.

We are currently improving and extending two facets of the SM :

- We are attempting support many DBMS functions using the hypernode data structure. For example, persistence of hypernodes in the current version is achieved by an explicit command that is sent to the SM manager during a transaction. We are currently implementing a different mechanism whereby persistence is achieved through *reachability*, as in PS-ALGOL [ATK83a] and FAD [BAN87]. The reachability tree which describes the whole hypernode database and the hypernodes that are derived from a given root node, can itself be maintained as a hypernode. Other examples are clustering which can use a placement tree, also a hypernode, and versioning that can be maintained as a graph data structure.

- Optimisation to buffering sets of hypernodes and prefetching mechanisms can improve the overall performance of the system significantly. We are currently working on implementing different policies for buffering and prefetching in order to support specific applications such as hypertext.

6 Acknowledgements

We are grateful to Carol Small for her useful comments on this paper and to George Loizou for many fruitful discussions. The work we describe here forms part of the Hypernode Project, which is supported by S.E.R.C grant no. GR/G 26662.

References

[AST76] M. M. Astrhan et al, "System R: Relational Approach to Database Management", ACM Transaction on Database Systems, 1(2), pp 97-137, 1976.

[ATK83] M. P. Atkinson, K. J. Chisholm and W. P. Cockshott, "CMS - A Chunk Management System", Software - Practice and Experience, 13, pp 273-285, 1983.

[ATK83a] M. P. Atkinson, P. J. Bailey, K. J. Chisholm and W. P. Cockshott, "An Approach to Persistent Programming", The Computer Journal, 26(4), pp 360-365, 1983.

[BAN87] F. Bancilhon, T. Briggs, S. Khoshafian and P. Valduriez, "FAD, a Powerful and Simple Database Language", Proc. 13th VLDB, Brighton, pp 97-105, 1987.

[BAY77] R. Bayer and K. Unterauer, "Prefix B-Trees", ACM Transactions on Database Systems, 2(1), pp 11-26, 1977.

[CAR86] M. J. Carey, D. J. DeWitt, J. E. Richardson and E. J. Shekita, "Object and File Management in the EXODUS Extensible Database System", Proc. 12th VLDB, Kyoto, pp 91-100, 1986.

[CON90] M. P. Consens and A. O. Mendelzon, "Graphlog : A Visual Formalism for Real Life Recursion", Proc. of ACM Symposium on Principles of Database Systems, Nashville, Tennessee, pp 404-416, 1990.

[DES88] A. Deshpande, D. Van Gucht, "An Implementation for Nested Relational Databases", Proc. 14th VLDB, Los Angeles, pp 76-87, 1988.

[GAR89] G. Gardarin and P. Valduriez, "Relational Database and Knowledge Bases", Addison-Wesley, 1989.

[GRA78] N. Gray, "Notes On Data Base Operating Systems", Operating Systems: An Advanced Course, Springer-Verlag, 1978.

[GYS90] M. Gyssens, J. Paredaens and D. V. Van Gucht, "A Graph-Oriented Object Model for Database End-User Interfaces", Proc. of the ACM SIGMOD , Atlantic City, pp 24-33, 1990.

[HAR88] D. Harel, "On Visual Formalism", Communications of the ACM, 31(5), pp 514-530, 1988.

[HOR87] M. F. Hornick and S. B. Zdonik, "A Shared, Segmented Memory System for an Object-Oriented Database", ACM Transaction on Office Information Systems, 5(1), pp 70-95, 1987.

[HUD89] S. E. Hudson and R. King, "CACTIS : A Self-Adaptive, Concurrent Implementation of an Object-Oriented Database Management System", ACM Transaction on Database Systems, 14(3), pp 291-321, 1989.

[KAE81] T. Kaehler, "Virtual Memory for an Object-Oriented Language", BYTE, pp 378-387, 1981.

[KIM88] W. Kim, N. Ballou, H. -T. Chou, J. F. Garza, D. Woelk and J. Banerjee, "Integrating an Object-Oriented Programming System with a Database System", Proc. OOPSLA 88, pp 142-152, 1988.

[KIM90] W. Kim, J. F. Garza, N. Ballou and D. Woelk, "Architecture of the ORION Next-Generation Database System", IEEE Transactions on Knowledge and Data Engineering, 2(1), pp 109-124, 1990.

[KHO86] S. N. Khoshafian and G. P. Copeland, "Object Identity", Proc. OOPSLA 86, pp 406-416, 1986.

[KHO90] S. N. Khoshafian, M. J. Franklin and M. J. Carey, "Storage Management for Persistent Complex Objects", Information Systems, 15(3), pp 303-320, 1990.

[KUS87] K. Kuspert, P.Dadam and J. Gunauer, "Cooperative Object Buffer Management in the Advanced Information Management Prototype", Proc. 13th VLDB, Brighton, pp 483-492, 1987.

[LEV90] M. Levene and A. Poulovassilis, "The Hypernode Model and its Associated Query Language", Proc. 5th Jerusalem Conference on Information Technology, 1990, pp 520-530.

[LEV91] M. Levene and A. Poulovassilis, "An object-oriented data model formalised through hypergraphs", Data and Knowledge Engineering, 6(3), pp 205-224.

[NIE89] J. Nielsen, "Hypertext and Hypermedia", Academic Press, 1989.

[POU90] A. Poulovassilis and M.Levene, "A nested-graph model for the representation and manipulation of complex objects", Research Note RN/90/86, Dept. of Computer Science, University College London, December 1990.

[SCH90] H.-J. Schek, H.-B. Paul, M.H. Scholl and G. Weikum, "The DASDBS project: Objectives, Experiences, and Future Prospects", IEEE Transaction on Knowledge and Data Engineering, 2(1), pp 25-43, 1990.

[STO81] M. Stonebraker, "Operating System Support for Database Management", Communications of the ACM, 24(7), pp 412-418, 1981.

[STR86] B. Stroustrup, "The C++ Programming Language", Addison-Wesley, 1986.

[TOM89] F. W. Tompa, "A Data Model for Flexible Hypertext Database Systems", ACM Transactions on Information Systems, 7(1), pp 85-100, 1989.

[ULL88] J. D. Ullman, "Principles of Database and Knowledge-Base Systems", Computer Science Press, 1988.

[ULL91] J. D. Ullman, "A Comparison of Deductive and Object-Oriented Dtabases", Proc. 2nd DOOD, Munich, pp 263-277, 1991.

[VAL86] P. Valduriez, S. Khoshafian and G. Copeland, "Implementation Techniques of Complex Objects", Proc. 12th VLDB, pp 101-109.

[VEL89] F. Velez, G. Bernard and V.Darnis, "The O_2 Object Manager: An Overview", Proc. 15th VLDB, Amsterdam, pp 357-366, 1989.

VIEWS AND FORMAL IMPLEMENTATION IN A THREE-LEVEL SCHEMA ARCHITECTURE FOR DYNAMIC OBJECTS*

Gunter Saake and Ralf Jungclaus

Abt. Datenbanken, Techn. Universität Braunschweig
Postfach 3329, W-3300 Braunschweig, FRG
E-mail: {saake|jungclau}@idb.cs.tu-bs.de

Abstract

The three-level schema architecture proposed as part of a framework for database standardization supports data independence resulting in a database architecture being flexible and adaptable to changes. Dynamic object bases differ from classical database models in their integrated description of structure and behaviour of objects. The arguments for introducing the different schema levels for database applications hold for object bases, too, and may help to structure large object-oriented applications. This paper discusses the transfer of the three-level approach to an object-oriented approach for describing dynamic objects. Requirements for description formalisms for the external, conceptual and internal level lead to desired language features for object-oriented system specification languages.

1 Introduction

Large database applications like information systems tend to become very complex both in terms of the database schema and the application software. Such applications are used by several user groups that make different demands upon the data access. Therefore, different *database views* are offered to different user groups and applications. Such views are also needed to control access rights and enforce data security. Changes of the database realization must be separated from the database interface because the interface is used by several applications and thus its stability is of great importance.

For classical value-oriented database models like the relational model, the *three-level schema architecture* of the ANSI/X3/SPARC group [DAFTG86] introduced a schema architecture supporting the separation of external views, the central conceptual database schema and its implementation (cf. fig. 1). Each external view is associated with an external schema describing the database objects as presented to a specific application (or user group).

---

*This work was partially supported by CEC under ESPRIT BRA WG 3023 IS-CORE (Information Systems – COrrectness and REusability) and by Deutsche Forschungsgemeinschaft under grant no. Sa 465/1-1.

The current research in object-oriented databases and active databases leads to the notion of *object bases* containing both passive and dynamic/active objects as basic building blocks of a database application [SSE87, SFSE89]. This new approach to database technology has its roots in several fields of research:

- *Object-oriented databases* now under development and formalization at several sites are mainly based on new database structuring techniques originally required by non-standard applications [Bee90, Dit88, ABD+89]. They usually support object-centered clustering of data, object identity and inheritance of object properties. Object specific methods (for updates) are realized in some systems [D+91] but are not covered by most current data model formalization approaches [Bee90].

- *Object-oriented design* focuses on the integrated design of structure and dynamics encapsulated into object units [Boo90] but lacks up to now a formal semantics.

- *Object-oriented programming languages* like Simula, Smalltalk, Eiffel or C++ concentrate on the computational aspects of objects as independent units of computation having a local memory and communicating solely through method calling/message passing. The basic elements of computation are methods manipulating the local object variables in a conventional operational way.

The idea of *dynamic object bases* combines these approaches into one framework supporting structured and persistent database objects as well as object dynamics in terms of update methods. The aim of this paper is to discuss a three-level schema architecture for an abstract concept of dynamic objects (i.e., objects evolving over time) and the resulting demands on description languages. To realize such a schema architecture, we have to introduce several formalisms and languages :

- We need a *formal concept of objects* to define the semantics of an object base both on the conceptual and implementation level.

- Conceptual object base schemata must be defined using a language that enables an *implementation-independent abstract description* of object bases.

- A formal concept of *object interfaces* is required to define external schemata as views on an object base.

- Finally, we need a formal concept of *object implementation* to define the relation between conceptual schema and internal schema.

This work has been motivated by the lack of approaches to formally specify updates and dynamic evolution in (object-oriented) data models so far. On the other hand, the issue of data independence in structural databases has been covered in a suitable way by the three-level architecture proposal.

Our aim is to present a discussion of these requirements in the object-oriented framework and their consideration by language features in an object-oriented conceptual language. In particular, we will discuss a three-level schema architecture using the Oblog

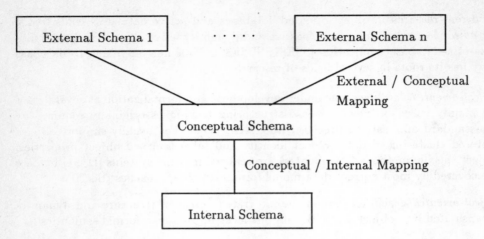

Figure 1: Schema structure of the three-level architecture.

model of dynamic objects firstly described in [SSE87]. The Oblog model bases on a formal semantical model regarding objects as observable processes [SE90, EGS90, ES91, SJE91, ESS92]. The conceptual modelling language TROLL presented in [JHSS91, JSH91, JSHS91, JSS91, SJ91, HJS92] is used as the description language for object base schemata. We start with the conceptual level and show how the structure and behaviour of objects can be conceptually specified. In Section 5, we introduce language features to specify *access interfaces* to objects modelled on the conceptual level in order to define external views. As an example for a specification on the internal level, we show in Section 6 how a representation of a relational implementation of the conceptual level can be specified. In general, our approach for mapping conceptual objects to the internal level is to (re-)specify the services provided by (existing) database systems in terms of our language and to implement conceptual objects formally using base objects.

This contribution is meant as a discussion of basic concepts related to a three-level schema architecture for object bases rather than a comprehensive presentation of concrete language features.

2   Basic Idea of Three-Level Architecture

The three-level schema architecture for databases can easily be explained using Figure 1. This architecture organizes the schema in three different levels :

- The central *conceptual* schema represents the conceptual view on the complete database using an abstract data model schema. 'Abstract' data model means that the conceptual schema abstracts from implementation details.

- The *internal* schema describes the implementation details in terms of the implementation platform used (the DBMS). This may require a change of the used data model. Typical description issues for classical DBMSs are access paths and their realization.

- The *external schemata* describe several views on the conceptual schema specific to particular applications or user groups.

This schema architecture induces a family of *transformations* which must be formally defined to guarantee a correct usage of the database :

- The *schema transformation* is the link between levels. The conceptual schema must be implemented in terms of the implementation platform concepts, and the external schemata must be defined as views on the conceptual schema.

- The schema transformation induces a *query transformation* that transforms a query on an external view to an executable internal query expression. This usually goes together with a query optimization step. The result of a query must be retransformed to fit to the external schema.

- A critical issue is the transformation of *database updates*. In particular, powerful set-oriented database update mechanisms along with arbitrary external view definitions cannot be handled in the general case (view update problem). However, updateable views are inevitable features of databases organized according to the three-level architecture.

We will concentrate on schema and update transformation, because the definition of set-oriented object query algebras and their optimization is an active research area which can certainly not be worked out adequately in this paper.

In the context of dynamic objects, we have to solve several problems if we want to use the three-level architecture to organize an object base :

- We need a formal object description mechanism to describe the semantics of object bases on the three levels. A formal approach is necessary because otherwise we are not able to define formal and correct transformations !

- We need formal transformation concepts for objects which handle both structure *and* behaviour of objects in a suitable way.

- We have to decide which modeling approach to choose for which level. For the conceptual and external levels, we need abstract and descriptive object specification mechanisms. On the internal level, we need an operational language which, however, must fit to the formal semantics of the conceptual schema — otherwise we are not able to define correct transformations.

Our approach uses dynamic objects for defining the conceptual and internal level but using different abstraction degrees for these levels. We use object *interfaces* for the external level. Object interfaces do not create new objects but offer an access interface to existing objects. For the realization of the conceptual object society we introduce language features for formal implementation of objects over objects. These concepts are explained in more detail in the following sections. We start with introducing the basic concepts of a formal object model which is a necessary prerequisite if we want to talk about correctness of transformations and implementations.

3 An Abstract Object Model

In this paper, we will use a model-oriented view of dynamic objects. The concept of object evolved from evaluating several approaches to system development towards their use for an integrated description of all relevant static and dynamic aspects of the UoD. Formalizations of this concept can be found in [SE90, EGS90, Wie90, ES91]. We will recapitulate some basic concepts of the underlying semantic structures only.

Arbitrarily structured values and type-specific operations have been investigated in the abstract data type approach (see e.g. [EM85]). However, this approach aims at describing values and corresponding functions and thus does not include concepts of state, state transitions, temporal evolution, and persistence. Semantic data models enable the description of complex database entities, abstractions, and structural relationships between entities (cf. [UD86, HK87, PM88]). Many of them fail, however, to provide adequate means to include state transitions and temporal evolution.

Proposals for object-oriented data models strive to overcome these deficiencies. They support object classification, the notion of state by providing immutable object identifiers, and they allow integrated description of local state information and operations on the state of an object (cf. [ABD+89, Bee90]). Operations alone, however, are still not suitable to describe temporal evolution of objects.

In object-oriented programming languages, some additional emphasis is put on communication between objects through message passing, encapsulation, and limited capabilities of representation of temporal evolution [Weg87, Mey88].

In our view, the most important benefit from the object-oriented approach is the encapsulated integration of local structure and behaviour in objects.

An object can be regarded as an observable communicating process encapsulated by an access interface. Observations consist of reading its attribute values, object changes over time are driven by occurrences of its events. An event occurrence may be initiated by the object itself (active object) or as a result of a communication with another object (event calling). Both the values of attributes and the possible parameters of events are *data values* in the sense of abstract data type values.

The basis for a formalization of such an object concept are values structured using the concept of abstract data types (ADT's) [EM85, EGL89]. Data values are elements of the carrier set of some ADT. An ADT is defined by a carrier set for data values along with data type specific functions on this set.

For the formalization of object signatures, we use the notion of a signature from the ADT framework. An object signature consists of attribute and event symbols. Attributes are null-ary functions into a certain domain (a data type), events are functions with parameters and a special event sort as domain. The object signature defines the alphabet for an object specification in a formal framework.

The next step is the formalization of object evolutions using linear processes in a process framework. The reason we only consider linear processes is that we do not want to have intra-object concurrency, i.e. our objects are the units of concurrency. A possible choice is to adopt the life cycle model [JSS91] which defines a process as the set of possible snapshots of events. A snapshot is a set of concurrently occurring events. Special attention must be paid to events that create and destroy an object. Therefore we require the first snapshot in a life cycle to include at least one *birth* event. If the life cycle is finite, a *death* event is included in the last snapshot. Note that death events are not required, thus there may be objects that exist infinitely.

The last point to formalize for the specification of simple objects is the *observation of current object properties*. This is done by introducing an observation structure fixing attribute values for each reachable state of an object. A reachable object state is given by any finite prefix of possible object life cycles. The observation structure can be described as a mapping from object states (life cycle prefixes) to attribute-value relations [SSE87, ESS90].

Up to now we have only sketched a formalization of single objects. Another topic is the definition of object composition. Component relation between objects is modeled using structure preserving mappings between objects, the so-called object morphisms [ESS90, EGS90], which can be be compared to process combination known from process theory. As a special case we have inclusion morphisms where the mapping is supposed to be injective. Inclusion morphisms can be used to explain the *embedding of subobjects* into objects, i.e. aggregation of objects. The embedded objects are regarded as subprocesses in the enclosing composite object, where only events local to the subobject may have effects on attribute observations (of the subobject attributes).

The step from single objects to sets of objects is done by introducing an identification mechanism for object instances. Again we use ADT's to describe object identifiers. A class type defines a set of identifiers along with a prototype object model (an object template). An object class then consists of a class type and a set of object instances together with a mapping from a set of object identifiers to actual object instances.

The basic mechanism to support communication between objects is event calling. When an event e_1 calls another event e_2, then whenever e_1 occurs, e_2 must also occur simultaneously (but not vice versa). Thus, event calling is an asymmetric synchronization on event occurrences inside an object, which itself can be composed from several objects using object inclusion. Because of the definition of object embedding, calling is the only way an embedded object can be manipulated by the embedding one.

A more elaborated formalization of these ideas can be found in [JSS91, SJ91, JSH91]. For recent developments towards a more sophisticated semantic domain for object systems see [ES91, ESS92].

4 The Conceptual Level — Specification of Object Societies

The conceptual schema is the center of the three-level architecture for object bases. On this level, the complete object base must be described in an implementation-independent fashion. This task puts some requirements upon a description formalism used on this level :

- Objects must be described in an *abstract* way, i.e. independently from their later implementation. This holds both for objects from the UoD and for objects used for application tasks.

- The conceptual schema must be complete in terms of restrictions on objects, be it constraints on object properties, restrictions on object updates or restrictions on long-term object evolution, because it is the central description of the object base being the reference both for the implementors as well as for application developers.

- As mentioned already, a formal semantics is an indispensable property of a language for specifying a conceptual model, because otherwise transformations to the other levels cannot be formalized.

We will use the Oblog object model as semantical framework for conceptual schema descriptions. Let us now show how objects and object classes are specified in the TROLL-language presented in more detail in [JHSS91, JSHS91]. We will recapitulate some basic features of TROLL only. As an example, consider an object class representing departments:

object class DEPT
   identification id: string;
   template
     attributes
       est_date: date;
       manager: |PERSON|;
       employees: set(|PERSON|);
     events
       birth establishment(date);
       death closure;
       new_manager(|PERSON|); assign_official_car(|CAR|,|PERSON|);
       hire(|PERSON|); fire(|PERSON|);
     valuation
       variables P: |PERSON|; d: date;
       [establishment(d)]est_date = d;
       [new_manager(P)]manager = P;
       [hire(P)]employees = employees ∪ {P};
       [fire(P)]employees = employees \ {P};
     permission
       variables P: |PERSON|;
       { sometime(after(hire(P)))} fire(P);
       { **for all**(P: |PERSON|): sometime(P in employees) ⇒
          sometime(after(fire(P))) } closure;
end object class DEPT;

The **valuation** rules describe the evolution of the attribute observations. They describe the effect of event terms on attribute values in terms of a data-valued term evaluated before the event occurrence which determines the new attribute value. The **permission** rules describe permitted sequences of events and thus restrict the set of possible sequences over the alphabet of events to admissible sequences. Additional features of the language not described here include arbitrary constraints on attributes, liveness requirements (i.e.

goals to be achieved by the object in an active way) and activity, i.e. events that may occur on the object's own initiative whenever their occurrence is possible.

An object in TROLL is thus a unit encapsulating data and evolution. *Encapsulation* means that local data can solely be manipulated by local events which can be seen as basic operations on the state of an object and that the internal state can be observed by attributes only. In contrast to the view of encapsulation in object-oriented programming, we allow attribute values to be read by other objects, i.e. they are part of the object's interface. In a certain sense, we can see attributes as a read-only interface for queries and events as the manipulation interface offered by an object. We may, however, hide more information by explicitly defining interfaces to objects (see Section 5).

Another touchy issue in object-oriented approaches is *inheritance*. TROLL supports two different kinds of inheritance: *Syntactic inheritance* means reusing specifications, *semantic inheritance* means *inclusion of encapsulated objects*. That is, attributes of the inherited object may not be changed by events not local to the inherited object. Events local to the inherited object may, however, be triggered from the outside. In TROLL, subclass hierarchies determine patterns of *semantic* inheritance.

Subclasses in our model are either *specializations* or *phases*. Specialization is static, i.e. the specialized object is born as a special kind of the base object and remains of this special kind for its entire life (consider e.g. a woman as specialization of a person). An object being a special kind just for a part of its life has special properties only when it is in this role (consider e.g. a manager as a special kind of person). Note that both concepts are based on semantic inheritance.

The following specification fragment defines the class MANAGER of which the instances are phases of PERSON-instances:

object class PERSON
    identification
        Name: string;
        BirthDate: date;
    template
        attributes
           Salary: money;
           ...
        events
           ...
           become_manager;
end object class PERSON;

object class MANAGER
    role of PERSON;
    template
        attributes
           OfficialCar : |CAR|;
        events
           birth PERSON.become_manager;
           ...

```
    constraints
        Salary ≥ 5.000;
    ...
end object class MANAGER;
```

In TROLL, complex objects may be constructed using *aggregation*, i.e. composition of objects from sets or lists of objects as well as from single objects. The concept of aggregation is based on semantic inheritance, too: the components of a complex object are semantically inherited, i.e. they are included in a property-preserving way. Aggregation in TROLL is discussed in more detail in [JSHS91].

Consider for example the object representing **TheCompany**, which is a complex object having a list of departments as component:

```
object TheCompany
    ...
    template
        components
            depts : LIST(DEPT);
    ...
end object TheCompany;
```

An object society is a (possibly large) collection of objects that *interact*. Interaction is performed by *event calling*. To call an event means to force *synchronous* occurrence of the called event by the occurrence of the calling event. In TROLL, explicit *relationships* between objects serve as communication channels to structure communication between independent objects.

Consider e.g. the promotion of a person P identified by the identifier P.oid to become a manager of a department D. The event **new_manager(P.oid)** of the department object calls the event **become_manager** of the corresponding person object:

```
relationship Promotion between PERSON P, DEPT D;
        D.new_manager(P.oid) >> P.become_manager;
end relationship Promotion;
```

Note that event calling is also used for interactions with inherited objects inside complex objects. An important extension of event calling is *process calling* enabling an event to call a finite sequence of other events treated as a transaction unit [SE90].

5 The External Level — Object Society Interfaces

The external level of the three-level architecture define *access interfaces* to an existing object base modelled on the conceptual level. In principle, we may change the object / data model for these external schemata. We present the definition of external schemata as object societies in the sense of the Oblog approach because other data or object model proposals can be expressed in terms of TROLL objects, if we add further restrictions. For example, if we allow only flat attributes and forbid single-standing objects and complex objects, we have objects realizing a relational database view.

The basic idea of external schema definition is to give an access interface to existing objects. That is, we do not define new objects by defining views. In terms of the TROLL approach, we define *new interfaces* to existing objects by defining attributes, events and components (interfaces for derived objects). Thus, external object interfaces are very similar to conceptual schema objects, but their internal semantics is given by a transformation of the signature components to an implementation in terms of conceptual objects.

As mentioned before, an *object (class) interface* is mainly a mechanism for controlling access to objects in an object base. Access control for a single object is achieved by defining a restricted interface for the object, e.g. by performing a projection on the attributes and events of the object. Furthermore, we allow a restricted form of deriving new attribute values and events. This projection can be defined for single objects as well as for all instances of an object class. The following examples show the principles of defining object interfaces.

The first example is an interface to an object class PERSON defined for the use of the salary department. Only attributes and events being of interest for this department are shown in the interface signature.

interface class SAL_EMPLOYEE
encapsulating PERSON
      attributes
          Name: string;
          IncomeInYear(integer): money;
          Salary: money;
      events
          ChangeSalary(money);
end interface class SAL_EMPLOYEE;

The semantics of this interface definition is a restriction of the *access* to PERSON objects as it is done in relational databases by a projection view. Please note that the projection definition does not only restrict the observation of attributes but also the possible modification events being offered to the view users. This kind of projection can be used to restrict the access to complex object components, too.

The object's external keys (for PERSONs the values of Name and BirthDay) are not generally preserved by an interface definition, but the internal object identity is preserved since we do not derive new objects. This implies that we in general do not have a set of interfaces but a multiset.

As an example for an interface with *derived attributes and events* we have the interface class SAL_EMPLOYEE2 where the additional attribute CurrentIncomePerYear is derived from the value of the attribute Salary and only a restricted way of changing salaries is offered.

interface class SAL_EMPLOYEE2
encapsulating PERSON
      attributes

```
        Name: string;
        derived CurrentIncomePerYear: money;
        Salary: money;
    events
        derived IncreaseSalary;
    derivation
        derivation rules
            CurrentIncomePerYear = Salary *13.5;
        calling
            IncreaseSalary >> ChangeSalary(Salary *1.1);
end interface class SAL_EMPLOYEE2;
```

The derivation part is usually hidden to the users. For the derivation of attribute values we have the full power of the object query algebra QUAL defined for the Oblog model [SJ90, SJS91]. QUAL resembles well known concepts of database query algebras handling values (not objects !). Algebra terms are evaluated locally to the encapsulated object. For the derivation of events we can use arbitrary *process calling* [SE90]. Thus, the derived event may be evaluated by a finite process defined over the local events of the encapsulated object.

Furthermore, object class interfaces allow the selection of a subpopulation of an object class. To define a selection, we allow arbitrary QUAL terms of sort **boolean**. The variable SELF denotes the currently observed instance. The following interface class RESEARCH EMPLOYEE selects only those persons working for the research department.

```
interface class RESEARCH EMPLOYEE
encapsulating PERSON
selection where SELF.Dept = 'Research';
        attributes
            Name: string;
            Salary: money;
        events
            ChangeSalary(money);
end interface class RESEARCH EMPLOYEE;
```

In the semantic domain of TROLL, one may implicitly define an *aggregation object* identified by the identification of its parts [EGS90, SE90] over each two objects. Therefore, we can easily extend our view mechanism to support *join views*:

```
interface class WORKS_FOR
encapsulating PERSON P, DEPT D
selection where P.oid in D.employees;
        attributes
            DeptName: string;
            PersonName: string;
        derivation
            derivation rules
```

```
        DeptName = D.Id;
        PersonName = P.Name;
end interface class WORKS_FOR;
```

In a join view, we typically introduce variables to identify the participating object instances (which is, however, not necessary in our example). These variables can be used in the (optional) selection clause and in derivation rules. As said before, the internal object identity is preserved by the view and therefore even derived updates can be offered in the view definition without semantic difficulties.

The semantics of interfaces is in principle only an *authorization* for *restricted object manipulation* and *attribute value retrieval*. It has nothing to do with object copies — it is only a restricted view on existing objects. We can regard interface definitions as a mechanism to select objects for manipulation. The manipulations themselves are encapsulated within the objects, therefore we do not have to describe the concrete manipulations but the restrictions for using them correctly.

As a last point on object views we want to discuss the relation of our interface concept to view concepts for object-oriented data models [Day89, SLT90]. The basic idea in [SLT90] is to use object preserving queries as a way to define views. This partly corresponds to our interface declaration as an access mechanism to existing objects instead of deriving new objects as discussed in [Day89]. The main difference to both proposals is that these structure–oriented approaches do not consider object events and behaviour in their formalisms as first class concepts — for example, projection views in [SLT90] consider attributes only. To handle dynamic objects in our sense, these approaches have to be extended by explicit handling of update events similar to the approach presented above.

6 The Internal Level — Formal Implementation of Objects

The internal level contains a more concrete, i.e. operational, description of database structures and update transactions. Update transactions are the implementation of object events, and data structures are realizations of object society observations.

Most of the currently used description formalisms for internal schema definitions lack a formal semantics, which is a necessary feature for correct implementations. We propose to define an *object-oriented interface* to existing database management systems as the target of a formal implementation which enables us to stay in the object world presented for the conceptual schema, and as a result the semantics of both levels are defined using the same formalism. The relation between both levels is then described using *formal implementation of objects over objects* [ES89, SE90]. That is, we propose to regard the internal level as an *abstract* internal level that uses the language TROLL for the *formalization* of services provided by concrete database management systems. This way, it is also possible to integrate several (heterogeneous) databases using a canonical model.

As an example, we implement the object class EMPLOYEE on top of an object emp_rel describing a database relation of a relational database. The object class EMPLOYEE is very simple to keep the implementation example small. EMPLOYEE objects are identified (like PERSONs) by their name (EmpName) and birthday (EmpBirth) and have a current salary (Salary). As update events we have hire and fire of an employee (HireEmployee and FireEmployee) and a change of their salary (IncreaseSalary).

The implementation of the class EMPLOYEE is done using one object emp_rel managing a set of tuples storing the data. Please note that this is just one alternative of implementing the class EMPLOYEE – we could also have specified the relation as a class of which the instances are the current tuples in this relation.

```
object emp_rel
template
    data types string, date, integer;
    attributes
        Emps : set(tuple(ename:string, ebirth:date, esalary:integer));
    events
        birth CreateEmpRel;
        UpdateSalary(string, date, integer);
        InsertEmpl(string, date, integer);
        DeleteEmpl(string, date);
        death CloseEmpRel;
    valuation
        variables n:string, b:date, s:integer;
        [CreateEmpRel] Emps = {};
        [InsertEmp(n,b,s)] Emps = insert(Emps, tuple(n,b,s));
        {in(Emps,tuple(n,b,s))} ⇒
            [DeleteEmp(n,b)] Emps = delete(Emps, tuple(n,b,s));
    permissions
        variables n:string, b:date, s:integer;
        { exists(s1:integer) in(Emps,tuple(n,b,s1))} UpdateSalary(n,b,s);
        { Emps = {} } CloseEmpRel;
    interaction
        variables n:string, b:date, s:integer;
        ChangeSalary(n,b,s) >> ( DeleteEmp(n,b); InsertEmp(n,b,s) );
end object emp_rel;
```

The operators **in**, **insert** and **delete** are operations defined for the parameterized data type constructor **set**. The keyword **tuple** is used for the data type constructor (the 'record of' construct of programming languages) as well as for the tuple creation operation.

The interfaces (i.e., the object signature) of such implementation objects can be derived automatically from a given relational schema. For example, the semantics of update operations are semantically modelled by a sequence consisting of an insert and delete operation in a set of tuples under the requirement to satisfy the key constraints. In general, there are a number of update events generated from a given relational schema. It should be mentioned that this relation object itself may be implemented for example by an other object using a B-tree or a hash table access method leading to a hierarchy of implementations.

To define the relation between `emp_rel` and `EMPLOYEE`, we define as a next step the implementation of an object class `EMPL_IMPL` on top of the single object `emp_rel` representing the relational implementation.

```
object class EMPL_IMPL
identification
      data types date, string;
      EmpName : string;
      EmpBirth : date;
template
   including emp_rel as employees;
   attributes
      derived Salary;
   events
      birth HireEmployee;
      derived IncreaseSalary(integer);
      death FireEmployee;
   constraints
      derivation rules
         Salary =
            count(project[esalary]
                  (select[ename = EmpName and ebirth = EmpBirth] (employees)))
   interaction
      variables n:integer;
      HireEmployee >> employees.InsertEmpl(self.EmpName, self.Empbirth, 0);
      FireEmployee >> employees.DeleteEmpl(self.EmpName, self.Empbirth);
      IncreaseSalary(n) >>
         employees.UpdateSalary(self.EmpName, self.Empbirth, self.Salary + n);
end object class EMPL_IMPL;
```

The object class `EMPL_REL` realizes the implementation of 'employee' instances onto the single object realization. Therefore derived attributes are computing using arbitrary local queries and events are derived by interpreting them by events on the implementation base. In general, events are interpreted by *transactions* composed of base events. To compose transactions, TROLL offers a process language offering language features like sequence, choice and iteration [JSHS91]. Since implementations can be composed leading to implementation hierarchies, the transaction model has to offer nested transactions of variable nesting level.

The last step of the implementation is to hide implementation details (encapsulation) by defining an interface class `EMPL` for `EMPL_IMPL`.

```
interface class EMPL
encapsulating EMPL_IMPL
      attributes
         EmpName: string;
         EmpBirth: date;
         Salary: integer;
```

```
      events
          IncreaseSalary(integer);
          HireEmployee;
          FireEmployee;
end interface class EMPL;
```

To show the correctness of our implementation, we have to prove that all properties of the original **EMPLOYEE** specification can be derived from **EMPL**, too. It is outside the scope of this paper to present a proof theory for formal object implementation. Basic concepts for a proof theory for object specifications can be found in [FSMS90, FM91].

Such an implementation may use several base objects to implement an abstract object, for example if normalization of relations becomes necessary to realize nested structures. In general, a formal implementation consists of two steps :

1. First of all, a complex object (or a class of complex objects) is constructed consisting of all base objects needed for the implementation.

2. An object (class) interface defines the encapsulation of implementation details.

Formal implementation of objects over objects enables consistency checks and formal verification because it is done in the same formal framework [FSMS90, SE90]. A necessary prerequisite is the definition of an object-oriented interface to existing database management systems. Our example gives hints how to achieve this for relational databases. Object-oriented database management systems offer such an interface and can therefore be directly used as target systems for the internal level.

7   Conclusions

In this paper, we discussed a three-level architecture for object-oriented database applications. This architecture requires explicit transformations of object structure *and* object behaviour. In contrast to classical data models, external object behaviour views (i.e., the update interfaces to an object base) must be defined explicitly because of the object-oriented paradigm of integrating structure and behaviour.

Topics of future research include full integration of complex object aggregation both in interface definitions and formal implementations, the formalization of the necessary framework for nested transactions in implementation hierarchies, and the development of methods and tools supporting consistency checking and verification of implementation steps.

Acknowledgements

Thanks to Thorsten Hartmann and Cristina Sernadas, who collaborated in the definition of the TROLL specification language. Hans-Dieter Ehrich and Amílcar Sernadas developed basic ideas of objects and object descriptions. Last but not least we thank the anonymous referees for very constructive reviews that helped to improve the presentation of our ideas.

References

[ABD+89] Atkinson, M.; Bancilhon, F.; DeWitt, D.; Dittrich, K. R.; Maier, D.; Zdonik, S. B.: The Object-Oriented Database System Manifesto. In: Kim, W.; Nicolas, J.-M.; Nishio, S. (eds.): *Proc. Int. Conf. on Deductive and Object-Oriented Database Systems*, Kyoto, Japan, December 1989. pp. 40–57.

[Bee90] Beeri, C.: A Formal Approach to Object Oriented Databases. *Data & Knowledge Engineering*, Vol. 5, No. 4, 1990, pp. 353–382.

[Boo90] Booch, G.: *Object-Oriented Design*. Benjamin/Cummings, Menlo Park, CA, 1990.

[D+91] Deux, O. et al.: The O_2 System. *Communications of the ACM*, Vol. 34, No. 10, 1991, pp. 34–48.

[DAFTG86] Database Architecture Framework Task Group (DAFTG) of the ANSI/X3/SPARC Database System Study Group: Reference Model for DBMS Standardization. *ACM SIGMOD Records*, Vol. 15, No. 1, 1986, pp. 19–58.

[Day89] Dayal, U.: Queries and Views in an Object-Oriented Data Model. In: Hull, R.; Morrison, R.; Stemple, D. (eds.): *Proc. 2nd Int. Workshop on Database Programming Languages*, Oregon Coast, 1989. Morgan Kaufmann, San Mateo, Ca, pp. 80–102.

[Dit88] Dittrich, K. R. (ed.): *Advances in Object-Oriented Database Systems*. Lecture Notes in Comp. Sc. 334. Springer Verlag, Berlin, 1988.

[EGL89] Ehrich, H.-D.; Gogolla, M.; Lipeck, U.W.: *Algebraische Spezifikation abstrakter Datentypen*. Teubner, Stuttgart, 1989.

[EGS90] Ehrich, H.-D.; Goguen, J. A.; Sernadas, A.: A Categorial Theory of Objects as Observed Processes. In: deBakker, J.W.; deRoever, W.P.; Rozenberg, G. (eds.): *Proc. REX/FOOL Workshop*, Noordwijkerhood (NL), 1990. LNCS 489, Springer-Verlag, Berlin, 1991, pp. 203–228.

[EM85] Ehrig, H.; Mahr, B.: *Fundamentals of Algebraic Specification I: Equations and Initial Semantics*. Springer-Verlag, Berlin, 1985.

[ES89] Ehrich, H.-D.; Sernadas, A.: Algebraic Implementation of Objects over Objects. In: deRoever, W. (ed.): *Stepwise Refinement of Distributed Systems: Models, Formalisms, Correctness (Proc. REX'89)*, Mood (NL), 1989. LNCS 394, Springer Verlag, Berlin, 1989, pp. 239–266.

[ES91] Ehrich, H.-D.; Sernadas, A.: Fundamental Object Concepts and Constructions. In: Saake, G.; Sernadas, A. (eds.): *Information Systems – Correctness and Reusability. (Workshop IS-CORE '91, ESPRIT BRA WG 3023, Selected Papers)*, London, 1991. TU Braunschweig, Informatik-Bericht 91-03, 1991.

[ESS90] Ehrich, H.-D.; Sernadas, A.; Sernadas, C.: From Data Types to Object Types. *Journal on Information Processing and Cybernetics EIK*, Vol. 26, No. 1-2, 1990, pp. 33–48.

[ESS92]   Ehrich, H.-D.; Saake, G.; Sernadas, A.: Concepts of Object-Orientation. In: Studer, R. (ed.): *Proc. of the 2nd Workshop of "Informationssysteme und Künstliche Intelligenz"*, Ulm (FRG), 1992. IFB 303, Springer-Verlag, Berlin, 1992, pp. 1–19.

[FM91]   Fiadeiro, J.; Maibaum, T.: Temporal Reasoning over Deontic Specifications. *Journal of Logic and Computation*, Vol. 1, No. 3, 1991, pp. 357–395.

[FSMS90]   Fiadeiro, J.; Sernadas, C.; Maibaum, T.; Saake, G.: Proof-Theoretic Semantics of Object-Oriented Specification Constructs. In: Meersman, R.; Kent, W.; Khosla, S. (eds.): *Object-Oriented Databases: Analysis, Design and Construction (Proc. IFIP WG 2.6 Working Conference DS-4*, Windermere (UK), 1990. North-Holland, Amsterdam, 1991, pp. 243–284.

[HJS92]   Hartmann, T.; Jungclaus, R.; Saake, G.: Aggregation in a Behavior Oriented Object Model. In: *Proc. ECOOP'92*. Springer, LNCS Series, Berlin, 1992. *To appear.*

[HK87]   Hull, R.; King, R.: Semantic Database Modeling: Survey, Applications, and Research Issues. *ACM Computing Surveys*, Vol. 19, No. 3, 1987, pp. 201–260.

[JHSS91]   Jungclaus, R.; Hartmann, T.; Saake, G.; Sernadas, C.: Introduction to TROLL – A Language for Object-Oriented Specification of Information Systems. In: Saake, G.; Sernadas, A. (eds.): *Information Systems – Correctness and Reusability. (Workshop IS-CORE '91, ESPRIT BRA WG 3023, Selected Papers)*, London, 1991. TU Braunschweig, Informatik-Bericht 91-03, 1991.

[JSH91]   Jungclaus, R.; Saake, G.; Hartmann, T.: Language Features for Object-Oriented Conceptual Modeling. In: Teory, T.J. (ed.): *Proc. 10th Int. Conf. on the ER-approach*, San Mateo, 1991. pp. 309–324.

[JSHS91]   Jungclaus, R.; Saake, G.; Hartmann, T.; Sernadas, C.: Object-Oriented Specification of Information Systems: The TROLL Language. Technical Report 91-04, TU Braunschweig, 1991.

[JSS91]   Jungclaus, R.; Saake, G.; Sernadas, C.: Formal Specification of Object Systems. In: Abramsky, S.; Maibaum, T. (eds.): *Proc. TAPSOFT'91 Vol. 2*, Brighton, 1991. LNCS 494, Springer-Verlag, Berlin, 1991, pp. 60–82.

[Mey88]   Meyer, B.: *Object-Oriented Software Construction*. Prentice-Hall, Englewood Cliffs, NJ, 1988.

[PM88]   Peckham, J.; Maryanski, F.: Semantic Data Models. *ACM Computing Surveys*, Vol. 20, No. 3, 1988, pp. 153–189.

[SE90]   Sernadas, A.; Ehrich, H.-D.: What Is an Object, After All? In: Meersman, R.; Kent, W.; Khosla, S. (eds.): *Object-Oriented Databases: Analysis, Design and Construction (Proc. IFIP WG 2.6 Working Conference DS-4*, Windermere (UK), 1990. North-Holland, Amsterdam, 1991, pp. 39–70.

[SFSE89]   Sernadas, A.; Fiadeiro, J.; Sernadas, C.; Ehrich, H.-D.: The Basic Building Blocks of Information Systems. In: Falkenberg, E.; Lindgreen, P. (eds.): *Information System Concepts: An In-Depth Analysis*, Namur (B), 1989. North-Holland, Amsterdam, 1989, pp. 225–246.

[SJ90]   Saake, G.; Jungclaus, R.: Information about Objects versus Derived Objects. In: Göers, J.; Heuer, A. (eds.): *Second Workshop on Foundations and Languages for Data and Objects*, Aigen (A), 1990. Informatik-Bericht 90/3, Technische Universität Clausthal, pp. 59–70.

[SJ91]   Saake, G.; Jungclaus, R.: Specification of Database Dynamics in the TROLL-Language. In: Harper, D.; Norrie, M. (eds.): *Proc. Int. Workshop Specification of Database Systems*, Glasgow, 1991. Springer-Verlag, London, 1992, pp. 228–245.

[SJE91]   Saake, G.; Jungclaus, R.; Ehrich, H.-D.: Object-Oriented Specification and Stepwise Refinement. In: *Proc. IFIP TC 6 Int. Workshop on Open Distributed Processing*, Berlin, 1991. North-Holland, Amsterdam. *To appear.*

[SJS91]   Saake, G.; Jungclaus, R.; Sernadas, S.: Abstract data type semantics for many-sorted object query algebras. In: Thalheim, B.; Demetrovics, J.; Gerhardt, H.-D. (eds.): *Proceedings 3rd. Symp. on Mathematical Fundamentals of Database and Knowledge Base Systems MFDBS-91*, Rostock, 1991. LNCS 495, Springer-Verlag, Berlin, 1991, pp. 291–307.

[SLT90]   Scholl, M.; Laasch, C.; Tresch, M.: Views in Object-Oriented Databases. In: Göers, J.; Heuer, A. (eds.): *Proc. 2nd Workshop on Foundations of Models and Languages for Data and Objects*, Aigen, Austria, 1990. Informatik-Bericht 90/3, TU Clausthal-Zellerfeld, Germany, pp. 37–58.

[SSE87]   Sernadas, A.; Sernadas, C.; Ehrich, H.-D.: Object-Oriented Specification of Databases: An Algebraic Approach. In: Hammerslay, P. (ed.): *Proc. 13th Int. Conf. on Very Large Databases VLDB'87*, Brighton (GB), 1987. Morgan-Kaufmann, Palo Alto, 1987, pp. 107–116.

[UD86]   Urban, S. D.; Delcambre, L.: An Analysis of the Structural, Dynamic, and Temporal Aspects of Semantic Data Models. In: *Proc. Int. Conf. on Data Engineering*, Los Angeles, 1986. ACM, New York, 1986, pp. 382–387.

[Weg87]   Wegner, P.: Dimensions of Object-Based Language Design. In: *OOPSLA Conference Proceedings*, Orlando, FL, 1987. ACM, New York, 1987, pp. 168–182. (Special Issue of SIGPLAN Notices, Vol. 22, No. 12, November 1987).

[Wie90]   Wieringa, R. J.: *Algebraic Foundations for Dynamic Conceptual Models*. PhD thesis, Vrije Universiteit, Amsterdam, 1990.

THE MEIKO COMPUTING SURFACE:
A PARALLEL & SCALABLE OPEN SYSTEMS
PLATFORM FOR ORACLE

Andrew Holman,
Meiko Limited,
650 Aztec West,
Bristol BS12 4SD.

Abstract

The Meiko Computing Surface is a massively parallel distributed memory computer system based on multiple SPARC processors. Each Sparc module has its own local memory and interacts with other modules and the parallel filing systems through a high performance scalable internal network.

Meiko in conjunction with Oracle have implemented the ORACLE parallel server (ORACLE V6.2) and toolset for the Computing Surface. The ORACLE parallel server fully exploits the distributed memory multiprocessing architecture of the Computing Surface, providing a cost effective and scalable high performance RDBMS and application server.

The implementation of the ORACLE parallel server, ORACLE toolset and applications is the result of over 18 months of close collaboration between Meiko and Oracle. Following an intensive beta test phase at selected sites and a rigorous QA and validation process within Oracle, the development was announced as full product status in October 1991. The solutions now available from Meiko and Oracle provide a uniquely flexible and scalable environment which is in tune with new business practices and organisational trends. As an enterprise-wide IT infrastructure, the Computing Surface can be tailored to the precise requirements of the business.

- A predictable level of service can be provided at all times and to all classes of user because the workload can be balanced evenly across the system.

- Conflicting workloads such as transaction processing and information systems can be support concurrently without one affecting the performance of any other.

- The system is responsive to change - capable of accommodating new applications and functions and growing to meet new demands.

This paper discusses the development, key features and benefits of the Meiko Computing Surface and details the implementation of the ORACLE parallel server.

Introduction

The general purpose, commercial, large scale system market has historically been dominated by proprietary mainframe systems. Until recently, the technological limitations and immaturity of the hardware and software environment offered by Open Systems computing has largely prevented the penetration of such systems into very large scale computer applications.

This position is changing rapidly as the commercial pressures which have driven Open Systems into the mid-range computer market are being felt even at the top end of the computer marketplace. Such commercial pressures, in combination with the rapid maturation of Open Systems functionality and performance, have created the opportunity for genuine mainframe-class computing based on an Open Systems platform.

The Meiko Computing Surface represents the first of a new class of computer system. It combines the benefits of distributed computing with the management control, functionality, and performance traditionally provided by large mainframe class proprietary systems. A unique design allows it to deliver flexibility and price/performance normally only associated with smaller machines, whilst providing scalability and overall system performance which cannot be matched by any machines founded on older generation technology. The design is upgradable over time, being implemented to allow the easy incorporation of newer, more powerful technologies as they emerge. It guarantees protection of the original investment by continuing to provide the user with a leading edge, cost effective computing resource.

The Meiko Computing Surface design strategy is founded on the following basic components:

- Processing capabilities provided by standard, commodity microprocessors and I/O sub-systems, capable of integrating new technology as it becomes available.

- Total commitment to Open Systems Software Standards.

- Compatible, fine grained scalability from deskside to mainframe/supercomputer.

- Parallel processing technology to provide the power needed, whatever the workload.

By adopting this strategy, the Computing Surface will become recognised as the definitive solution to the computing problems of the 90s and beyond.

There are great pressures on all organisations to be more customer orientated, to provide an ever increasing array of new products and services, to react faster to change and to provide better return on investment.

Many organisations recognise that flexibility of approach in a dynamic environment is a key success facilitator. That flexibility is founded on knowledge, that knowledge on information. Increasingly the most valuable asset of any organisation is its knowledge base. The organisations which will be successful are those that make better use of their knowledge base.

The need for an organisation to access its data in the most flexible way has prompted a large scale migration of databases from a hierarchical to a relational form. This combined with increasing levels of on-line transaction processing (OLTP) and demand for more complex information and decision support systems requires the provision of massive levels of computer power, well beyond that of today's fastest mainframes.

At the same time organisations are demanding these levels of performance, commercial imperatives require substantial cost reductions in their IT infrastructures. It is these diametrically conflicting needs that solutions from Meiko address.

Meiko, in partnership with Oracle, have implemented the ORACLE Parallel Server (ORACLE RDBMS V6.2) and toolset for the Computing Surface. The ORACLE Parallel Server fully exploits the distributed memory multiprocessing architecture of the Computing Surface, providing a cost effective and scalable high performance RDBMS and application server.

The implementation of the ORACLE Parallel Server, ORACLE toolset, and applications is the result of several years of close collaboration between Meiko and Oracle. Following a beta test phase at selected sites, and a QA and validation process within Oracle, the development was announced as full product status in October 1991.

This paper discusses the development, key features, and benefits of the Meiko Computing Surface, and details the implementation of the ORACLE Parallel Server.

The Development of Multiprocessor Architectures

Today's highly parallel computers employ multiple processors, sometimes many hundreds, all operating simultaneously to solve data and compute intensive problems. The Meiko Computing Surface is an example of such an architecture; it is a distributed memory parallel computer. Each Computing Surface processing module has its own powerful processor and local memory, together with communication processors to allow message passing to other processing elements in the machine.

A wide variety of computer architectures exist today. The traditional or Von Neuman architecture is based on a processor-memory pair connected by a bus (Figure 1). Although the performance of these systems has improved dramatically through advances in the underlying technology, they are still limited by the power of the single processor.

More powerful computers are now available with multiple processors, each operating independently. These machines are classified as Multiple Instruction Multiple Data (MIMD) systems. MIMD systems are highly flexible and are applied to a wide range of commercial applications. MIMD is now the dominant architecture of high performance computer systems.

There are two distinct MIMD architectures:

- Shared memory systems or Symmetric Multiprocessing (SMP).

- Distributed memory multiprocessor systems (DMPP).

Fig. 1   Single Processor Architecture

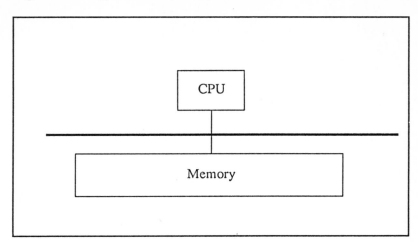

Symmetric Multiprocessors

A natural extension to single processor systems is achieved by connecting more processors to the same bus (Figure 2). All these processors share and must compete for access to the common memory/bus system and a single operating system image.

To support these processors the bus and memory systems must offer very high performance, and are often constructed from exotic and expensive technology. Even so, as each additional processor is configured, both the system's processing efficiency and its cost effectiveness decrease rapidly. This diminishing return is such that SMP systems rarely offer useful performance improvements beyond 4 to 8 processors.

The shared memory architecture of SMP systems is not scalable and limits the maximum attainable performance.

Fig. 2   SMP Architecture

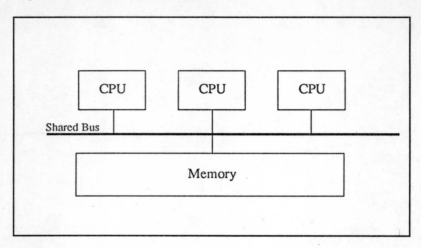

Most of today's mid-range and mainframes systems have an SMP architecture, and as a result suffer from poor scalability and limited performance. Although SMP machines have become commonplace through the 1980's and early 1990's, they will be rapidly superseded by systems which are inherently more scalable.

Distributed Memory Systems

In distributed memory computers each processor has exclusive access to its own private memory system. As more processors are added, both the processing power and the bus/memory bandwidth increase linearly. Since there is generally only one or a few processors connected to each bus/memory system, more cost effective memory technology can be used. In order that multiple processing elements can co-operate, a means for passing data between them must be provided. The communication medium, or interconnect, is a key feature of the distributed memory architecture.

Networks of workstations (Figure 3) or clustered computers (Figure 4) can be considered as distributed memory systems, however the communications medium (Ethernet, for example) is of limited fixed bandwidth and so, like the SMP common bus/memory architecture, constrains the scalability of these systems.

Fig. 3   Network System

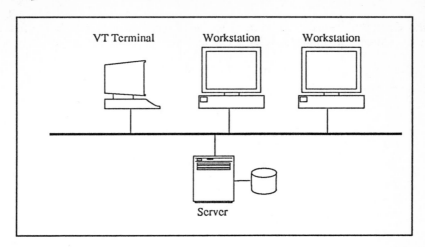

Fig. 4   Cluster System

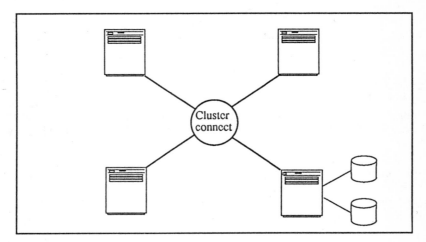

The Meiko Computing Surface

The Meiko Computing Surface (Figure 5) is a massively parallel distributed memory system, with a high performance, fully scalable, internal communications medium.

Fig. 5   Meiko Computing Surface

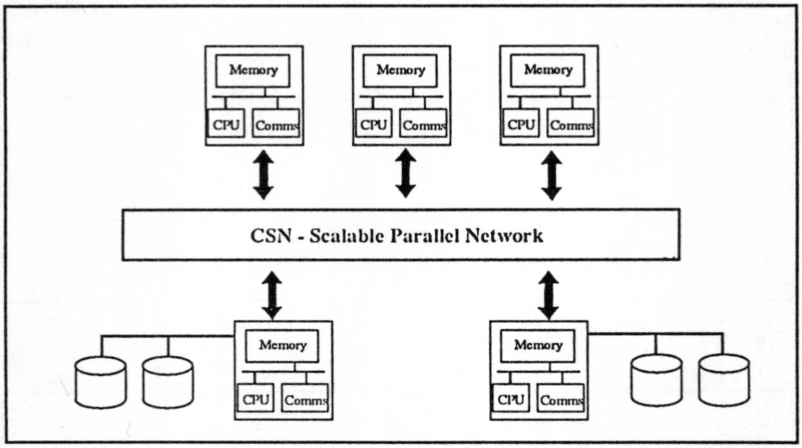

The system comprises multiple modules, each having a processor with exclusive access to its own dedicated local memory. The processor does not have to compete for access to its memory with any other processors in the system. This approach, in contrast to the SMP architecture, allows very cost effective commodity memory technology to be deployed.

For multiple processors in a distributed memory parallel system to be exploited on a single task (for example a RDBMS) they must be able to co-operate, in order to co-operate they need to communicate. The capabilities of the inter-processor communication medium are critical in the provision of a fully scalable computer system.

In addition to the processor and memory, each module in the Computing Surface has dedicated communication processors, each providing multiple network links. These links are used to construct a very high performance parallel internal network known as the Computing Surface Network (CSN). As the CSN is an internal and reliable network, very efficient light-weight communication protocols are used; this both reduces the overhead associated with protocol processing and ensures efficient sustainable high performance communication rates. Advanced network routing facilities allow multiple modules to communicate with each other along parallel and independent paths through the CSN.

The system software interface to the CSN provides explicit support for a client/server approach to software design and implementation. Systems and application software are constructed as a collection of client and server processes. The CSN interface provides an abstraction of the physical communication medium to the client and server processes allowing them the key flexibility to be located arbitrarily within the machine.

As modules are added to a Computing Surface, the processing power, memory bandwidth, and the CSN performance all increase linearly and proportionately, providing a fully scalable computer system.

Fig. 6   Computing Surface Scalability

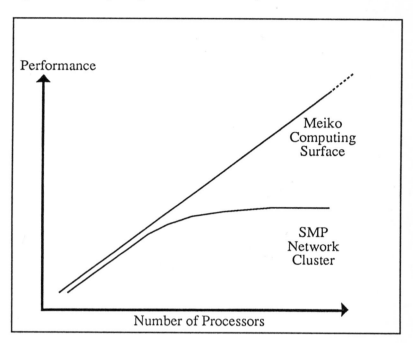

The Computing Surface provides massive absolute scalability (Figure 6), and can be configured in any size from a small desk-side system with a few processors to an enterprise class facility with tens or hundreds of processors.

By exploiting commodity micro-processor, memory, disk and peripheral technology combined with a fully scalable architecture, the Meiko Computing Surface provides the same competitive price/performance for an entry level system as it does for systems with a performance beyond that of today's fastest mainframes (Figure 7). The Meiko Computing Surface can deliver the same functionality and performance as mainframe systems and beyond, but at a fraction of the cost.

104

Fig. 7   Computing Price/Performance

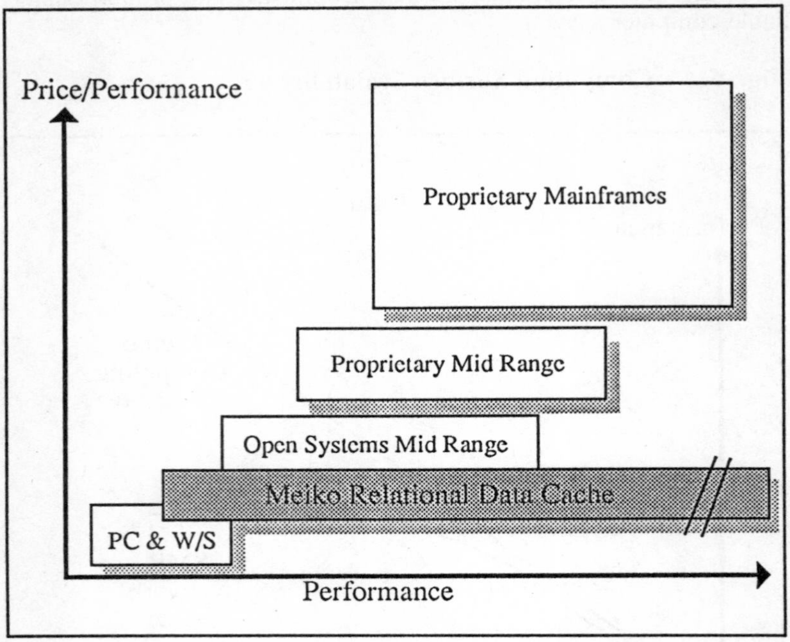

Price/Performance

Proprietary Mainframes

Proprietary Mid Range

Open Systems Mid Range

Meiko Relational Data Cache

PC & W/S

Performance

SPARC Processor Modules

Computing Surface systems for ORACLE are based on multiple SPARC processor modules. The SPARC processor is an Open System design initially developed by Sun Microsystems, and now adopted by a number of major computer system vendors. With many major chip manufacturers innovating and developing within the SPARC definition, the continued availability of higher performance processors at lower cost is guaranteed. As these processors become available, they can easily be integrated into the Computing Surface with no impact on system and application software.

The SPARC processor is well suited to the demands of a multi-process multi-user environment, and as such is a key platform for the future. Apart from the large number of applications currently available, SPARC technology is advancing rapidly as more and more companies worldwide develop SPARC-compatible hardware and software products.

Each SPARC module within the Meiko Computing Surface runs the latest version of Solaris (formerly known as SunOS), perhaps the most widely accepted Unix operating system. The SPARC/Solaris combination is one of the major target platforms for third party software developers. Any software conforming to the SPARC/Solaris application binary interface (ABI), can be run without modification on any ABI compliant platform. This Open System standard means that any one of over 3000 third party applications can run on the Meiko Computing Surface.

Importantly for ORACLE on the Computing Surface, SPARC/Solaris is one of Oracle's major porting platforms, ensuring the continued availability of all latest developments of the ORACLE RDBMS, tools, and applications.

Meiko's SPARC modules support a wide range of third party peripherals, for example optical juke boxes and high performance, high capacity backup units. Many of the industry standard network protocols are supported, for example TCP/IP, DECNET and SNA over Ethernet, FDDI and token ring.

Floating Point Modules

High performance floating point processing modules (based on the Intel i860 for example) are available for the Computing Surface. These modules are typically used for scientific and engineering applications. Within the Computing Surface a large floating point capability can be closely coupled with a high performance ORACLE database, making the Computing Surface a unique system for applications having both RDBMS and data analysis components, such as geographic information systems (GIS) and seismic data processing.

ORACLE Parallel Server on the Computing Surface

With the launch of ORACLE for the Meiko Computing Surface, the benefits of a distributed memory parallel machine are available to mainstream IT users.

Meiko were the first organisation in the world to make the ORACLE Parallel Server available on a massively parallel platform. The implementation of the ORACLE Parallel Server, with the ORACLE toolset and applications, is the result of several years of close collaboration between Meiko and Oracle. Following a beta test phase at selected sites, and a QA and validation process within Oracle, the development was announced as full product status in October 1991.

This partnership between Meiko and Oracle has yielded a high performance implementation of ORACLE which can easily accommodate large networks of users, large databases, many hundreds and thousands of transactions per second (with sub-second response times), and corporate management and executive information systems.

The system offers a predictable level of service to all types of user, a feature only possible with a distributed memory parallel architecture, where the workload can be balanced and managed across all the processors. Conflicting workloads, such as transaction processing and decision support, can be separated within the system so that neither impacts the performance of the other whilst sharing a coherent view of a single database.

The ORACLE Parallel Server

An ORACLE instance is the system code and shared memory which acts as the gateway to the database. The key components of an instance are:

- A single shared memory area, known as the System Global Area (SGA). This is a cache where data is buffered while being read or modified.

- The background and shadow processes which provide system and process monitoring, manipulate data structures in the SGA, and perform database I/O.

The unique innovation of the ORACLE Parallel Server is the ability for multiple instances, each running on separate SPARC nodes in the Computing Surface, to execute transactions concurrently and independently on a single database. Key features of the ORACLE Parallel Server are:

- One or more instances can be started on each processing node in the system.

- Each instance has its own SGA and background processes.

- All instances share the same database files, control files, and redo log files.

- All instances can execute transactions concurrently and independently against the same database.

- Multiple instances accessing a single database in shared mode use an external lock manager to ensure that all the SGAs remain consistent and coherent.

- Specific to the Computing Surface, the database can be striped over many disks.

Applications (for example, SQL*PLUS and SQL*FORMS) access an ORACLE instance through an inter-processor communication (IPC) mechanism known as the two-task architecture. In the two-task architecture, each application task starts a corresponding shadow process. The shadow process is part of the instance, and is used to access the SGA on the application's behalf (Figure 8).

Fig. 8 ORACLE Instance

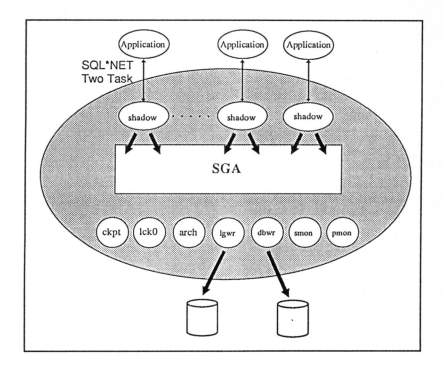

The two-task architecture is exploited by SQL*NET to provide client/server location transparency, allowing applications and instances to run anywhere within the system arbitrarily. The application can even run on a workstation that is connected to a Computing Surface by Ethernet. SQL*NET supports application connection over a variety of protocols, such as TCP/IP and DECnet over Ethernet, pipe on shared memory, and the Computing Surface Network, CSN.

Connection of many applications to multiple instances within the Computing Surface fully exploits the parallel data paths and high performance of the CSN.

ORACLE Support Services

Meiko have invested substantial effort in the design and implementation of a parallel lock manager and parallel filing system to support ORACLE on the Computing Surface (Figure 9). These parallel services are critical in the provision of a fully scalable system; not only must the underlying hardware architecture be inherently scalable but also the system software which runs on it.

The parallel lock manager is used by multiple ORACLE instances to maintain all the SGAs in a coherent and consistent state. Clearly, as the number of processors running ORACLE instances increases, so the demand on the parallel lock manager increases. Meiko's parallel lock manager is fully scalable and can be run over multiple processor nodes, ensuring that lock processing does not become a performance limiting bottleneck.

The parallel file server provides a fast and scalable I/O subsystem. The file server's performance can be scaled as more ORACLE instances are added, an essential requirement to maintain data throughput.

Fig. 9   Oracle Support Services

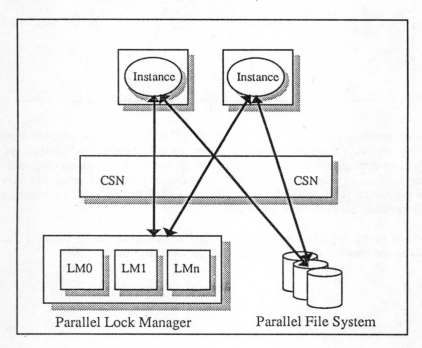

The Parallel Lock Manager

The ORACLE Parallel Server uses an external lock manager service to maintain all the SGAs of a multi instance system in a coherent and consistent state. Only one instance can update a database block at a time. Each ORACLE instance can have an independent connection to multiple lock manager nodes over the CSN.

When an instance wants to update a database block it requests an exclusive lock from the lock manager. If the lock is granted, the instance is able to read the block from the parallel disk subsystem into its SGA where it can be modified. ORACLE employs a lazy locking scheme; an instance will not release a lock held on a block unless the SGA is full and the instance needs to free space to read other blocks, or another instance wants to update the block.

For an instance to update a database block that is already locked by another instance, a mechanism known as 'block pinging' occurs. The instance waiting to update the block requests an exclusive lock from the lock manager. When the lock manager finds that another instance already holds an exclusive lock, it sends a blocking asynchronous trap (AST) to that instance. The instance holding the lock receives the AST, writes the block to disk, and releases its lock. The second instance is granted the exclusive lock and reads the block from the database. As the read of the block occurs soon after the write, the block is likely to be held in the filing system cache, ensuring that block pinging is highly efficient.

Copies of the same block can be held by multiple instances in each of their SGAs for read only. When an instance wants to update the block, an AST is sent to all instances holding read locks causing them to be released.

The parallel lock manager is orthogonal to ORACLE's database locking mechanism. The parallel server supports full unrestricted row level locking, allowing multiple transactions on different processors to modify different rows in the same data block, without ever waiting for each other to release a lock.

The implementation of a fully scalable parallel lock manager with deadlock detection is the result of a significant development effort and investment by Meiko, and is a key component in providing mainframe levels of transaction processing performance and beyond.

Parallel File Server

In order to exploit the potential of a massively parallel ORACLE RDBMS, it is necessary to provide a fast and scalable I/O subsystem; indeed, the design of the disk subsystem is critical to the overall performance of an ORACLE system.

Meiko have implemented a parallel filing system which is exploited automatically by ORACLE instances. The parallel I/O subsystem is based on multiple disk controllers, each with a dedicated high performance processor and large data cache. The parallel I/O subsystem provides multiple independent data paths from disks to the ORACLE instances via the CSN.

The Database Administrator (DBA) is able to specify a striped file with the CREATE DATABASE or CREATE TABLESPACE commands. Striping allows database files, tablespaces (including the system tablespace), and redo log files to be placed over all the disk drives available. File striping ensures uniform access over the whole parallel file system by all the ORACLE instances, so maximising the benefit of concurrent disk I/O and bandwidth.

The specification of a striped file is particularly straightforward, for example, the creation of a 100 Mbyte tablespace over 8 disks as follows:

```
CREATE TABLESPACE eg_tablespace DATAFILE
'dbs {16,BASE:0,7 }:example.dbf' SIZE 100M;
```

This will place the first 16 blocks of the file on the filing system dbs0:, the second 16 blocks on dbs1:, the third on dbs2: and so on.

Once the DBA has striped the database files, the applications are completely unaware that striping has been used. In other systems file striping must be done manually, and database files can not be placed on multiple disks with such fine granularity as on the Computing Surface. The ability to stripe files automatically over many disks significantly eases the DBA's task of eliminating disk bottlenecks and hot spots.

Meiko's parallel filing system is based on SCSI, the industry's dominant disk and peripheral interface standard. Disks for this popular standard are available as commodity items from many manufacturers who are continuously developing higher performance and capacity devices at lower costs.

Application Processing

The most significant goal of the Open System approach is the protection of on-going investment in applications by providing a high degree of portability and interoperability across a wide range of platforms.

In addition to running multi-instance ORACLE on the Computing Surface, further processing resource can be allocated to ORACLE and other Unix based applications. These applications benefit from high performance connections to the ORACLE instances over the CSN. Since SPARC modules are used for these applications, many thousands of applications are immediately available to run on the Computing Surface. Any application developed for the Meiko Computing Surface will run in binary form on other SPARC ABI compliant platforms and will have source level compatibility with other Unix systems.

Resource Management - Partioning and Load Balancing

A benefit of the Computing Surface's distributed memory multi-processor architecture is the ability to partition or *firewall* the machine into separate groups or domains of processors. Each group of processors can be assigned to the needs of a specific user community.

The load balancing mechanism developed by Meiko is the key technology allowing multiple SPARC processors and instances to be viewed as a single logical resource by users and applications (Figure 10). Load balancing also ensures that all work, both front-end application and backend database processing, are spread evenly amongst the available resource, thereby maximising the system's efficiency.

Fig. 10   Load Balancing

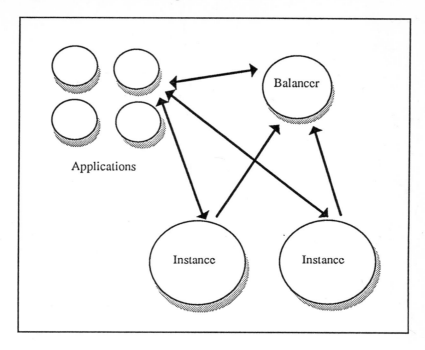

Multiple load balancers can be used in a single system, each with an associated group of processors. Specifically for ORACLE, several instances can be grouped into a *class*, with each class having a single load balancer. Users and applications do not connect to individual instances but to balancers. When a connection is made to a balancer, it redirects the connection to the least loaded instance in its class.

A unique benefit of the Meiko's system is the ability to separate conflicting workloads, such as OLTP and decision support, so that neither impacts the performance of any other, whilst maintaining a coherent view of a single database (Figure 11). Traditional technology has attempted to provide this functionality by using multiple computer systems each with their own copy of the database. This approach requires substantially more complex system management and administration, for example the transfer of large data volumes between machines, and results in out of date information and inconsistent databases.

Fig. 11 Processor Grouping

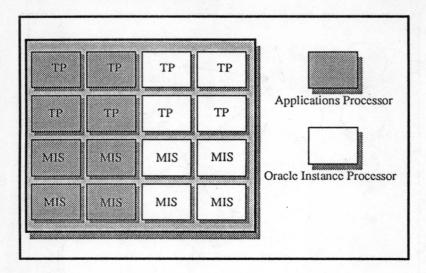

The Meiko Computing Surface is unique in its ability to deliver such levels of control. Groups and classes of processors and instances allow the machine to be partitioned in a flexible way to guarantee all users a predictable performance.

Resilience

The architecture of the Meiko Computing Surface is inherently resilient. The system can provide a graceful degradation in service, rather than a catastrophic loss of the whole system as is the case for shared memory technologies.

The failure, due to hardware or software errors, of one or more instances of an ORACLE parallel server does not bring down the whole database. Another instance that is still running automatically performs on-line recovery for the failed instances.

When an instance fails, the system monitor background process of another instance detects the failure, automatically rolls forward all changes the failed instance committed and recorded in the redo log, and rolls back any incomplete transactions. No data is lost from transactions already committed by the failed instance.

Current disk technology typically has a 250,000 hour mean time between failure (MTBF), which is outstanding for such high performance mechanical devices. Despite this, for any large database server the disks and their power supplies are usually the most unreliable part of the whole system.

Meiko addresses this critical data reliability and availability issue by supporting an emerging and important standard known as RAID (Redundant Array of Inexpensive Disks). RAID arrays are available in a range of configurations the choice of which is determined by the operational performance, capacity, reliability and availability requirements. The RAID-5 configuration is considered best suited for supporting large high performance relational database systems. In RAID-5, data and parity information are placed on a subsystem of 5 disk drives. If a disk in a RAID-5 system fails, the RAID controller rebuilds its data using the data and parity from the remaining functional drives and the system continues to provide an uninterrupted service. For example in a 100 disk system the use of RAID-5 can reduce the chance of losing data in one operational year from 99.7% to 0.4%.

Conclusion

A new era of IT is unfolding.

The Open Systems solutions now available from Meiko and Oracle provide a uniquely flexible and scalable environment which is in tune with new business practices and organisational trends.

As an enterprise-wide IT infrastructure, the Computing Surface can be tailored to the precise requirements of the business.

• The absolute, fine grained scalability of the Meiko Computing Surface allows systems to be configured with performance levels beyond that of today's fastest mainframes.

• By exploiting commodity components, Meiko can deliver equivalent function and performance of mainframe technology at a fraction of the cost.

• A predictable level of service can be provided at all times and to all classes of user; the workload can be balanced evenly across the system.

• Conflicting workloads, such as transaction processing and information systems, can be supported concurrently without one affecting the performance of any other, whilst accessing a single corporate database.

• The system is responsive to change; capable of accommodating new applications and functions, and growing to meet new demands.

Meiko's new IT systems provide a high performance ORACLE environment which cannot be outgrown.

References

1   Computer Architectures: A Quantitative Approach.
Hennessy and Patterson

2   ORACLE for the Meiko Computing Surface.
Installation and User Guide. Oracle

3   ORACLE RDBMS Database Administrator's Guide.
(Version 6.0). Oracle

4   ORACLE RDBMS version 6.2.
Database Administrator's Guide - Addendum. Oracle

5   Database Management Systems for Parallel Computers.
ORACLE Technical paper - John Spiers, June 1990.

6   Principles of Distributed Database Systems.
Prentice-Hall: M. Tamer, Patrick Valduriez.
1991 ISBN 0-13-715681-2

A STUDY OF A PARALLEL DATABASE MACHINE AND ITS PERFORMANCE THE NCR/TERADATA DBC/1012

Jon Page
Professional Services Manager
NCR/Teradata
Alwyn House
31, Windsor St.
Chertsey
Surrey KT16 8AT

ABSTRACT

Parallel processing has long been recognised as a highly efficient method of applying large amounts of computing power to specialised applications. The world of commercial computing however, has for the most part, failed to supply suitable work to justify the creation of commercial parallel systems. The advent of the relational model, with its parallel language - SQL - and the need to hold large amounts of data, has given this opportunity. This paper introduces some of the benefit to be gained from large scale parallel hardware using the Teradata DBC/1012 database computer, currently in use at many large commercial organisations, as a prime example.

INTRODUCTION

The advantage of the relational approach to data management is that objects of importance to a business can be represented in tables which are both simple to understand and unambiguous in content. With such tables, questions such as who is buying which product or which product is the most popular for a particular class of customer can be answered through the use of the standard Structured Query Language (SQL), with no knowledge of the physical format of the data.

Relational data storage and access is now available through relational database management systems (RDBMS) on all computing environments from Personal Computers through to the largest Mainframe systems. However their benefit is perhaps most dramatically seen, when the relational facility is applied to very large volumes of data, perhaps those typically found in large retail or finance organisations. For marketing staff, the ability to examine the full detail of all transactions occurring over several years may be a requirement in order to analyse in depth, the buying patterns of the customers. In this case the tables grow to extremely large sizes, and tables holding hundreds of millions of rows are not uncommon. Flexibility and the ease of data manipulation, become imperative.

The challenge set to all computer and RDBMS manufacturers who wish to supply solutions to such problems, is to build a system which can handle these large volumes of data for both pre-defined and ad-hoc queries arising from both batch and on-line systems. The combination of complex ad-hoc requirements and high OLTP performance cannot be achieved by conventional computing architectures. This paper seeks to illustrate a parallel architected Database machine, that has proved time and time again, that the goals above can be achieved in a commercially viable way.

MICROPROCESSOR DOWNSIZING

The table below shows the relative growth of Mainframe and microprocessing power during the 1980's. The faster growth rate of the microprocessors has arisen because of their increasing complexity in terms of both word-length and instruction set, whereas their alternative, the Mainframe processors, are limited to fixed architectures. Microprocessors leverage technology by gaining both speed and complexity benefits as technology shrinks in size.

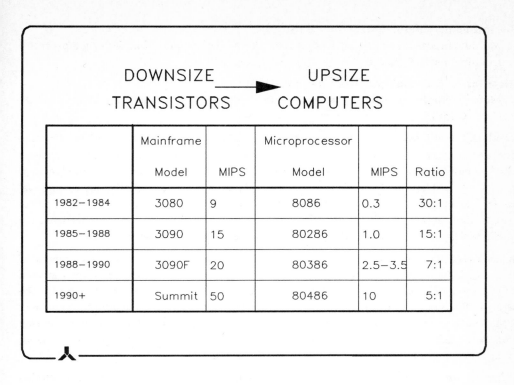

DOWNSIZE ➤ UPSIZE
TRANSISTORS   COMPUTERS

	Mainframe		Microprocessor		
	Model	MIPS	Model	MIPS	Ratio
1982–1984	3080	9	8086	0.3	30:1
1985–1988	3090	15	80286	1.0	15:1
1988–1990	3090F	20	80386	2.5–3.5	7:1
1990+	Summit	50	80486	10	5:1

Fig 1. Computer Downsizing

The challenge however, is to be able to devise an architecture which can harness the power of these new devices for special applications, such as relational databases.

It has long been recognized that for any given state of processor technology, limited by the size of electronic components and the speed of mechanical components such as disks, the route to high power systems comes from replication. The nature of this replication governs the nature of the applications which such a system can process efficiently.

Computer systems making use of replication are generally categorised according to the Instruction/Data stream classification, as shown below:

Single Instruction Single Data Stream
The classic Von Neumann computer, with a simple processor operating on one instruction at a time (e.g. IBM 7090)

Multiple Instruction Single Data Stream (MISD)
Pipelined single processor systems, with separate parts of several instructions being processed in parallel for a single program (e.g. IBM 3083, ICL 3900)

Single Instruction Multiple Data Stream (SIMD)

Multiple processors operating synchronously on a single application, with each processor handling a set of data (e.g. AMT DAP, Goodyear MPP)

Multiple Instruction Multiple Data Stream (MIMD)

Multiple processors operating independently on individual sets of data (e.g. Denelcor HEP, Cray X-MP)

Conventional multiprocessing systems such as the IBM 3090/600, with 6 CPU's operating independently, may be considered as MIMD systems, but the convention used above assumes that the complete power of the system can be harnessed to a single program (multiprocessing) rather than to aid multiple job streams (multiprogramming). Until recently, no commercial computer was available which successfully used MIMD techniques to provide very high power for single applications. All the SIMD and MIMD systems described above originate from the scientific world, with no equivalent systems for the general commercial workload.

With the advent of Relational Databases, which give the possibility of rapid development of flexible management information systems, the need for commercial computer power has risen rapidly. For typical marketing applications, where millions of customer records need to be joined to millions of order records, the power of a single conventional CPU using software-based RDBMS's such as Ingres, Oracle or DB2, is inadequate. The challenge, therefore, is to develop a parallel architecture specifically to handle this relational processing. As with scientific systems, the interconnection of the processors is of prime importance.

Relational processes are a combination of operations on single tables and operations combining tables (Join, Union, Intersect, Minus). Since the relational model allows such flexible access to data, any network of processors, designed to work in harmony when answering relational queries must be capable of supporting movement of data rows between all processors in the system, because to join rows, demands that they be on the same processor (or at least, in shared memory).

The enormous sizes of some existing relational databases also dictate that the system must combine both solid state and disk technology, with parallelism, to provide high CPU power and high bandwidth to the disks. A picture emerges therefore of a sophisticated computer utilising parallel processing mechanisms to give access to enormous amounts of relationally held data.

DBC/1012 CHARACTERISTICS

In order to meet these challenges families of Database Machines have arisen each bringing unique characteristics to solve the problems so far described. These machines vary from the Oracle Accelerators back-ending VAX/Oracle systems, to ICLs well established CAFS engine, sold today, largely aimed at improving the performance of Ingres. The older Britten Lee systems were sold successfully for many years and are now owned and marketed by NCR/Teradata as the Server series. However, the most powerful of these systems used today in the commercial arena, is without doubt the NCR/Teradata DBC/1012, which is a dedicated relational database machine, based on a parallel processing architecture. It is the market leader amongst database machines in current commercial usage, having a presence in the worlds major airlines, finance institutions and retail chains. In fact the DBC/1012 was originally designed to meet the needs of Citibank in New York who required a system capable of holding up to 1 Terabyte (10^{12}) bytes of data, accessed through many host systems, to act as a single data store for all customer information. The DBC/1012 is now accompanied in the NCR/Teradata product range by a similar product, the NCR 3600 and both of these machines will be the forerunners of the massively parallel UNIX based NCR 3700 computer destined for the marketplace in the near future.

A fundamental characteristic of the DBC/1012, as we have seen, is that is utilises standard microprocessor technology in a system designed purely for relational database processing. Its design ensures that it is never constrained by any particular architecture or hardware limitations, but we should remember that this specialised design ensures that it can in no way be considered a general purpose computer.

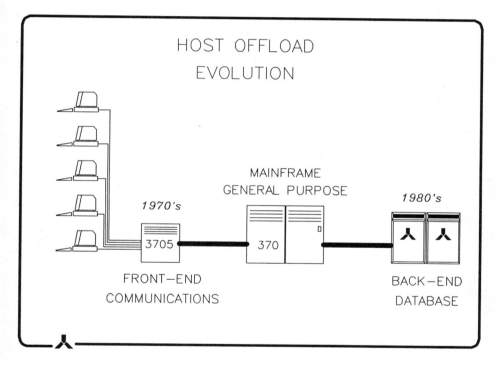

Fig 2. Host Offload

In fact the DBC/1012 does not function in a 'stand alone' mode, but requires at least one general purpose system to connect to and house its user population. This is called the 'host' system, and the job of the DBC/1012 is to off-load from this system, all the work associated with relational database management and access. This off-loading from a centralised and general purpose 'host' machine is not a new idea. Fig 2 shows that for many years we have been off-loading communications processing from our mainframes using specially designed Front End Processors - doesn't it make as much sense to offload the DBMS work?

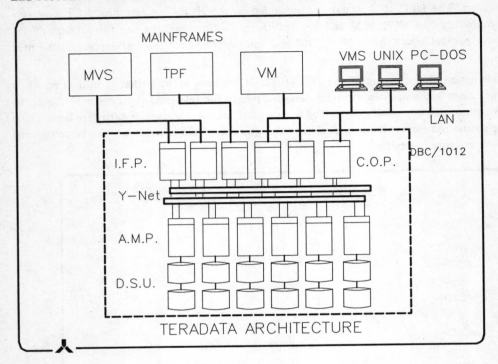

Fig 3. The DBC/1012 Architecture

Fig 3 shows the basic components of the DBC/1012. The system consists of three types of processors, all using the same basic technology.

The three types of processor are:

Access Module Processor (AMP)

The AMP is the database engine of the DBC, which manages database rows held on its associated disk storage units (DSU's). The AMP handles all aspects of database access, searching, updating etc.

Interface Processor (IFP)

The IFP has the role of managing the flow of requests and results between the DBC and an IBM, Bull or Unisys Block Multiplexor Channel. The IFP accepts SQL requests from the host system, chooses the appropriate sequence of actions, passes the actions to the AMP's to be processed, then returns the results to the host.

Communications Processor (COP)

The COP has essentially the same function as the IFP, but instead of handling a block multiplexor channel, attaches directly to an Ethernet, and through this network to PC's, various Unix minicomputers and workstations, and the DEC VAX system operating under VMS.

HOW DOES THE DBC/1012 WORK?

As described above, one of the prime objectives of a parallel system is to be able to deliver the complete power of the system to a single 'query'. For this to be possible using a relational operation, the tables participating in the query must be available to all the processors in the system. On the DBC/1012 each table is hash-distributed to all AMPs, so that each AMP receives an equal portion of the rows. This enables a query that requires all rows to be accessed, such as a full table scan, to be processed in parallel by all the AMPs. As shown below, the power of the DBC/1012 is thus directly proportional to the number of AMPs in the system.

One of the initial design objectives of the DBC/1012 was that it should be a single corporate data store, capable of being accessed through many different host systems. Figure 3 shows a configuration attached to three IBM hosts, under the VM, TPF and MVS operating systems, and a network of PCs and minicomputers. As illustrated, this connectivity is made possible by the IFP and COP processors.

As well as providing physical connections, the IFP and COP systems also handle any data conversions required between the DBC/1012 and the hosts, such as ASCII to EBCDIC, IEEE to IBM floating point, and byte conversions to the Bull system. All operations performed inside the DBC/1012 are identical, regardless of the host from which the request originated.

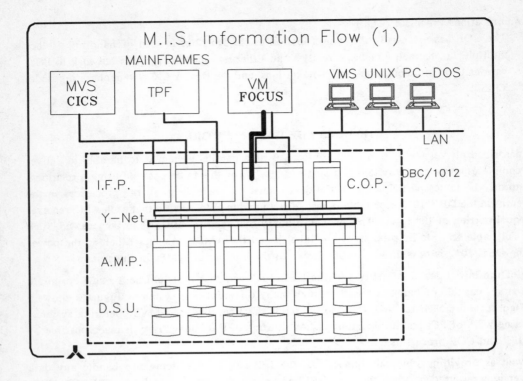

Fig 4. Origination of an MIS Request

The simplest way to explain the operation of the DBC/1012 is to follow the route of a query (transaction) from the user attached to an application on one of the host systems. Fig 4 shows a Management Information System query being generated by the user of a FOCUS system running under VM.

FOCUS will automatically generate the required SQL to formulate the query using the definitions stored within its own data dictionary, in the same way as it would for DB2 or SQL/DS. In the DBC/1012 case, the SQL is passed to the DBC/1012 via the host connection (channel). The SQL, still in its textual form, is received by the IFP.

The IFP handles the initial stage of SQL operation by parsing the SQL statement to validate that it is a legal statement and that the user has the access rights to perform the requested action. Assuming a valid statement, the IFP then chooses the optimum access path to process the request. The choice of such an optimum access path is based on a simple costing algorithm. The optimiser will generate as many access plans as it can to answer any query and associate a cost with each, prior to picking the cheapest and generating executable 'steps' from it. When dealing with large amounts of data, and processing complex SQL queries, it is very important that the costs associated with specific plans are accurate. To assist, the DBC/1012 allows for the collection of detailed statistics describing the demographics of data stored in its tables. Such information will record the number of rows in the table, the number of distinct values, and the maximum and minimum values on a column by column basis. In addition to these figures the optimiser will also sort the data and divide it into several partitions before calculating, for each partition, the maximum and minimum values, the number of rows, number of distinct values, the most common value and the number of rows having that most common value. Such detailed statistics enable the optimiser for example, to swap between indexed access and full table scans dependent on the data values supplied in WHERE constraints.

The IFP does not, itself, hold any of the relational data, and at this stage must hand the steps of the request to the AMPs for the actual database operations.

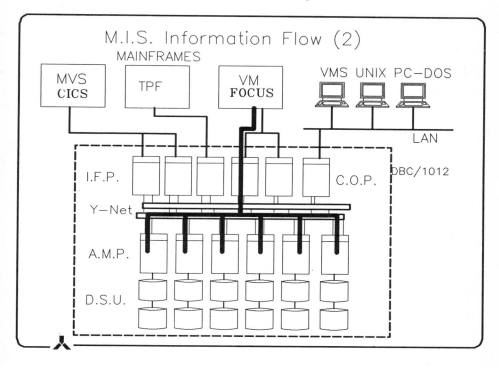

Fig 5. Executing Data Retrieval

The architectural feature which enables the DBC/1012 to combine the power of multiple processors in answering a single SQL query, is the method of distributing data across all the processors. If we wish to make all the AMPs contribute to the processing of a request, they must all share part of the data.

In fact, the data for each relational table in the system is spread equally across all processors and disks, through the use of a special algorithm and the definition of a 'primary index' for each table. It is the value of a rows primary index that will determine the AMP that will store it. For example, on a 10 processor system, each AMP will hold 10% of each and every table. Because the data is evenly spread, each processor can contribute equally to handling the request, as shown in Fig 5.

The IFP hands each stage (step) of the request to all the AMPs, which then work independently on their own portions of the data. If movement of data is required for complex relational join operations, this is carried out automatically through the Y-Net.

When every AMP has finished its task, which may include selection, joining, sorting and formatting of the data, the IFP manages transmission of the result set back to the host system. Special logic within the Y-Net ensures that partial result sets, which may have been sorted on the individual AMPs, are correctly merged on their way back to the host.

The complete process, from host to IFP to AMP and back via the IFP to the host, is designed to meet the original criterion of host offload, since the DBC/1012 has removed from the host all aspects of relational database handling, from parsing through to final result presentation.

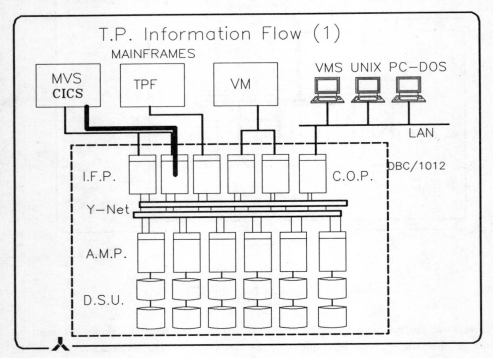

Fig 6. The TP Request

The case described above, where the parallel processing capability is brought to bear on a large MIS query, can be distinguished from the case of simple transactions such as found in high volume On-Line Transaction Processing Systems. Here, access is typically required to single rows (records), accessed by keys (indexes). In this case the requirement is to handle many simple transactions simultaneously, rather than large complex transactions.

The DBC/1012 architecture is designed to handle multiple simple transactions through the same distribution technique and multiprocessing system as used for the complex transactions.

Figure 6 shows a transaction arising from a a high volume MVS/CICS system, where the original application may well be a COBOL programme with embedded SQL. As before, the transaction is passed, untranslated, to the IFP. During the analyse of the request, the IFP will have determined that the request is for an indexed retrieval, and generates the appropriate single AMP step.

This step, as before, is sent to the Y-Net, but this time is routed, through the distribution algorithm, directly to the AMP that contains the target row. All other AMPs are unaffected by the transaction.

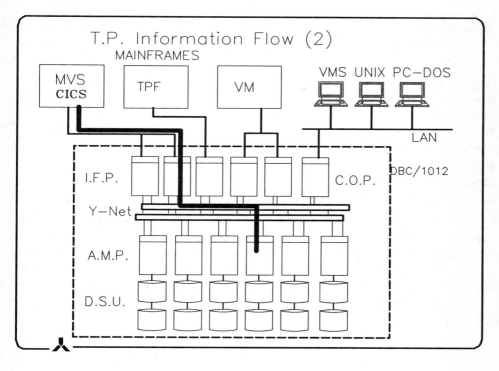

Fig 7. Retrieving a Single Row

The target AMP is usually able to retrieve the row in a single disk access, or even directly from its data cache memory or non-volatile RAM (an optional extra). The result row, or rows, are formatted and sent back to the IFP and then to the calling application.

We can see therefore, a real simplicity in the answering of these different families of transaction. Of course, the truth is that these machines are used primarily for the execution of very large complex queries. In order to perform the required joins and sorts needs more complex mechanisms than those so far explained. For example, nearly all complex queries involve the joining of many tables. On a distributed parallel architecture, with no shared memory, this will often cause data to move over the Ynet onto different processors, because of the fact that to join two rows, both must be on the same AMP at 'join time'.

Optimisation therefore is key to good performance, and the DBC/1012 can utilise several types of merge, product and nested joins to arrive at the correct answer. Such activities may, as already noted, involve data transfer, and this may be the duplication , redistribution or local copying of a table.

In fact, the number of ways in which the DBC/1012 can execute a given query, is a measure of the sophistication of its optimiser. In order to examine the final execution path of a query, an EXPLAIN facility is provided that can report exactly how a given query will be executed, and includes in its diagnostic text:

> Locking requirements
> Temporary space requirements
> Temporary file row counts
> Relative run times
> Number of rows in result set
> Access method
> Join method
> Generation of common and parallel steps

Figure 8 shows such an Explain which illustrates the type of output available. Here we can see the joining of two tables TABA and TABB with an equi-join. The rows of each table are physically distributed across all AMPs based on the values in the COL1 column of each table (the primary index of each table). To join TABA to TABB on the equi-join of TABA.COL1 = TABB.COL2 (COL2 is a non primary index column in TABB) involves a redistribution of TABB in order to get the rows from each table to be joined, on the same AMPs. When this is achieved, TABA and TABB can be merge joined.

SAMPLE (ABRIDGED) EXPLAIN

1) First we lock TABA for read and we lock TABB
2) Next we do an all—AMP RETRIEVE step from TABB
by way pf an all—rows scan into Spool 2 which is
redistributed by hash code to all AMPs
We do a SORT to order Spool 2 by row hash
estimated size of Spool 2 is xxxx rows and the
estimated time for step is xxxx seconds
3) We do an all—AMP join step joining TABA
to Spool 2 using a merge join into Spool 1
The estimated size of Spool 1 is xxxx rows.
The estimated time for this step is xxx seconds
4) Finally we send out an End Transaction

Fig 8 A Sample EXPLAIN

The movement of data involved in answering such a join, can take the form of redistribution or duplication, and only involves copies of the original data. Ynet speeds of 12 MBytes per second aid such movement, but with careful physical database design any such need for data transfer can be minimised.

In terms of locking, Teradata uses a standard method of taking object locks and ensures consistency by the implementation of a simple set of rules. Dirty reads are allowed, and are often required in systems of this size. The objects that can be locked include database, tables and ROWID (a near approximation to row level).

Since each processor in the system is a complete, independent computer system, each is capable of full multiprogramming of tasks, and thus the system is able to handle many transactions simultaneously. In this way the DBC/1012 can be configured to give any required level of transactions per second. However performance is not the only issue.

On a conventional Database system, each database or table resides on a specific set of disks, often with different tables on different disks. In the case of a disk failure, a portion of the database will become inactive. For the DBC/1012, where each table is contained partially on each AMP, and hence on at least one of the DSUs on each AMP, failure of a single AMP or DSU would render the table unavailable for operations which require full table scanning.

The DBC/1012 software system holds the solution to this problem and ensures high data availability in the DBC/1012. Each row, as described above, is allocated to an AMP through a hashing algorithm. If the user selects the Fallback option, at the level of a database or individual table, the Y-Net uses a second hashing map to direct each row to a second, fallback AMP, thus providing complete data replication. For update operations both rows will be updated simultaneously. For select operations, the primary copy of the row will be used. If the primary AMP is unavailable, all operations will automatically use the fallback copy of the row. Facilities are provided to bring the primary table up to date when the failed AMP is re-introduced into the system.

Fallback requires by its very definition, twice the disk space that is required in its absence. It does however result in very high availability figures. As the DBC/1012 moves into the future and evolves into the NCR/Teradata 3600 and 3700 series machines, then Redundant Arrays of Independent Disk (RAID) technology will be utilised. In combination with a Customer Replaceable Unit (CRU) design and on-line redundant disks, time between data loss figures will be quoted in the hundreds of years.

DBC/1012 SOFTWARE

As we have seen, the DBC/1012 is a completely self-contained database management system, handling all aspects of the relational model including SQL queries, database creation, maintenance and security as well as physical management of the system. Since the DBC/1012 may be accessed by many external host systems, all the database management must be internal to the DBC/1012 itself. The Teradata system also provides facilities on the various host systems to permit access to the database.

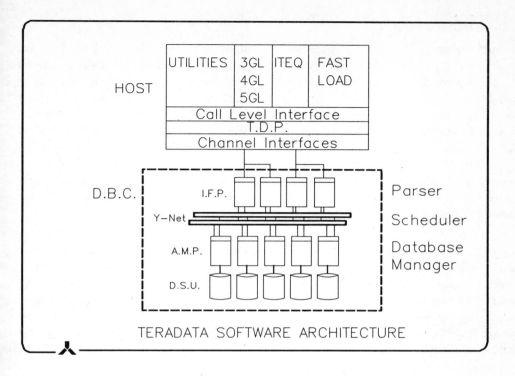

Fig 9. DBC/1012 Software

Figure 9 shows the structure and location of the main components of the DBC software system, together with their physical locations.

DBC/1012

Teradata Operating System (TOS)
SQL parser, optimiser, dispatcher

HOST (IBM)

Teradata Director Program (TDP)*
Call Level Interface Software*
Various SQL pre-processors*
CICS and IMS interfaces
Bulk loading and Archiving facilities
Interactive Teradata Enquiry system (ITEQ)*
Batch Teradata Enquiry system (BTEQ)*

Products indicated with * are also available on LAN-connected PC, Unix and VAX/VMS systems.

But what about software?

In a simplistic way we should remember that the traffic across the channel or LAN interface from the host to the DBC/1012 is SQL and the traffic returning to the host consists of result rows. Other products such as Intellect and NOMAD, that generate SQL from their own enquiry languages, can thus also communicate with the DBC/1012 and use it as a database server. Such products can post-process the result set returned from the DBC/1012 to provide functionality such as cross-casting, and graphics which are not available from pure SQL. In this way the DBC/1012 takes maximum advantage of the development of existing 4GL systems, and the 4GL vendors can make efficient use of the enormous power available from the DBC/1012 with the minimum of development effort. We should note here that this way of utilising third party software is different from the norm in that the software itself does not actually run on the Database Machine.

The figure below lists various products that can currently communicate directly with the DBC/1012. Some of these use the Teradata Call Level Interface (CLI is a Teradata specific Application Programming Interface) to achieve such communication, whilst others require a Gateway to make the DBC/1012 mimic the proprietary database distributed with the specific product. Still others use industry accepted Application Programming Interfaces such as those found in the SQLBase, SQLServer and SQL*Connect products. Support for Dynamic Data Exchange (DDE) protocols allow workstation based Windows applications such as Excel, to talk directly to the DBC/1012.

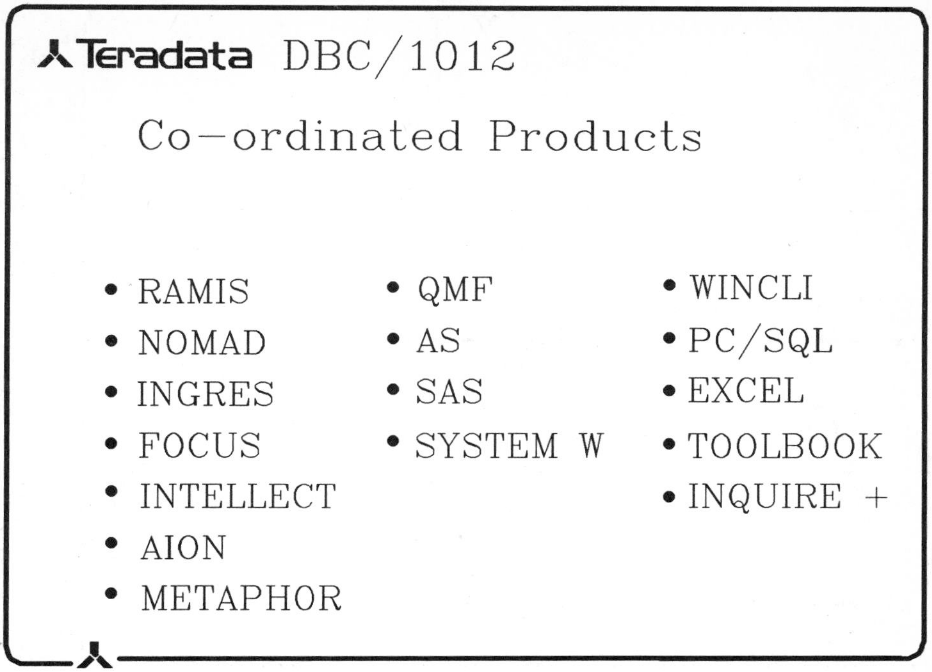

人 Teradata DBC/1012

Co—ordinated Products

- RAMIS
- NOMAD
- INGRES
- FOCUS
- INTELLECT
- AION
- METAPHOR

- QMF
- AS
- SAS
- SYSTEM W

- WINCLI
- PC/SQL
- EXCEL
- TOOLBOOK
- INQUIRE +

Fig 10. DBC/1012 Coordinated Products

GETTING SQL TO THE DBC/1012

The software architecture shown previously implies that any application using the DBC/1012 requires a combination of host and DBC/1012 processing. The balance between these two determines the extent to which the DBC/1012 can fulfil its promise of providing host offload.

As a test of this principle, a series of benchmark runs were performed for a UK banking customer. The customer had a standard series of complex FOCUS management information reports running on an Amdahl Mainframe. The reports were taking excessive amounts of CPU time and were giving rise to long run times.

In order to ascertain any advantage that the DBC/1012 could bring, the reports were run as supplied, against the FOCUS database running on the Mainframe, and the results were noted as a reference point. For a second series of tests, the database was converted into relational form and loaded onto the DBC/1012. The reports were run again from the Mainframe, but all data access was done via a channel interface to the DBC/1012 resident Focus database.

Teradata/Focus
Host Offload

	FOCUS HOST Elapsed	FOCUS HOST CPU	FOCUS/DBC Elapsed	FOCUS/DBC CPU
1	6 hours	390 secs	14 mins	2 secs
2	4 hours	280 secs	22 mins	3 secs
3	2 hours	150 secs	9 mins	9 secs
4	4.5 mins	9 secs	3 mins	3 secs

Fig 11. Processing Offload

The table shown above gives the before-and-after performance figures in terms of run times and the amount of CPU work performed by the host. To some extent the run times are artificial, since the DBC/1012 times could be reduced by a considerable factor, either by upgrading the processor type, or by increasing the number of processors. The important factor is the amount by which the host CPU has been reduced, since this limits the ultimate speed improvement to be gained through off-loading the database work.

The first query shows that for a large report, of the 390 CPU seconds originally taken by FOCUS on the Mainframe, 388 seconds were in the database part of the work, which is off-loaded to the DBC/1012, and in fact, the queries show that the more complex they are (many joins, aggregations and sorts), the more effective the host offload and the greater percentage reduction in elapsed time.

DBC/1012 PERFORMANCE

The next diagram shows some statistics gathered when a DBC/1012 was working as a fast TP system with a Mainframe transaction driver. The figures were taken in 1988, following the announcement by IBM of DB2 V2, with increased performance on a 3090-600E with ESA. The IBM system, with a CPU loading of more than 85%, achieved around 438 simple enquiries per second for the 'credit check' benchmark.

The same tests were run on a 43x143x143 Model 2 DBC/1012 (43 IFPs, 143 AMPs and 143 DSUs), attached to an Amdahl Mainframe. The system exceeded 1100 TPS, with the AMPs only 25% busy. A second test, with an MIS workload in the background, still achieved over 1000 TPS. A sort process, which had taken 2 hours on an empty 3090-300, ran in under 12 minutes at low priority concurrently with the above tests.

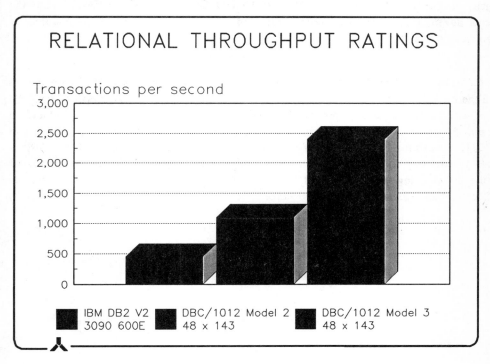

Fig 12. Transaction Throughput

Later that year, Teradata announced the Model 3 system, with performance 2.5 times faster for the TP workload. It was estimated that over 2500 TPS could have been achieved with such a DBC/1012. Already a Model 4 exists that is capable of a further 3 fold performance increase, but I still include the example to clearly illustrate the enormous benefits to be achieved by harnessing large numbers of processors together, so that they might all work in partnership with each other.

This last point is fundamental to questions regarding performance in general. Because the DBC/1012 exhibits such linear performance characteristics, it is possible to have whatever performance is required by adding hardware (within reason!). If we imagine for example, that a Model 4 AMP can scan 6,000 rows (100 bytes in length) in a second, then it is easy to see that to achieve 600,000 rows per second would need a 100 AMP system. There are several systems bigger that this in the world today. Similarly, if a single AMP could do 1 TPS (whatever that transaction involved), then a 100 AMP system could be expected to deliver 100 of those transactions in a second. Of course cost is a factor, and it has been calculated that for the equivalent priced IBM Mainframe, a DBC/1012 could be purchased with seven times the processing power, four times the data scan rate and using just two thirds of the mainframes required floor space.

LEVERAGING CURRENT TECHNOLOGY

One of the objectives of the DBC/1012 architecture was to be able to achieve high growth rates through the use of microprocessor technology. The next diagram shows the growth of the CPU power of a single processor as technology has moved through the Intel series of products, to the current 80486 processors. By the early 1990's, the power of the basic processors used in the DBC/1012 has grown by a factor of more than 30 since its introduction in 1985. Further advances toward the new P24 chip will allow greater performance by a simple process of increasing the clocking speed to around 60 MHz and the product lines future will remain to be tied to Intel as it moves into the 3700 range.

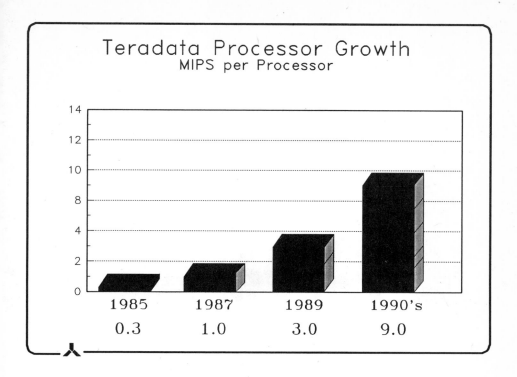

Fig 13. Intel Processor Growth

Disk technology has also made rapid advances over the years, and these have been incorporated by Database Computer vendors. The original DBC/1012 systems used Eagle technology, with up to 4 500MB drives in a single cabinet. The Model 3 uses up to 16 1.2GB drives in the same physical cabinet, giving a tenfold increase in usable storage, and a 12 fold increase in throughput. The latest Model 4 uses discs over *twice* this capacity, giving 16 2.5GB drives in the same cabinet. As already mentioned RAID technology will soon be available.

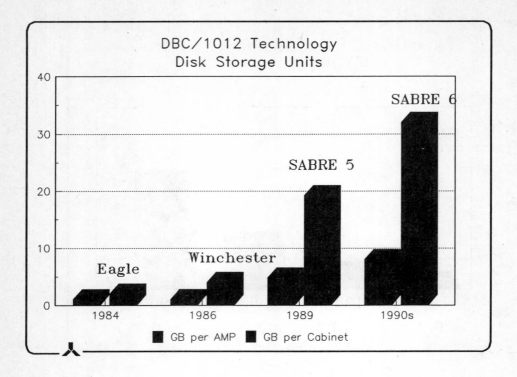

Fig 14. Disk Growth

FUTURES

It's been mentioned elsewhere that the communications paths to a DBC/1012 are found in its ability to talk channel protocols through IFPs and LAN protocols through COPs. Increasingly though, this is not enough. To participate in a truly 'open' environment, the ability to understand SQL must be enhanced by a UNIX environment through which to deliver it. The point has not been lost at NCR/Teradata and both the DBC/1012 and its sister, the NCR 3600, will have front end processors running Unix by this summer. Such processors, still based on Intel technology, will enhance the connectivity of hosts to these database machines, and provide full application development environments. Local disc storage and the ability to run Sybase and Parallel Oracle will enable the machines to be used for sophisticated OLTP and Decision Support systems.

However there will still be requirements for processing outside the scale of even the DBC/1012. Text, image and voice will bring requirements for the management of tens and hundreds of Terabytes of data. Computers to meet these challenges are already being developed at NCR

CONCLUSION

We have seen in this paper how the largest commercially available Database Machine has brought to market massive capabilities in the area of raw power, speed and connectivity. Certainly one can expect to see other offerings in this market, and examples springing to mind include systems from White Cross Systems and the Meiko Computing Service. Sequent have long been in the race, and whilst they offer a machine with many hardware similarities to the DBC/1012, there shared memory architecture and lack of any easy mechanism of delivering massive power to single SQL queries, puts it at a disadvantage for the support of MIS type queries against massive databases.

To summarise, the DBC/1012 had many design objectives to be met in its initial conception. This paper has sought to explain how objectives have been met, and how this new capability can be easily incorporated into an information architecture.

REFERENCES

[1] Page J: Relational Databases - Concepts, Selection and Implementation
    ISBN 1-85058-140-1: Sigma Press 1990

[2] Teradata Systems Manual: Rel 4.1.1/4.1.2: C10-0001-10

[3] Teradata Reference Manual: Rel 4.1.1/4.1.21: C03-0001-10

[4] W Inmon: Third Wave Processing Database Machines for Decision Support Systems: QED Information Sciences: 0-89435-335-7

[5] Advanced Information Systems 91: 19-21 March 91: Learned Information
0-904933-78-4

[6] S Reddaway: Text Retrieval on the AMT DAP: Second International Specialist Seminar on The Design and Application of Parallel Digital Processors: 18-19 April: IEEE Book of Abstracts

CONTROL OF A LARGE MASSIVELY PARALLEL DATABASE MACHINE USING SQL CATALOGUE EXTENSIONS, AND A DSDL IN PREFERENCE TO AN OPERATING SYSTEM

Mike Unwalla, Jon Kerridge
Department of Computer Science
University of Sheffield
PO Box 600, Mappin Street
Sheffield, S1 4DU
England
Tel: (+44) - 742 - 768555
Email: m.unwalla@uk.ac.shef.dcs

ABSTRACT

The IDIOMS parallel database machine supports large applications where integrated OLTP and MIS is required. It can be considered a relational engine, and SQL is used as the MIS query language. We make some comparisons between IDIOMS and other database machines. We justify why IDIOMS does not use an operating system, and why a Data Storage Description Language (DSDL) is used to control data placement. Our implementation extends the SQL2 information schema tables. These extensions, which are described in detail, can be used by a Data Dictionary process to control resource allocation and data access. General principles behind further extensions which can be used to improve data partitioning are discussed. By means of examples, we show how our extensions support multi-column partitioning, and how, with such a partitioning strategy, MIS query access time can be reduced.

1. INTRODUCTION - MOTIVATION AND OVERVIEW

The application domain of the IDIOMS (Intelligent Decision making In On-line Management Systems) machine is combined On-line Transaction Processing (OLTP) and Management Information Services (MIS). The machine is specifically geared to the relational paradigm, and can be considered an SQL engine. It has been designed to support applications where the storage requirement is measured in at least tens of gigabytes of data, and probably hundreds.

OLTP is a mission-critical service, and takes priority over MIS queries. However, within this constraint, it is possible to service MIS queries concurrently. This is a considerable improvement over the typical industrial situation, in which MIS queries are sent to a Data Processing department for processing, where turn-round times may stretch to many weeks. We are working closely with a number of industrial companies, and many of the assumptions on which we base our design are a reflection of current and perceived future requirements.

For MIS queries we choose not to worry about data inconsistency because MIS cannot get an exact picture of the OLTP data unless the whole database is locked (or there is some form of version control). Clearly, we cannot lock the whole database in order to get a consistent snapshot. Given this practical constraint, there is therefore no point in worrying about consistency at the individual tuple level. For all practical purposes, small inconsistencies in MIS queries are irrelevant, although it is vital that the OLTP data is consistent and integral at all times.

Due to the mission critical nature of OLTP processing, there is likely to be a dense index on OLTP data to optimise access to that data. However, IDIOMS does not maintain indices for the MIS system, since MIS queries generally involve range searches on columns, or access columns which are not suitable for indexing. For example, an index on gender is not likely to be very useful, and a column containing age data is likely to be accessed by range for which an index is useless. Furthermore, the cost of maintaining indices can be high. The IDIOMS machine therefore scans a table partition serially identifying the rows that satisfy a query predicate. Once the selected rows have been identified an in-memory sort can be undertaken on particular columns so that subsequent processing of relational operations can be more efficiently undertaken. The in-memory sort mechanism also permits the elimination of duplicates (ie the DISTINCT operation).

Initial research has shown that over a set of typical MIS queries only a few columns have any associated selection predicates. Clearly, it is these columns which should be partitioned. The partitioning (or indexing) of other columns serves no purpose, since if there is no selection predicate, all rows are required. Of course, when discussing selection predicates, we refer to the underlying logical query tree, rather than the superficial SQL query.

The underlying design principle of the IDIOMS machine is that of taking a parsed query tree and using it to construct a dataflow graph where the nodes specify the operations to be undertaken. This is shown in section 6. [KERR91a] contains full details of the design of the IDIOMS machine. The basic architecture consists of storage processors and associated disks, relational processors, and a communications ring. Storage processors (S) are of two types, those that hold OLTP data, and those that hold MIS data, eg summary tables. OLTP disks are connected to transaction processors, which service OLTP queries. Each table or partition that is stored on disk has an associated Table Handler (TH) that implements SQL statements (select, update, insert, delete). We also have specific processes to deal with referential constraint processing and selections that refer to a column which has a unique constraint. Each Relational (R) processor has two associated input buffers, labelled B0 and B1, and an associated Insert (I) processor which is used to send intermediate results back to the communications ring. Figure 8 is a schematic of the machine which shows just those parts pertaining to the flow of data for MIS queries.

A simple concurrency control strategy is used, which permits more than one SELECT query on a table partition, and provided that there is sufficient relational processing power available, this should not lead to degradation of response times for individual queries. Only one INSERT, UPDATE or DELETE operation is permitted at one time on each partition. Thus we implement a table partition locking strategy, which for an MIS based system is not unreasonable. Further research is required to implement a row level or column level locking strategy in a shared-nothing parallel database machine.

2. COMPARISONS WITH OTHER DATABASE MACHINES

This section briefly comments on some aspects of IDIOMS, and makes comparisons with a few well-known database machines.

2.1 Database machines, and dataflow models

A well accepted logical model of a shared-nothing database machine (DBM) is that it consists of storage devices, processing elements, and an interconnection network, and the physical implementation of IDIOMS clearly follows this. It is possible to combine the logical functions of processor nodes and storage nodes on the same device; the Bubba team do just this [BORA88]. The advantage of reduced communications traffic is offset by the disadvantage that the processing power of the machine becomes dependent on the storage requirements/capability. In our design, we can scale both the storage and the processing capacity independently.

As with other designs, such as Gamma [BORA88] and Bubba, MIS query execution follows the dataflow model. In other words, as soon as an operation can input from the required data stream(s), the operation will normally commence. Advantages of this strategy are that intermediate data does not have to be saved to disk, and that there are minimal delays, because processing does not need to wait until the previous operation is complete. In order to do this, it is necessary to have sufficient processors available to be used for different operations. Additionally, we will physically optimise the dataflow execution by ensuring wherever possible that if operation X sends data to operation Y, then X and Y will be carried out on physically adjacent processors.

2.2 OLTP/MIS mix

The major aim of IDIOMS is to service both OLTP and MIS queries concurrently, even for complex MIS queries. Teradata, for example, deal with an OLTP/MIS mix [REED90], but only one MIS query can be dealt with at a time, whereas IDIOMS can service multiple MIS queries concurrently.

Consider the Teradata machine, where each disk contains both MIS and OLTP data, with the result that "some DSU [disk] capacity must also be reserved for spool space for sorts" [REED90]. Clearly, this reserved space is wasted most of the time. Furthermore, this sharing of disks by OLTP and MIS data implies that while OLTP is reading/writing, MIS must wait, because there is only one physical disk arm on each disk.

By careful design we ensure that this problem cannot arise. We have two sets of disks, one reserved specifically to store OLTP data, and the other for MIS data such as summary tables, resulting in minimal interference between OLTP transactions and the access of purely MIS data. The design ensures that the OLTP disks have spare access capacity, which is used by MIS queries that require access to OLTP data. Although OLTP disks can be read by MIS, OLTP transactions have priority on disk access. Clearly, OLTP transactions can be accessing one set of disks, while MIS queries requiring only MIS data are accessing another set.

2.3 Partitioning and placement strategies

Teradata has a partitioning strategy that is superficially similar to that of IDIOMS, in that "data in each DBC/1012 table is stored evenly across all AMPs [access module processor]. This parallelism is, in fact one of the system's most significant benefits" [REED90]. However, Teradata choose a hybrid partitioning strategy based on the hashing of the primary key, whereas our data is range partitioned. The issues of partitioning strategies have been discussed in detail in [KERR91b], and our conclusion is that range partitioning is superior to hash partitioning in our application domain. OLTP accesses typically are 'single hit', using a key value. With a hash partitioning strategy, if we wish to go directly to the tuple, we would still need a dense index for each partition. Similarly, MIS accesses are not helped by hash partitioning, because MIS queries often involve ranges of values and neither indices nor hashing techniques help with such queries.

With reference to placement of partitions, the Bubba team state, "... we should identify the relations involved in this nonlinear operation (N-M join) and reduce their DegDecl [degree of declustering]" [COPE88]. Their reasoning is that message costs dominate, and are of the order $O(DegDecl^2)$. We argue that this is not the answer. Message costs may be reduced by doing this, but surely, the problem is inherent in the operation ie an M-N join requires M*N comparisons. Indeed, in an attempt to overcome this, hash and range-partition based joins have been proposed eg [RICH89], [DEWI90], where one logical join is physically implemented as a set of joins between partitions, and the results merged.

Boral states that data placement must be static because of the amounts of data involved [BORA88]. As far as allocation of space to partitions is concerned, we agree. However, our placement strategy allows migration of data between partitions, with the constraint that the migration rate is low.

Some researchers have developed complex partitioning and placement strategies eg [SACC85], [CERI82]. At this stage we consider that the complexity of these is such to preclude their use in very large industrial applications.

Currently we are developing a cost model which will enable us to determine suitable partition ranges. Factors involved include data skew, dependencies between data values and tuple heat, update rate, and update value/partition range ratio. Basically the tradeoff is that smaller partitions result in reduced scan time, but increased migration rate. This migration necessitates the update of the OLTP index, in addition to the raw migration costs. For this reason we cannot have a large number of partitions, and we should ensure that those columns which we do partition are the ones which give the greatest scan time saving over all MIS queries.

3. DSDL VERSUS OPERATING SYSTEM

In previous work [KERR91b] we have given detailed reasons for the rejection of a general purpose Operating System, and the use of a Data Storage Description Language (DSDL) in IDIOMS. Below, we summarise our findings.

The role of an operating system is essentially the allocation of resources (memory, processing time, use of peripherals). Most of the functions provided are not needed for a dedicated machine, and additionally, the transputer [INMO88], which we are using as the hardware base, is able to provide those facilities which we do require. Memory is allocated statically at compile time, and is thus dealt with by language compilers. This is not a major restriction given the size of real memory that can be made available. Further, the problems of memory fragmentation and garbage collection do not occur. Processing time is allocated by means of a micro-coded process scheduler built into the transputer. This scheduler provides the two scheduling modes required to support database processing [SHAR91], namely a high priority non-preemptive mode suitable for OLTP, and a low priority mode, which time-slices between processes, and is suited to MIS. There are no peripherals to control, apart from storage disks, which have their own (possibly shared) disk controller. The access interface which we have constructed can be easily modified to deal with any type of disk, thereby enabling easy incorporation of new faster disk technology.

There is a fundamental mismatch between the file organisations normally provided by an operating system (serial and random) and those needed by a database system. Thus most systems claiming portability implement their own storage access mechanism using low level operating system calls. The database implementor is faced with the task of designing a special purpose data access method in any event. This is precisely what happens in the IDIOMS machine, except that the additional system software interface is omitted thereby improving efficiency. A further problem with file systems is that the generation of multi-volume files is very difficult to manage. A large database will usually have tables which span many disk volumes. The control of what data is placed upon which disk volume usually cannot be finely controlled.

Our conclusion is that an operating system does not help with the efficient operation of a database machine, especially when it is built with transputers. The only aspect which requires control is the actual placement of rows to a particular unit of data storage. This is achieved by the DSDL [KERR91c].

The whole reason for using SQL is that (MIS) data is accessed by content rather than a navigational technique. The DSDL naturally expresses the partitioning of data by content over the data storage. This has the advantage that the search space of a query can be reduced if a predicate in the query refers to a column which is used to partition the data. For example, rows containing personal details can be partitioned by gender. Queries referring to a particular sex will only need to be sent to the required partition. A partial DSDL specification, relating to our example partitioning (figure 4) discussed later, is shown in figure 6.

A further aspect of (OLTP) database access is that sophisticated indexing strategies are used. Such strategies are not normally provided by operating systems. We have included this capability in the DSDL.

4. PARSER/DATA DICTIONARY

The Parser/Data Dictionary (P/DD) is the heart of the control mechanism of IDIOMS, and consists of a set of processes and data structures (SQL tables). It resides on the host as a central resource, not a replicated one, because global control is needed for resource allocation, and a replicated directory structure is not strictly scalable, inasmuch as the size of **each** instance is proportional to the number of nodes.

4.1 Parser/data dictionary process.

The parser/data dictionary process consists of sub-processes, viz parser, data dictionary, query optimiser/allocator. All of these are logically separate, although they interact closely. The Parser takes an MIS query in textual form, parses and validates it, and an internal representation is generated. The query optimiser/allocator requests information from the Data Dictionary, and uses this to generate the 'best' access plan [MURR91], considering the processing resource available, partitioning, and heuristics on previous hit rates of queries.

4.2 The data dictionary

The basic required functions of the Data Dictionary (DD) are to:

a) hold information that is specified in the DSDL - eg partitioning predicates, volume page size, access mechanisms, replication.
b) relate storage predicates to query predicates, and inform the optimiser of these.
c) control the machine - allocate processing and selection resources, and schedule the resources.
d) keep statistics to aid
   i. the optimiser - eg hit rates, partition cardinality.
   ii. the database administrator.

In order to do this, a set of tables, which are an extension of SQL catalogue tables, are used.

4.3 SQL catalogue tables and extensions

The data dictionary contains a set of tables, which hold information on various aspects of the system. Although they are all integrated, for convenience we group them under a number of headings; SQL DDL catalogue, DSDL, Resource Control, Statistics. The latter three groups are known collectively as SQL Catalogue Extension tables. All these tables are based on SQL2 [ISO90], but implement only SQL version 1 (SQL1) with Integrity Enhancement [ISO89].

For any given database system, all the information that is specified in the DSDL is stored in the DSDL tables, and the schema definition is stored in the DDL tables. Statistics tables, and Resource Control tables are discussed in sections 4.4 and 4.5 respectively. Entity Relation (Chen) diagrams for DSDL and Resource Control tables (attributes are not shown) are given in figures 1 and 2. The DSDL tables link into the SQL DDL tables via a Foreign Key reference from STORAGE_AREA to TABLES.

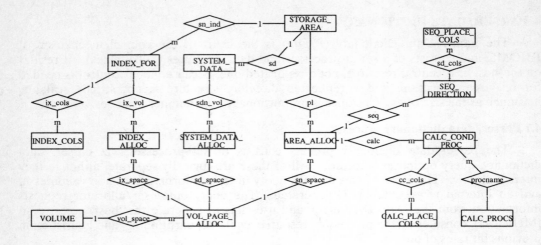

figure 1. Entity relation diagram for DSDL tables

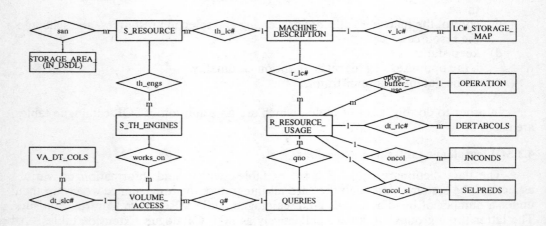

figure 2. Entity relation diagram for Resource Control tables

Note that although for convenience we have used the symbol # in some identifiers, strictly, this is not allowed in SQL2.

4.4 The use of statistics tables

Statistics tables store statistics on queries and on accesses to the database. In addition to aiding the optimiser to generate an access plan, statistics may also be used to aid longer term optimisations. For example, machine resource usage statistics can tell us if more relational processors are needed for the given number of disks available and the queries needing servicing.

Statistics on queries enable us to refine our heuristics for access plan determination. For example, if one column is predominant in selection predicates, this indicates that some access optimisation should be made on this column - perhaps partitioning, storage in physically sorted order, or in extreme cases, even an index. We envisage that a process could periodically scan the statistics tables, and generate appropriate messages to a database administrator.

Initial partitioning of data is based on an analysis of previous MIS queries on the application data, or expected MIS queries if no previous queries are available. Those columns which have selection predicates on them are candidate partitioning columns. It may be that these are never seen as part of the data returned, indeed, they may not even be initially projected from the base relation. Note how with this analysis, we do not need the concept of query type. Although the analysis takes place before the system is operational, this initial collection of statistics on MIS queries will be contained within the overall collection.

Statistics on the access patterns which arise can be compared with query statistics. Differences in patterns between the two indicate areas where changes to access methods/partitioning might be appropriate.

These aspects are areas of current research, and will be the subject of future publications.

4.5 Resource control tables

4.5.1 Design details

The interconnection network that is used in a system is immaterial to the operation of the Resource Control tables, except that logically close resources should also be physically close (in terms of message hops needed to communicate). This means that our work can be generalised to other database machines which are based on dataflow concepts, and which use the shared-nothing architecture.

There are two types of sequences, intra-, and inter-query. SEQ# in the tables (see figure 3) refers to intra-query sequencing, whilst Q# itself gives an implicit order to the resource allocation between queries, assuming that all MIS queries have the same priority. SEQ# increases only if a resource is queued, and the number is specific to an instance of a resource.

figure 3. Resource Control table usage

The entire filled tables are not shown, due to limitations of space. | indicates that data is incomplete.

QUERIES

Q#	USER
1	Mike

MACHINE DESCRIPTION

LC#	LC_ENG_TYPE
0	MIS
1	MIS
2	MIS
3	OLTP
4	OLTP
5	OLTP
—	
23	OLTP
24	R
25	R
—	
29	R
30	P/DD
31	MISFE

VOLUME ACCESS

Q#	SLC#	SEQ#	TH#	TH_ENG#
1	8	1	1	1
1	9	1	1	1

R RESOURCE USAGE

Q#	RLC#	SEQ#	B0_FROM	B0_FROM_SEQ#	B1_FROM	B1_FROM_SEQ#	OPNAME	SELPRED
1	27	1	9	1	8	1	JOIN	branch = '99-22-11' AND age > 63 AND age < 66
1	28	1	9	1	5	1	JOIN	branch = '99-22-11' AND age > 58 AND age < 61
1	29	1	27	NULL	28	1	UNION	branch = '99-22-11'
1	31	1	29	NULL	NULL	NULL	NULL	

DERTABCOLS

Q#	RLC#	SEQ#	COLPOS	FROM_BUFFER_COL	FROM_COL	NEW_COL_TYPE
1	27	1	1	0	2	CHAR
1	27	1	2	0	1	INT
1	27	1	3	1	2	CHAR
1	27	1	4	1	3	CHAR
1	27	1	5	1	4	CHAR
1	27	1	6	1	5	CHAR
1	27	1	7	1	6	CHAR
1	27	1	8	1	7	CHAR
1	28	1	1	0	2	CHAR
1	28	1	2	0	1	INT
1	28	1	3	1	2	CHAR
1	28	1	4	1	3	CHAR
1	28	1	5	1	4	CHAR
1	28	1	6	1	5	CHAR
1	28	1	7	1	6	CHAR
1	28	1	8	1	7	CHAR

LC STORAGE MAP

LC#	VOLNAME	VOL_REP
0	MIS_ST	1
1	MIS_ST	2
2	MIS_ST	3
3	OLTP_ST	1
4	OLTP_ST	2
5	OLTP_ST	3
—		
23	OLTP_ST	21

OPERATIONS

OPNAME	TYPE
SELECT	UNARY
UNIQUE_SEL	UNARY
PROJECT	UNARY
JOIN	BINARY
UNION	BINARY
DIVISION	BINARY
DIFFERENCE	BINARY

JNCONDS

Q#	RLC#	SEQ#	B0_JNCOL	B1_JNCOL	THETA
1	27	1	1	1	=
1	28	1	1	1	=

S_RESOURCE

SLC#	TH#	SN
3	1	cust_st
4	1	cust_st
5	1	cust_st
6	1	cust_st
7	1	cust_st
8	1	cust_st
9	1	insure_st
10	1	cust_st
—		

Similarly for Storage Logical Columns (SLC) 11 to 23.

S_TH_ENGINES

LC#	TH#	TH_ENG#	TH_ENG_TYPE
5	1	1	SELECT
5	1	2	SELECT
5	1	3	UPDATE
5	1	4	INSERT
5	1	5	DELETE
—			

VA_DT_COLS

Q#	SLC#	SEQ#	COLPOS	FROM_COL	NEW_COL_TYPE
1	5	1	1	1	INT
1	5	1	2	10	CHAR
1	5	1	3	4	CHAR
1	5	1	4	5	CHAR
1	5	1	5	6	CHAR
1	5	1	6	7	CHAR
1	5	1	7	8	CHAR
1	8	1	1	1	INT
1	8	1	2	10	CHAR
1	8	1	3	4	CHAR
1	8	1	4	5	CHAR
1	8	1	5	6	CHAR
1	8	1	6	7	CHAR
1	8	1	7	8	CHAR
1	9	1	1	3	INT
1	9	1	2	5	CHAR

Where a binary relational operation is followed (in the query tree) by Select or Project, both the operations are likely to be performed on the same processor. This does not go against the dataflow principles of our design, and there is a definite disadvantage (ie an extra communications cost) in performing the operations on separate processors.

Logical Columns (LC) are used in the tables merely as a convenient way of identifying processors, and they have no significance apart from this. Each storage processor, and each relational processor and associated buffers, is considered as a logical column. The output of a logical column is a derived table in SQL terms. The column definitions of a derived table (see DERTABCOLS) from a UNION, INTERSECT, or DIFFERENCE relational operation are replicas of the column definitions of the data entering input buffer B0.

Where a Select operation retrieves all tuples from disk, the predicate is indicated with an asterisk. This is in preference to using NULL, or an empty string, because it shows that the predicate is known. Additionally, it conforms to SQL notation.

4.5.2 Functions of the resource control tables

MACHINE_DESCRIPTION defines the type of the Logical Columns (LC) of the machine.

QUERIES relates Query number (Q#) to user_id. Each query is given an internally generated identifier.

OPERATIONS is a list of (not necessarily purely relational) operations that are allowed, along with an indication of the arity of the operation.

R_RESOURCE_USAGE specifies the operations that occur on the Logical Columns that are defined as R. The input buffer usage is checked against the operation's arity.

DERTABCOLS (derived table columns) defines the structure of the output data stream of a relational processing Logical Column. The output data structure is derived from the input stream(s). Column NEW_COL_TYPE is needed here, since the domain of a derived column can be different from the domain(s) of its input column(s). For example, inputs may be two dates or times, and the output will be an interval - clearly, a domain change has taken place. In SQL2 it is possible to specify a domain change using the CAST operation.

VA_DT_COLS (volume_access derived table columns) defines the structure of the output data stream from a storage processor. A column to describe new column type is necessary here, because although the domain of a projected column does not change, its position in the derived table will probably be different from that of the base table.

JNCONDS (Join conditions) defines the condition, and the (single) columns of the two input streams, on which the Join takes place.

SELPREDS (Select predicates) defines the predicates on which a relational select operation works. It is applicable only to Relational processing engines, not Selection engines, as these are dealt with by the table VOLUME_ACCESS.

S_RESOURCE relates Storage Name (ie the name associated with a data partition) to Table Handlers (TH), on each of the (storage) Logical Columns.

S_TH_ENGINES defines the available Table Handler engines, and their type, for each Table Handler.

VOLUME_ACCESS holds information on the Table Handler engine usage, and the selection predicate, if any, that is applied. The page location of the relevant Storage Name is held in the DSDL tables.

LC_STORAGE_MAP relates (storage) Logical Column to a physical volume. There is a FOREIGN KEY reference to the DSDL table VOLUME, which defines volumes.

5. PARTITIONING EXAMPLE

We now show our multi-column partitioning strategy in detail. Consider an artificially simple database for a bank, which consists of just two relations.

CUSTOMER(C#, BRANCH, INITIAL, LASTNAME, ADDR_L1, ADDR_L2, CITY, POSTCODE, AGE, SEX)

INSURANCE(POLICY#, BRANCH, C#, P_DATE, P_TYPE, PREMIUM)

The Primary Key is underlined, and there is a Foreign Key relationship between INSURANCE and CUSTOMER on (BRANCH, C#). Note that BRANCH equates to bank sort code, the first two digits of which identify the bank, the third and fourth identify the region, and the last two identify branch within region.

The first step to partitioning in our system is to decide how many Transaction Processors are required to service the OLTP queries (these are not shown on figure 8). Let us assume that we need three - this means that we need **at least** three physical partitions on three separate disks. In order to guarantee an even access rate for OLTP, we ensure that each of the OLTP partitions is of approximately equal size. We have no worries about overall partition "heat", as we assume that although access frequency to individual tuples varies greatly, on average heat will balance out within and across partitions.

Nothing precludes further partitioning of data. If we know that MIS queries on our database typically use age and sex in selection predicates, then we are justified in physically partitioning data on these attributes. This does **not** mean that we are creating a non-relational system, as the concept "relational" refers entirely to the method of specifying queries. To improve MIS access further, we allocate each of the sub-partitions to a disk, even though they are accessed by the OLTP system as if they were all on a single disk (the OLTP dense index spans a number of physical disks). This is illustrated by figure 4. In practice, we could have more age partitions, but for clarity and simplicity, these are not shown. The DSDL allows us to specify such partitioning (figure 6). Note that this is not a complete specification, a full example is given in [KERR91b].

Any column that is used for partitioning, and that contains data that changes (eg age) necessitates the use of data migration. The basic options are that either a process regularly scans data and relocates appropriate tuples, or that data is moved when it is updated. The first option means that much work may be needed, even if it is found that data does not need to be moved. The latter means that although OLTP would not be affected, MIS might not give as accurate a picture as with the former option. Zorner discusses the issues of data migration in the context of DSDLs [ZORN87]. Many of our ideas regarding the DSDL are based on the work of the BCS Database Administration Working Group, reported by Zorner.

Note that any partitioning strategy we choose in order to aid optimisation of MIS queries has minimal effect on OLTP access (there is of course the issue of migration). We aim to keep the cardinality of the sub-partitions approximately equal, so that MIS scan time of these is equal. However, even if the cardinality became unequal, this would not lead to any OLTP problems with different access rates to partitions, because what is important is the OLTP access rate to the Transaction Processing logical partitions. This is not affected by sub-partitioning cardinality inequalities, because of the OLTP index which spans the sub-partitions.

Finally, we point out that this is a practical system which will be used in a commercial environment. We aim for robustness, and therefore we do not envisage vast numbers of partitions as being an appropriate strategy. The main reasons for this are that increasing numbers of partitions leads to an increase in the probability of migration, and many partitions would require a multiplicity of physical join operations with resulting complexity of sequencing and routing.

6. PIPELINED MIS QUERY

At a given branch (99-22-11), select all customers who are likely to retire soon (ie male > 63, female > 58), and who have insurance with the bank. The SQL for this is:

```
SELECT      P_TYPE, C#, SEX, LASTNAME, ADDR_L1, ADDR_L2,
            CITY, POSTCODE
FROM        INSURANCE, CUSTOMER
WHERE       CUSTOMER.BRANCH = '99-22-11' AND
            CUSTOMER.BRANCH = INSURANCE.BRANCH AND
            CUSTOMER.C# = INSURANCE.C# AND
            ((SEX = 'm' AND AGE BETWEEN 64 AND 65) OR
            (SEX = 'f' AND AGE BETWEEN 59 AND 60))
```

Figure 5 shows a logical query tree for this, figure 7 shows an access plan, figure 8 indicates the flow of data around the machine, and the actual table usage is shown in

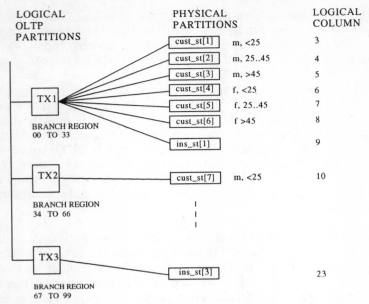

figure 4. sub-partitioning of OLTP partitions

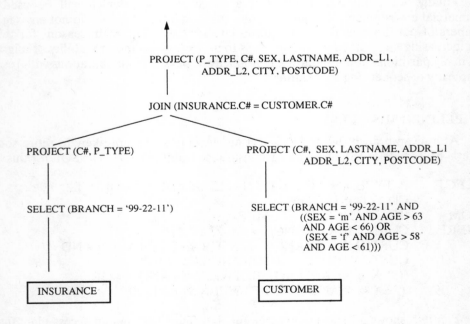

figure 5. query tree for example query

figure 6. DSDL partitioning specification

The partitioning specification for the first seven disks only is shown. The reader should be able to generalise for the other disk partitions.

STORAGE AREA cust_store PAGE SIZE IS 1024 BYTES SIZE IS 10000 PAGES PARTITIONED
        INTO 18

IF branch BETWEEN '99-00-00' AND '99-33-99' AND SEX = 'm' AND AGE < 25
        THEN PLACEMENT SERIAL WITHIN PARTITION 1

IF branch BETWEEN '99-00-00' AND '99-33-99'
        AND SEX = 'm' AND AGE > = 25 AND AGE < = 45
        THEN PLACEMENT SERIAL WITHIN PARTITION 2

IF branch BETWEEN '99-00-00' AND '99-33-99' AND SEX = 'm' AND AGE > 45
        THEN PLACEMENT SERIAL WITHIN PARTITION 3

IF branch BETWEEN '99-00-00' AND '99-33-99' AND SEX = 'f' AND AGE < 25
        THEN PLACEMENT SERIAL WITHIN PARTITION 4

IF branch BETWEEN '99-00-00' AND '99-33-99'
        AND SEX = 'f' AND AGE > = 25 AND AGE < = 45
        THEN PLACEMENT SERIAL WITHIN PARTITION 5

IF branch BETWEEN '99-00-00' AND '99-33-99' AND SEX = 'f' AND AGE > 45
        THEN PLACEMENT SERIAL WITHIN PARTITION 6

IF branch BETWEEN '99-34-00' AND '99-66-99' AND SEX = 'm' AND AGE < 25
        THEN PLACEMENT SERIAL WITHIN PARTITION 7

The partitions are then allocated to physical disks using the ALLOCATE specification.

The INSURANCE table is also partitioned, but only three partitions corresponding to the three logical branch partitions are created. Each of these is then assigned to a separate disk.

STORAGE AREA insure_store PAGE SIZE IS 1024 BYTES SIZE IS 10000 PAGES PARTITIONED
        INTO 3

IF branch BETWEEN '99-00-00' AND '99-33-99' THEN PLACEMENT SERIAL WITHIN PARTITION 1
IF branch BETWEEN '99-34-00' AND '99-66-99' THEN PLACEMENT SERIAL WITHIN PARTITION 2
IF branch BETWEEN '99-67-00' AND '99-99-99' THEN PLACEMENT SERIAL WITHIN PARTITION 3

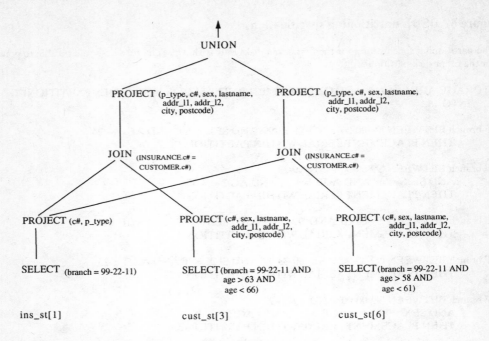

figure 7.   access plan for example query

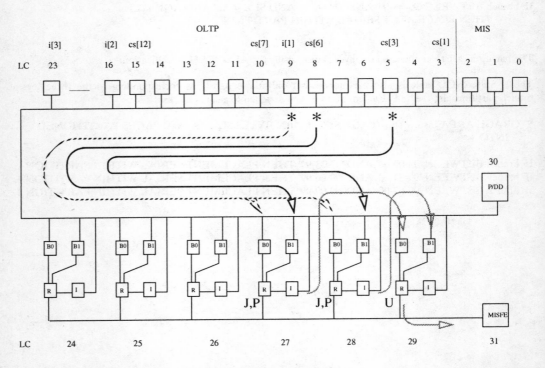

figure 8.   data flow for example query

figure 3. The reader can see that the operations Project and Select are done on the Selection engines (refer to VOLUME_ACCESS and VA_DT_COLS).

Note that the access plan (figure 7) is based on the partitioning of figure 4. For this reason, the SELECT predicates superficially appear incomplete. This is not the case, as the partitioning forces an implicit predicate. eg cust_st[3] (customer-store 3, on logical column 5) contains only rows for male customers.

The reader can see from this example that by means of suitable partitioning, it is possible to reduce greatly the amount of data that must be scanned in order to answer an MIS query.

7. FURTHER RESEARCH

One consideration is how to keep the number of message hops to a minimum. The physical location of relational processing resource is important, and we want tuples to be sent to physically adjacent sites if possible. This raises the question of whether, on completion of an operation, immediate (possible) re-allocation of processors is in fact the best option. It could be that it is better to keep clusters of processors together.

An access plan is generated using heuristics. It may be that derived tables become very large or very small, and therefore it might be appropriate to re-evaluate the execution strategy, and modify the remainder of the access plan. In other words, dynamic access plan modification allows changes to operator parallelism whilst a query is being evaluated.

For each MIS query, we could either allocate a fixed number of (available) relational processors (static allocation), or take resource as needed at each stage of the evaluation (dynamic allocation). Our initial work uses static allocation, because although dynamic allocation allows better utilisation of resources, it is considerably more complex than static allocation, and we can envisage situations in which evaluation becomes deadlocked with the dynamic strategy. Additionally, processor and memory costs are low, and the typical application environment is not cost sensitive at this level. Further work is required in this area.

Currently, our table design only allows for a single data stream for each MIS query to be sent to the Front End or the MIS disks. For implementations that can accept multiple streams this is clearly a limitation, and we are working on an enhanced table design to deal with this.

The collection of statistics to aid the database administrator to choose an optimal partitioning strategy is one of our goals. We envisage that once the requirements for the statistics have been established, automatic collection and evaluation could take place. Should re-partitioning be required, messages to this effect could be generated. We do not imagine that (in the near future) re-partitioning could be an automatic process, because partitioning requires semantic knowledge of the business system within which the database operates. By this we mean that, for example, although metrics could be used to derive an allocation strategy that "optimised" all queries, it might be a business decision that some have priority and others do not.

If a particular column is used for partitioning, then additional statistics will be held on it. Specifically, we aim to investigate the relationship between query predicates and partitioning values. It may be that small adjustments to partitioning values could lead to large savings in response time. For example, let us say that a certain class of query usually contains the selection predicate "age < = 21". If our partitioning strategy uses the ranges

> age < 21
> age > = 21 AND age < 50
> age > =50

then two partitions must be scanned. By changing the partitioning range (eg age < 22), we need only access one partition. This is possible, because, as discussed previously, we do not envisage having a large number of partitions for each partitioning column.

8. CONCLUSIONS

Various aspects of the IDIOMS machine have been compared with other designs. We have justified both the use of a DSDL and the rejection of an operating system within the IDIOMS implementation. Extensions to the SQL2 information schema have been described, in which partitioning and control information is stored. Proposals for the use of statistics tables have been suggested, which indicate how these could be used to gather information on MIS queries, in order to enhance the partitioning strategy. An example of multi-column partitioning has been given, along with an MIS query.

We have shown how multi-column partitioning based on attribute values can help to reduce the amount of work needed to retrieve data for MIS queries on OLTP data, and how the IDIOMS architecture matches this partitioning. Much work has been done by others in the field of data partitioning and placement, and many strategies have been devised to aid data retrieval. Our work is limited to a mixed Transaction Processing/MIS environment, and we make no claim for a universal solution. Furthermore, our partitioning strategy is limited by the semantics of the database itself. For example, a column that is frequently used in MIS queries, but which has a high update rate may not be a suitable partitioning column if the updates were to result in a high migration rate between partitions. From the work we have carried out so far, we believe that a practical multi-column partitioning strategy is viable for some applications.

We do not yet have experience of using our SQL catalogue extension tables in a working environment, and until we do, we cannot know how practical they are for storing control data.

The next stage of our work is to complete the cost model pertaining to our partitioning strategy, in order to obtain precise information on the costs and benefits. The problem of defining suitable partition ranges for each of the partitioning columns is complex, due to the relationships between the variables, and it may be that ranges will need to be determined using heuristics. In itself, the cost model will not suffice. We intend to implement our partitioning strategy using real data from our commercial collaborators, in order to evaluate our ideas.

We would like to thank the referees of this paper for their comments. Part of this research has been carried out under funding from SERC.

REFERENCES

BORA88   H. Boral, "Parallelism and Data Management", Proceedings 3rd International Conference on Data and Knowledge Bases; improving usability and responsiveness, Jerusalem, Israel, 28-30 June 1988.

CERI82   S. Ceri, M. Negri, G. Pelagatti, "Horizontal Data Partitioning in Database Design", Proceedings ACM SIGMOD International Conference on Management of Data, pp128-136, 1982.

COPE88   G. Copeland, W. Alexander, E. Boughter, T. Keller, "Data Placement in Bubba", SIGMOD International Conference on Management of Data, Chicago, Illinois, USA, June 1-3, 1988.

DEWI90   D. J. DeWitt, J. Gray, "Parallel Database Systems: The Future of Database Processing or a Passing Fad?", SIGMOD Record, vol 19(4), December 1990.

INMO88   Inmos Ltd., "The Transputer Data Book", 1988.

ISO89   ISO/IEC, "Information Processing Systems - Database Language SQL1 with Integrity Enhancement", ISO/IEC: 9075, (second edition), 1989.

ISO90   ISO/IEC, "Information Technology - Database Language SQL2", 2nd Committee Draft, ISO/IEC JTC1/SC21/WG3 - CD 9075, December 1, 1990.

KERR91a J. Kerridge, "The Design of the IDIOMS Parallel Database Machine", in Aspects of Databases, The Proceedings of the Ninth British National Conference on Databases, Wolverhampton, M. S. Jackson, A. E. Robinson (eds), 128-147, Butterworth Heinemann 1991.

KERR91b J. Kerridge, et al, "Table Placement in a Large Massively Parallel Database Machine", submitted for publication.

KERR91c J. Kerridge, S. North, M. Unwalla, R. Guiton, "A Data Storage Description Language for Database Language SQL", Sheffield University Department of Computer Science Research Report, CS-91-05, 1991.

MURR91   P. Murray, "Parallel Execution of SQL Queries", MPhil/PhDd transfer report, University of Sheffield, UK, September 1991.

REED90   J. R. Reeder, "Teradata Processor Technology in a Parallel Data Management Universe", The Relational Journal, pp16-20, Issue 10, July 1990.

RICH89   K. Richter, D. Grigoras, "Hash-Join Algorithms for SIMD-MIMD Computer Architecture", Computers and Artificial Intelligence, vol 8(4), pp369-384, 1989.

SACC85   D. Sacca and G. Wiederhold, "Database Partitioning in a Cluster of Processors", ACM Transactions on Database Systems, vol 10(1), pp29-56, March 1985.

SHAR91   G. Sharman, "The Evolution of Online Transaction Processing Systems", in occam and the transputer - current developments, J. Edwards (ed), IOS Press, Amsterdam, 1991.

ZORN87   A. L. Zorner, et al, "Draft SQL Data Storage Description Language", DBAWG - SP24.2, January 1987.

INTEGRATION OF MODAL LOGIC AND THE FUNCTIONAL DATA MODEL

D.R. Sutton and P.J.H. King.
Dept. of Computer Science,
Birkbeck College,
University of London.
Malet Street,
London WC1E 7HX.

Abstract

This paper argues that the treatment of incomplete information in conventional database systems is inadequate. It is not possible for users to formulate queries which clearly state what it is they want to know and the answers to queries are often misleading. These problems can be remedied by the use of modal logic which allows questions to be asked about what *might* be true and what *must* be true, rather than simply about what *is* true.

This paper presents a functional database language which seamlessly integrates propositional modal logic with the computationally complete functional data model of FDL, thus allowing incomplete information to be handled more effectively than in SQL or in more recent developments.

1. Introduction

The computationally complete functional data model of FDL [Poul90, Poul88] is an important recent development. However in the area of the handling of incomplete information it does not greatly improve upon relational database systems using SQL, the shortcomings of which we discuss in section 3. Our conclusion - that these shortcomings are a consequence of the use of truth functional logic - leads to a consideration of how propositional modal logic can be adapted to the functional database context.

The work we then describe could be viewed as a further development of FDL. However in addition to the incorporation of modal logic we have made a number of other, albeit relatively minor, changes to that language. We have therefore given the language described here a distinct name, Fudal. Moreover the implementation of Fudal is new and not a modification of the implementation of FDL.

In section 2 we survey the FDL development from which Fudal derives. Section 3 discusses the problems of incomplete information we seek to address. Section 4 discusses propositional modal logic and its adaptation to the functional database context. In section 5 we give a necessarily brief description of the syntax and semantics of Fudal, with examples, only going into detail when considering those points where Fudal differs from other functional languages and from FDL. Section 6 contains our conclusions.

2. The functional database language, FDL

FDL extends to computational completeness the functional data model, a development from the binary relational model. In the functional data model information is represented as entities and functions between them. Entities may be *scalar* meaning they have a value that can be written down, e.g. as a number or a string, or else *abstract* meaning that they do not. For instance a person's name is represented as a scalar entity but the person himself is represented as an abstract entity. The distinction between scalar and abstract entities is the same as that between lexical and non-lexical entities in NIAM [Verh82].

From a programming language viewpoint FDL is functional, polymorphic, strongly typed and persistent, with a novel pattern matching algorithm, facilities for defaults and integrity constraints, and for transaction management. All functions are treated uniformly whether defined extensionally, intensionally, or of mixed definition. From a database viewpoint the function definitions and declarations *are* the database, which is updated by their modification.

The motivation for the development of FDL, descriptions of its syntax and semantics, and examples of its use are given by King and Poulovassilis in [Poul90, Poul88]. The implementation of FDL is over a virtual memory content addressed triple store which itself is implemented using a modified form of Nievergelt's Grid File [Niev84] and conventional operating systems techniques for page and buffer management. A description of the implementations of FDL over this platform is given by Poulovassilis in [Poul92] and of the triple store itself in the PhD thesis of Derakhshan [Dera89]. An overview of the context of this work and its results is given by King et al in [King90].

A different development of FDL, termed PFL was described by Poulovassilis and Small in [Poul91]. This development abandons the functional data model and adopts a nested n-ary relational model whilst retaining the persistent functional programming approach. PFL does not, however, address the matter of incomplete information and suffers from the same defects as SQL and FDL as discussed in the next section.

3. Incomplete Information

Database systems such as SQL or FDL store imprecise information using null values. Different interpretations of null values are possible, but we restrict our attention here to the "as yet unknown" interpretation. Thus if a relational database contains the table:

Staffdata	
Name	**Salary**
John	15000
Michael	25000
Joanna	*null*

we interpret it as stating that John's salary is 15000, Michael's is 25000 and that, although Joanna has a salary, we do not know what it is.

3.1. Three valued logic

In SQL queries are interpreted using a three-valued logic in which the operators **and**, **or**, and **not** have the truth tables:

p	not p
T	F
M	M
F	T

p and q

	T	M	F
T	T	M	F
M	M	M	F
F	F	F	F

p or q

	T	M	F
T	T	T	T
M	T	M	M
F	T	M	F

where **T,M,** and **F** represent **True, Maybe,** and **False**. "Select" expressions retrieve only those tuples for which the "where" clause evaluates to **True** [Cham80].

This method can give results which run counter to our intuition [Codd79]. For instance

Select * from Staffdata
      where (Salary > 20000) or not (Salary > 20000)

should, intuitively, select every tuple in **Staffdata** because its "where" condition seems a tautology. This is not the case however, because when we test the "Joanna" tuple, the "where" condition will be evaluated as: **(null > 20000) or not (null > 20000) = Maybe or Maybe = Maybe** and hence the tuple will *not* be selected. In SQL's three-valued logic, the expression (*P* **or not** *P*) is *not* a tautology.

Two important points must be made:

(a)   We cannot "fix" this problem by changing the truth tables. Whilst, intuitively, **(null > 20000) or not (null > 20000)** should evaluate to **True**, the expression **(null > 20000) or not (null > 10000)** should evaluate to **Maybe** , which is what the three-valued logic actually gives. We cannot define truth tables which give the value of the first expression as **True** and that of the second as **Maybe** because, in *both* cases we end up evaluating **(Maybe or Maybe)**.

The problem is the assumption that (*A* **or** *B*) can *always* be evaluated by determining the values of *A* and of *B* and then consulting a truth table. When both *A* and *B* evaluate to **Maybe**, then sometimes **True** seems to be an appropriate result and other times **Maybe**.

A logical operator whose semantics can be described by a truth table is known as a *truth functor*. The three-valued logic of SQL is described as *truth functional* because *all* its logical operators are truth functors. The problem we illustrate results from the use of a truth functional three-valued logic. It does *not* result from the *particular* truth tables used and cannot be solved by using different tables or increasing the number of logical values.

(b)   The problem is not limited to tautologies, and can *not* be dismissed by saying that a user would not, in practice, introduce a tautology into a "select" expression. Consider the following example, adapted from one suggested by Vassiliou [Vass79], in which we imagine that a life insurance company maintains a database containing the table:

Risk_factors			
Name	**Male**	**Drinker**	**Driver**
John	Yes	No	No
Michael	Yes	No	Yes
Joanna	No	Yes	No
Chris	*null*	Yes	Yes

If the company decides that men who drive and women who drink are high risks, and creates a view containing only such people using

Create view High_risk
    as select * from Risk_factors
      where (Male = 'Yes') and (Driver = 'Yes') or
        (not (Male = 'Yes')) and (Drinker = 'Yes')

then, for the "Chris" tuple, the "where" condition will evaluate as **(Maybe and True) or (Maybe and True)** which gives **Maybe**, and hence this tuple will be excluded. However this is intuitively "wrong". We may not know Chris's sex but since Chris is both a drinker *and* a driver we do not need to know. Chris is necessarily high risk since if he is male then he is a male driver, and if she is not male then she is a non-male drinker.

Again, the problem is that the logic we are using is truth functional. We have an expression of the form (*A* **and** *B*) **or** (*C* **and** *D*) which we have evaluated by evaluating *A*,*B*,*C*,and *D*, and then using truth tables.

3.2. Incomplete information in FDL

FDL allows for two different types of null denoted by ? and @ . The first means "value as yet unknown", the second "not defined". Boolean expressions are evaluated according to a four-valued truth-functional logic. This means that many of the comments made about SQL apply equally to FDL. If we create an FDL analogue of the table **Risk_factors** above we have exactly the same problems when selecting out the "high-risk" cases.

Another complication arises because of the semantics of FDL's = operator. The expression (@ = @) evaluates to **True** as does the expression (? = ?). Thus if we have a database:

```
employee :: nonlex;
salary : employee -> integer;
debt : employee -> integer;
name : employee -> string;
create employee $a $b $c;
name $a <= "John";   debt $a <= 35000; salary $a <= 35000;
name $b <= "Joanna"; debt $b <= ?;     salary $b <= ?;
name $c <= "Michael";
```

and try to find the names of employees whose salary is equal to their debt, using :

```
[name x || x <- All_employee & (salary x) = (debt x)];
```

The result will be ["John", "Joanna", "Michael"] despite the fact that Joanna's salary and debt are unknown and Michael's are not defined.

Problems also arise when we consider equality between nulls in SQL. For instance, when removing duplicate tuples from a table, SQL will consider nulls to be equal, however when performing a join, nulls are not considered to be equal, i.e. SQL will not join two tuples if the attributes over which they are to be joined are both null.

3.3. Previous work on incomplete information

Many attempts have been made to address the problems outlined above. In general such attempts use the relational model and start from the premiss that a relation containing incomplete information can be interpreted as representing a set of relations each of which could be true in the real world and each of which contains no incomplete information. We shall refer to these as the *completions* of the relation.

Several new ways of representing incomplete information have been presented. "Maybe" tuples, representing information that is possibly true are used by Biskup [Bisk83] and Liu and Sunderraman [Liu90]. The latter also allow for sets of "indefinite" tuples of which at least one must be true. Keller and Wilkins [Kell85] allow for "set nulls" which represent the fact that an attribute is unknown, but that we can specify a set of values of which it is known to be a member. Morrissey [Morr90] allows attributes to be represented by "p-domains" and "p-ranges" indicating that it is known that the attribute value is, respectively, a member of a certain set or of a certain range.

Different ways of interpreting nulls have been explored by various authors. Imielinski and Lipski [Imie81, Imie84] have suggested that rather than a single null value, a countably infinite set of nulls should be used, the idea being that, although each null represents an unknown value, each occurrence of that particular null represents the *same* value. This approach resolves some of the problems associated with equality between nulls. Gottlob and Zicari [Gott88] make use of *open* nulls. If, for example, a relation **child_of** contains a tuple <**John,***open*> then, in a completion of the relation, this tuple is replaced by zero or more tuples with **John** as their first attribute, i.e. <**John,***open*> specifies an unknown number of children whose identities are also unknown. A similar idea is used by Biskup [Bisk83].

Once methods of representing incomplete information in a database have been proposed it is necessary to find an intuitively satisfying way of defining operations on such databases. If R is a relation containing incomplete information then an operation on R will generate a new relation R' which may also contain incomplete information. The "correctness" of this operation will depend on how the completions of R are related to the completions of R'. Ideally if, for example, R' is a projection of R then we would like the completions of R' to be exactly those relations that are generated by applying this projection to each of the completions of R. This notion of correctness is used in [Liu90], and a slightly less restrictive version of the same idea is explored in [Imie81, Imie84].

The use of multi-valued logic in relational databases is explored in [Codd86, Yue91, Gess91]. Lipski [Lips81] has explored the use of Modal Logic in information systems, and Prade [Prad84] has investigated the use of Zadeh's possibility theory.

The interaction of incomplete information and functional dependency is considered in [Date86, Vass80]. Formal approaches to the theory of nulls can be found in [Bisk81, Vass79, Reit84, Reit86].

4. Modal Logic

The purpose of Modal Logic [Chel80, Hugh72] is to allow us to reason about necessity and possibility. We consider here only systems of propositional modal logic. Formulae in such systems are formed using the ordinary propositional calculus, augmented by the two operators □ and ◇.

Broadly speaking □p means "p is certainly true" and ◇p means "p is possibly true". So for instance (□p)&(◇q) means "p is certainly true and q is possibly true". The exact meaning of these two operators is often clarified by reference to "possible worlds". For instance, in the system of modal logic known as S5, the expression □p means "p is true in all possible worlds" and ◇p means "p is true in at least one possible world". An interesting discussion of the various modal logics and of the different interpretations of possible worlds can be found in Frost [Fros86].

The use of modal logic allows us to express more clearly what we mean by a query. For instance, returning to the Staffdata table of section 3, when we pose the query

Select * from Staffdata
where (Salary > 20000) or not (Salary > 20000)

we expect every tuple in the table to be selected because we are interpreting the "where" clause as:

□((Salary > 20000) or not (Salary > 20000))

hence we are suprised that Joanna is not selected since her salary is certain to be either greater than 20000 or not less than 20000. If however we had interpreted the "where" clause as

□(Salary > 20000) or □(not (Salary > 20000))

it would seem perfectly reasonable to exclude Joanna since it is not certain that her salary is greater than 20000 nor is it it certain that her salary is *not* greater than 20000.

Our approach to adapting these ideas to to the functional database model is to regard the database (the function declarations and definitions) as modelling not just a single world in which each of the functions has a defined value but a number of possible worlds in which those values may be different. Thus if we know and record in the database that a person's age is either 19, 20, or 21, then that database represents at least three possible worlds, one or more in which the age is 19, one or more in which it is 20, and one or more in which it is 21. Clearly if their are many facts about which our knowledge is imprecise the number of possible worlds can undergo a combinatorial explosion. The handling of these situations in a practical way must be an important part of any such approach if it is to produce a usable database system.

In the remainder of this paper we describe the language Fudal which adopts a "possible worlds" approach to incomplete information. The operators we introduce permit meaningful queries to be asked about the "possible worlds" represented by by a Fudal database, that is about the incomplete information which that database contains.

5. The Language Fudal

Fudal handles incomplete information by introducing Modal operators into a functional language, along with a new kind of null value. Our approach combines the use of Modal Logic with the persistent functional programming approach of FDL. Fudal deals with abstract entities differently from FDL and makes what we consider to be some syntactic improvements. It could be regarded as a development of that language.

In this section we shall give a necessarily brief explanation of Fudal's syntax and semantics. We shall only go into detail when considering those points in which Fudal differs from other functional languages or from FDL. The reader may find it useful to refer to [Fiel88, Peyt87] and [Poul90] for more background information.

5.1. The use of Fudal

Fudal allows us to define functions and types and to evaluate expressions that contain these functions and types. In the sections that follow we shall show how function definitions may be used to specify the database extension and how queries may be represented as Fudal expressions.

5.2. Type Declarations in Fudal

Fudal's type structure contains:

(a)   The base types **integer**, **boolean**, and **string**.

(b)   Sum types, which may be used in a variety of ways. The most simple use they may be put to is to define types which are equivalent to enumerated types in C. For instance

student :: Matthew. Mark. Luke. John;

defines a new type **student** whose permitted values are those shown on the right hand side of the double colon. These values are referred to as *data constants* †. In section 5.6 we show how such types may be used to implement the functional model.

(c)   Function types, for instance the type declaration

factorial : integer->integer;
age : student->integer;

declares **factorial** to be a function which takes an **integer** argument and returns an **integer** result, and **age** to be a function whose argument is a **student** and whose result is an **integer**.

---

† A sum type may also contain elements which cannot be called data constants because they take arguments. However the reader will probably be able to understand the rest of this paper without troubling over this point.

(d)   Tuples, which are written using curly brackets, for instance {1,"Fudal",True} is an expression of type {integer,string,boolean},

(e)   Lists, which are written using square brackets For example [1,30,2,5] is an expression of type [integer], and [Luke, John] is an expression of type [student].

A list may be empty, in which case we write it as []. If it is not empty then we refer to its first element as its *head* and to the remainder of the list as its *tail*. For example the head of the list [1,2,3] is 1 and its tail is [2,3]. The head of the list [1] is 1 and its tail is the empty list [].

As in Lisp, a list with head **h** and tail **t** can be expressed as **Cons h t**, or as **h:t** (the colon being an infix form of the **Cons** constructor).

5.3. Definition of Functions in Fudal

In Fudal a function may be defined using several *equations,* the LHS of each equation consisting of the function name followed by a number of *patterns* which may contain variables, constants, or data constructors [Fiel88, Peyt87]. For example in the definitions:

factorial 0 = 1;
factorial x = x*factorial(x-1);

age Mark = 32;
age Luke = 45;

0, x, Mark, and **Luke** are all patterns. **x** is a variable, whilst the other three patterns consist of constants.

Functions are evaluated by *pattern matching*. That is to say that when the function is applied to an argument, or arguments, the evaluator determines which equations have patterns which "match" those arguments. A pattern which consists of a constant, such as **Luke**, will only match an argument which is equal to that constant. A variable matches any argument. If the pattern contains a mixture of constants, data constructors and variables then the situation is more complex, we shall give an example later in this section.

If only one equation matches the arguments to which a function is applied then it is used to evaluate this application. If there is more than one such equation then the evaluator will use a "best fit" algorithm to decide which equation to use. "Best fit" algorithms are described in detail in [Fiel88], the general idea being that if two patterns both match an argument then the algorithm will give preference to the pattern which is more specific to that argument, in the sense that the number of arguments that it *could* match is smaller. So, when evaluating (**factorial 0**) the first of the equations defining **factorial** will be used. If the evaluator cannot find any equations that pattern-match the arguments then an error is reported.

Patterns may have more subtle forms containing a mixture of constants, data constructors, and variables. For instance the definition

sum [] = 0;
sum (h:t) = h + (sum t);

uses the patterns [] and (**h:t**) and means "if the argument of **sum** is an empty list then return **0**, if it is a non-empty list with head **h** and tail **t** then return **h + (sum t)**". In the above definition **h** and **t** are variables, [] is a constant, and **:** is a data constructor.

5.4. "All" expressions

If a sum type **S** contains only data constants then the system will construct a built-in function **All_S** which takes no arguments and which returns a list containing all the data constants of that type. For instance **All_student** would evaluate to [**Matthew, Mark, Luke, John**].

5.5. List Comprehensions

A list comprehension is a pair of square brackets enclosing an expression which is followed by "filters" or "generators" each of which is preceded by a vertical bar. For instance

[x | x<-All_student | (age x) > 30];

evaluates to a list containing all the students whose age is greater than 30. In this expression **x<-All_student** is a generator, and **(age x) > 30** is a filter.

5.6. Implementation of the Functional model in Fudal

In Fudal each abstract entity is represented by a data constant rather than by an FDL "nonlex". So for instance a database containing information about two people might be created by entering:

person :: Person1. Person2;
name : person->string;
name Person1 = "Jane";
name Person2 = "Wendy";

The semantics of this is that **person** is a sum type containing, at present, two data constants **Person1** and **Person2** and that **name** is a function which maps these two constants, respectively, to **"Jane"** , and **"Wendy"**. If we subsequently want to add people to the database we can do so by means of Fudal's **!create** command. For example

!create person :: Person3.Person4;

adds two new constants, **Person3** and **Person4**, to the sum type **person**. Fudal also has a **!delete** command which may be used to remove constructors from a sum type.

5.7. Fudal Databases as Scripts

Any Fudal database can, at any time, be represented as a set of type declarations and function definitions written in Fudal, which we shall call a *script*. A script may not contain **!create** or **!delete** commands and thus is not in general the same as the the sequence of instructions that were entered to create, and subsequently modify, the database. For instance after the **!create** command above, the database would be represented by the script.

person :: Person1. Person2. Person3. Person4;
name : person->string;
name Person1 = "Jane";
name Person2 = "Wendy";

In the text that follows we shall often represent databases as scripts in this way.

5.8. Null Values in Fudal

In Fudal nulls take the form **Oneof L**, where **L** is a list, each of whose members is either a constant, or a range of constants in the form **c1 .. c2**. The equation **f x = Oneof L** indicates that the value of **f x** is not known, but must be a member of the list **L**. As an example, the script:

person :: John.Tracey.Michael.Julie;
age : person -> integer;
age John = 35;
age Tracey = Oneof [18..30];
age Michael = Oneof [33,35,37];
age Julie = Oneof [0..120];

Script 1

indicates that John's age is 35, Tracey's age is between 18 and 30, Michael's age is either 33,35 or 37, but we do not know which, and Julie's age is completely unknown, although we have assumed that no one is older than 120 (or younger than 0).

5.9. Errors and Partial Functions

If a function is applied to an argument for which there is no matching pattern then an error is reported. However there is a way of forestalling such an eventuality by using the operator **Defined**. An expression **Defined**(E) evaluates to **True** iff the expression E can be evaluated without a pattern-matching failure occurring. If such a failure does occur then no error is reported and **Defined**(E) evaluates to **False**.

5.10. Completions

We say that a *completion* of a database D is a new database in which every null value in D has been replaced by an "appropriate" value. An "appropriate" replacement for a null in the form **Oneof L** is any value in the list **L**. Thus a completion of script 1 is:

person :: John.Tracey.Michael.Julie;
age : person -> integer;
age John = 35;
age Tracey = 18;
age Michael = 37;
age Julie = 18;

5.11. Evaluation of Expressions in Fudal

If we consider any Fudal expression, for example let us take **(age Michael) +
5**, we may find that its value is different in different completions of the database. In such a
case Fudal will reduce the expression to **Oneof** followed by a list which contains the result of
reducing the expression in all completions, with duplicates removed. So, in the database of
script 1, this expression would be reduced to **Oneof [38,40,42]**.

5.12. Modal Operators

In Fudal, a boolean expression may contain the operators **Surely**, or **Maybe**. If
P is a boolean expression then **Surely** P evaluates to **True** iff P evaluates to **True** in *all* completions of the database, whereas **Maybe** P evaluates to true iff there is at least one completion in which P evaluates to **True**. In other words **Surely** and **Maybe** are similar to □ and ◇
in their semantics. So, for script 1, the expression **Maybe ((age Michael) == 33)** † evaluates
to **True** because there are completions of the database in which **((age Michael) == 33)** is
true, and **Surely ((age Michael) > 30)** also evaluates to **True** because **((age Michael) > 30)** is
true in *every* completion of the database.

5.13. Simple Examples Using Modal Operators

(a)   Using script 1 what query would give us the list of all people whose age *could*
be less than 35 ?

What we mean here is that we want the list of all people such that *in at least
one completion of the database* their age is less than 35. In other words a person **p** is in the list iff the expression

Maybe((age p) < 35)

evaluates to **True**. A query which will give us this list is

[p | p<-All_person | Maybe ((age p) < 35)]

which evaluates to **[Tracey, Michael, Julie]**.

(b)   What query would give us the list of people whose age is *known* to be greater
then 25 ?

What we mean here is that in *all* completions of the database **age p** is greater
than 25. That is

Surely ((age p) > 25)

evaluates to true. Hence an appropriate query is:

[p | p<-All_person | Surely ((age p) > 25)]

which evaluates to **[John, Michael]**

---

† Fudal uses the operator == to test for equality.

5.14. Expressing Conditional Possibilities in Fudal

We may want to express the fact that a certain state of affairs is possible only under certain circumstances. This can be done in Fudal using **if** expressions. Suppose that we wanted to express the facts that Tracey's age is in the range 18..30 and that *if Tracey's age is 21* then so is Julie's, but otherwise Julie's age could be anything between 0 and 120. These facts may be expressed as

age Tracey = Oneof [18..30];
age Julie = if (age Tracey == 21) then 21 else Oneof [0..120];

In the examples that follow we shall express conditional possibilities in this way. We shall also use the Modal Operators **Surely** and **Maybe** to express quite subtle queries about what we would be able to deduce if we knew that some given fact was true.

5.15. The representation of incomplete information

In Fudal an "as yet unknown" null may be represented as **Oneof[**$min..max$**]** where min and max are the minimum and maximum values which could be expected, e.g. if John's age is unknown we can represent this as **age John = Oneof[0..120]**. There is no "inapplicable" null in Fudal. If a function is inapplicable to a particular argument then it will have no defining equation for that argument. The operator **Defined** can be used to check whether a function is applicable to a given argument.

Consider the first of our examples in section 3 which in Fudal is specified by the script:

employee::John.Michael.Joanna;
salary:employee->integer;
salary John = 15000; salary Michael=25000;
salary Joanna = Oneof [7500...50000];

where we assume that all salaries are in the range 7500..50000
If for a query we use the list comprehension

[x|x<-All_employee|(salary x) > 20000]

then Fudal will give the result:

Oneof [[Michael],[Michael,Joanna]]

showing that for some completions of the database the result is **[Michael]** and for the others **[Michael,Joanna]**. However the query:

[x|x<-All_employee|Surely(salary x > 20000)]

would only give the result **[Michael]** since the query is now requiring the condition to be true in all completions of the database. Consider now the case we discussed where the condition was a tautology, i.e the query

[x | x<-All_employee | (salary>20000) or not (salary > 20000)]

There are two classes of database completions in relation to this condition, those for which **Michael** and **Joanna** satisfy the first term of the condition and **John** satisfies the second, and those for which **Michael** satisfies the first term and **John** and **Joanna** the second. Thus for all completions the result is **[John,Michael,Joanna]** which accords with our intuition. **Joanna** is not ignored as with FDL and SQL. Note that there would have been no difference had the condition been prefixed by the **Surely** operator since the condition evaluates to true for all instances of **x** in all completions.

The second of our examples in section 3 can be specified in Fudal by the script:

insured::John.Michael.Joanna.Chris;
male:insured->boolean;
drinker:insured->boolean;
driver:insured->boolean;
male Chris = Oneof [True,False]; drinker Chris = True; driver Chris = True; ...

where the elipsis denotes further function definitions as shown in our previous table. We could now define a function:

high_risk:insured->boolean;
high_risk x = ((male x) and (driver x)) or (not (male x) and (drinker x));

In the completions for which **male Chris** is **True** the expression **high_risk Chris** evaluates as:

(True and True) or (False and True)

whereas in those for which **male Chris** is **False** it evaluates as:

(False and True) or (True and True)

so that **high-risk Chris** will always be **True**. Thus the query:

[x|x<-All_insured|high_risk x]

will give the result

[Michael, Joanna, Chris]

as we would expect and **Chris** would not be omitted as with the corresponding SQL query.

5.16. Complicated Queries Expressed in Fudal

Suppose that we know that a murder has been committed either by a certain Colonel Mustard using a revolver or a rope in the study, or else by Miss Scarlett, in either the study or the drawing room, using a revolver or a piece of lead piping †. This situation may be represented by the following script:

person :: **Col_Mustard. Miss_Scarlett. Prof_Plum. Rev_Green;**
utensil :: **Lead_Piping. Revolver. Rope. Crowbar. Aubergine;**
scene :: **Study. Drawing_Room. Kitchen. Lounge. Library;**

murderer : person;
murderer = Oneof [Col_Mustard, Miss_Scarlett];

weapon : utensil;
weapon = if (murderer == Col_Mustard) then Oneof[Revolver,Rope]
           else Oneof [Revolver,Lead_Piping];

room : scene;
room = if (murderer == Col_Mustard) then Study
          else Oneof [Study, Drawing_Room];

in which we have arbitrarily limited the types **person, utensil** and **scene** to contain only those values indicated in the first three lines of the script.

(a)   Suppose that we wish to know whether it is possible that Colonel Mustard committed the murder using the lead piping. The query we should pose is:

Maybe((murderer==Col_Mustard) and (weapon==Lead_Piping));

which gives the answer **False**.

However if we wished to know whether it was possible that Colonel Mustard was the murderer and also possible that the crime was committed using the lead piping we would pose the query

Maybe(murderer==Col_Mustard) and Maybe(weapon==Lead_Piping);

to which the answer would be **True**.

The reason why we get different answers to these two queries is that there are completions of the database in which Colonel Mustard is the murderer and completions in which the lead piping is the weapon, thus the second query is indeed true, however the set of completions with Colonel Mustard as murderer and the set of completions with the lead piping as weapon are disjoint, hence the answer to the first query is false.

(b)   Suppose we were asked, "if Miss Scarlett is the murderer is it then certain that the weapon is the lead piping ?". If Fudal contained an implication operator →

† A possible situation in the board game "Cluedo".

then we could express this as the query

Surely((murderer==Miss_Scarlett)→(weapon==Lead_Piping));.

As Fudal does not contain such an operator we use the equivalence $p{\rightarrow}q \equiv$ **not** p **or** q, and express our query as:

Surely(not (murderer==Miss_Scarlett) or (weapon==Lead_Piping));.

which evaluates to **False**.

(c)　Suppose we were told that, if we knew what weapon had been used then, with the information already available to us, we would be able to deduce where the crime had taken place. What could the weapon then be?

Now for a utensil **w** to be a possible murder weapon under these conditions there must, first of all, be one or more completions of the database in which the weapon is **w**, in other words the expression **Maybe(weapon==w)** must be true. Secondly in all completions in which the weapon is **w** the scene of crime must be the same, in other words there must be some **r** such that the expression **Surely(not (weapon==w) or (room==r))** is true. So a query which gives us all the possible murder weapons under these condition is

[w | w<-All_utensil | Maybe(weapon == w) |
　　　r<-All_scene | Surely(not (weapon == w) or (room == r))];

which evaluates to **[Rope]**

Further examples in this vein may be found in [Sutt92].

6. Conclusions

In this paper we show that current database languages do not allow the user to clearly express queries on databases with incomplete information. Furthermore we demonstrate that the results of such queries are often not what one might expect. We argue that the use of modal logic allows such queries to be stated much more precisely and to be answered in a more intuitively satisfying manner. We show how modal logic can be integrated with functional programming techniques and with the functional data model.

Due to limitations of space, this paper has concentrated on introducing the main features of Fudal from a user standpoint and illustrations of its use. A previous paper [Sutt92] includes a discussion of the use and specification of inverse functions in Fudal. In a future publication we will present an implementation strategy for Fudal, based on transforming expressions involving modal operators into equivalent expressions which do not involve those operators. This strategy also enables us to specify a denotational semantics for the language.

The initial implementation of Fudal is giving us the opportunity to experiment with the language and with illustrative examples. Further work planned includes a review and revision of the syntax and semantics, a re-implementation, and experimental application to two or three realistic databases. One of our first priorities is to optimise the evaluation of Fudal queries. As we mention in section 4, if there are many facts about which our information is imprecise then the number of possible completions of the database undergoes a combinatorial explosion. It is not, in general, necessary to work through all these completions in order to answer a query on such a database, and even our initial implementation of Fudal does not actually do so. However there are many queries which would make our implementation work unnecessarily hard.

There are a wide range of situations in which the information contained in a database may be incomplete, either because the required facts are simply not known, as in, for example, historical or archeological research, or because of the practical difficulty of collecting information and entering it into a database. These situations give rise to problems which current database systems address in unsatisfactory manner. We believe that our work points the way to a practical resolution of these problems through the use of modal logic.

7. Acknowledgements

This work was carried out at Birkbeck College in the context of TriStarp, which has grant funding from the U.K. Science and Engineering Research Council (SERC). David Sutton holds an SERC CASE award with IBM UK laboratories Hursley as the co-operating body and also providing support. The authors are grateful to their colleagues in TriStarp for their helpful comments and encouragement and to the referees for their constructive criticism.

Appendix: Syntax of Fudal

instruction = query ';'|command ';'| statement ';'
query = expression
statement = definition|type_declaration|type_definition
definition = identifier {pattern} '=' expression
type_declaration = identifier ':' type_expression
type_definition = identifier {type_variable} '::' (sum_type|empty)
expression = constant | identifier | expression expression | expression infix_op expression |
        string | if_expression | '(' expression ')'| tuple_expression |
        explicit_list | list_comprehension | special_exp
constant = number | constructor
special_exp = 'Eval' expression| 'Defined' expression |
        'Maybe' expression | 'Surely' expression | Oneof' explicit_list
infix_op = '+'|'-'|'*'|'/'|'and'|'or'|'=='|'>'|'<'|'>='|'<='|'++'|':'
if_expression = 'if' expression 'then' expression 'else' expression
tuple_expression = '{' expression { ',' expression} '}'
explicit_list = '[' explicit_element {',' explicit_element} ']'
explicit_element = constant|constant '..' constant
list_comprehension = '[' expression {generator|filter} ']'
generator = '|' pattern '<-' expression
filter = '|' expression
pattern = constant|string|identifier|sum_pattern|tuple_pattern|list_pattern|'(' pattern ')'
sum_pattern = constructor {pattern} | pattern ':' pattern
tuple_pattern = '{' pattern {','pattern} '}'
list_pattern = '['pattern {',' pattern} ']'
type_expression = identifier|type_variable|list_type|tuple_type|function_type|
        '('type_expression')'
type_variable = '%'identifier
list_type = '[' type_expression ']'
tuple_type = '{' type_expression {','type_expression} '}'
function type = type_expression '->' type_expression
sum_type = constructor_type {'.'constructor_type}
constructor_type = constructor {type_expression}
string = '"' {character} '"'
identifier = lowercase {lowercase|uppercase}
constructor = uppercase {lowercase|uppercase} | nil
nil = '[]'
lowercase = any lower case alphabetic character
uppercase = any upper case alphabetic character
number = {digit}
digit = '0'|'1'|'2'|'3'|'4'|'5'|'6'|'7'|'8'|'9'
character = any ascii character
empty = ''
command = create_com|delete_com|quit_com|exit_com|type_com
create_com = '!create' identifier '::' sum_type
delete_com = '!delete' {identifier|identifier '::' sum_type}
quit_com = '!quit'
exit_com = '!exit'
type_com = '!type' expression

References

[Bisk81]   J. Biskup: "A Formal Approach to Null Values in Database Relations" in *Advances in Database Theory* Vol 1 (Eds. H.Gallaire, S.Minker, J.M.Nicolas), Plenum Press, New York, 1981, pp. 299-341.

[Bisk83]   J. Biskup: "A Foundation of Codd's Relational Maybe-Operations" *ACM Transactions on Database Systems,* Vol 8. No. 4, December 1983, pp. 608-636.

[Cham80]   Donald D. Chamberlin: "A summary of user experience with the SQL data sub-language" in *Proceedings, International Conference on Databases,* Heyden & Son 1980, pp. 181-203.

[Chel80]   Brian F. Chellas: "Modal Logic, an Introduction", Cambridge University Press, 1980.

[Codd79]   E.F. Codd: "Extending the Database Relational Model to Capture More Meaning" *ACM Transactions on Database Systems,* Vol. 4, No. 4, December 1979, pp. 397-434.

[Codd86]   E.F. Codd: "Missing Information (Applicable and Inapplicable) in Relational Databases" *SIGMOD RECORD,* Vol. 15, No. 4, December 1986, pp. 53-78.

[Date86]   C.J.Date: "Null Values in Database Management" *Relational Database, Selected Writings* Addison-Wesley, 1986, pp. 313-334.

[Dera89]   M. Derakhshan: "A Development of the Grid File for the Storage of Binary Relations", Ph.D. Thesis, Birkbeck College, Univ. of London, 1989.

[Fros86]   R.A. Frost: "Introduction to Knowledge Base Systems", Collins, 1986.

[Fiel88]   A.J. Field and P.G. Harrison: "Functional Programming", Addison-Wesley, 1988.

[Gess91]   G.H.Gessert: "Handling Missing Data by Using Stored Truth Values" *SIGMOD RECORD* Vol. 20, No. 3, September 1991, pp. 30-42.

[Gran79]   J.Grant: "Partial Values in a Tabular Database Model" *Information Processing Letters* Vol. 9, No. 2, August 1979, pp. 97-99.

[Gott88]   G.Gottlob and R.Zicari: "Closed World Databases Opened Through Null Values". *Proc. 14th International Conference on Very Large Databases,* 1988, pp. 50-61.

[Hugh72]   G.E. Hughes and M.J. Cresswell: "An introduction to Modal Logic", Methuen, 1972.

[Imie81]   T. Imielinski and W.Lipski: "On Representing Incomplete Information in a Relational Database", *Proc. 7th International Conference on Very Large Databases,* 1981, pp. 388-397.

[Imie84]   T. Imielinski and W.Lipski: "Incomplete Information in Relational Databases", *Journal of the ACM,* Vol 31, No 4, October 1984, pp. 761-791.

[Kell85]   A.M.Keller and M.W.Wilkins: "On the Use of an Extended Relational Model to Handle Changing Incomplete Information", *IEEE Transactions On Software Engineering,* Vol. SE-11, No 7., July 1985, pp.620-633.

[King90]   P.J.H. King, M.Derakhshan, A.Poulovassilis and C.Small: "Tristarp: an investigation into the implementation and exploitation of binary relational structures." *Proc. 8th British National Conference on Databases,* 1990, pp. 64-84.

[Lips81]   W. Lipski: "On Databases with Incomplete Information" *Journal of the ACM* Vol. 28, No. 1, 1981, pp. 41-70.

[Liu90]   K-C Liu and R.Sunderraman: "Indefinite and Maybe Information in Relational Databases" *ACM Transactions on Database Systems* Vol. 15, No. 1, March 1990, pp. 1-39.

[Morr90]   J.M. Morrissey: "Imprecise Information and Uncertainty in Information Systems", *ACM Transactions on Information Systems,* Vol. 8, No. 2, April 1990, pp. 159-180.

[Niev84]   J.Nievergelt, H.Hinterberger, and K.C.Sevcik: "The Grid File: An Adaptable, Symmetric, Multikey File Structure", ACM Transactions on Database Systems, Vol. 9, No. 1, March 1984, pp. 38-71.

[Peyt87]   Simon L. Peyton-Jones: "The Implementation of Functional Programming Languages" Prentice Hall, 1987.

[Prad84]   H.Prade: "Lipski's approach to incomplete information databases restated and generalized in the setting of Zadeh's possibility theory", *Information Systems,* Vol. 9, No. 1, 1984, pp. 27-42.

[Poul88]   A. Poulovassilis: "FDL: An integration of the Functional Data Model and the Functional Computational Model", *Proc. 6th British National Conference on Databases,* 1988, pp. 215-236.

[Poul90]   A. Poulovassilis and P.King: "Extending The Functional Data Model To Computational Completeness", in *Advances in Database Technology - EDBT '90,* 1990, pp. 75-91.

[Poul91]   A.Poulovassilis and C.Small: "A Functional Programming Approach to Deductive Databases" *Proc. VLDB 17,* 1991, pp. 491-500.

[Poul92]   A. Poulovassilis: "The Implementation of FDL, a Functional Database Language" *The Computer Journal* Vol 35, April 1992.

[Reit84]   R. Reiter: "Towards a Logical Reconstruction of Relational Database Theory" in *On Conceptual Modeling* (Eds. M.Brodie, J.Mylopoulos, J.W.Schmidt), Springer-Verlag, 1984.

[Reit86]   R.Reiter: "A Sound and Sometimes Complete Query Evaluation Algorithm for Relational Databases with Null Values" *Journal of the ACM,* Vol. 33, No. 2, April 1986, pp. 349-370.

[Sutt92]   D.R.Sutton and P.J.H.King: "Fudal: a functional database language based on modal logic.", to appear in *Proc. Congrès Inforsid 92,* 1992.

[Vass79]   Y.Vassiliou: "Null Values in Data Base Management. A Denotational Semantics Approach." *Proc. ACM SIGMOD,* Boston 1979, pp. 162-169.

[Vass80]   Y.Vassiliou: "Functional Dependencies and Incomplete Information" *Proc. 6th International Conference on Very Large Databases,* 1980, pp. 260-269.

[Verh82]   G.M.A. Verheijen and J. Van Bekkum: "NIAM· An Information Analysis Method" in *Information Systems Design Methodologies: A Comparative Review,* T.W.Olle et al. (eds.), North Holland, 1982.

[Yue91]   K-b Yue: "A More General Model For Handling Missing Information In Relational Databases Using A 3-Valued Logic" *SIGMOD RECORD,* Vol. 20, No. 3, September 1991, pp. 43-49.

THE RALEIGH ACTIVITY MODEL: INTEGRATING VERSIONS, CONCURRENCY, AND ACCESS CONTROL

M. H. Kay, P. J. Rivett and T. J. Walters[1]
ICL
Kings House, 33 Kings Road
Reading, Berks.

Abstract

Raleigh is an object-oriented database system being developed to support applications in software engineering (a dictionary or repository system) and in system management (a system configuration database). This paper describes Raleigh's activity model. The activity model provides a tightly-integrated solution to the requirements for version control, concurrency control, and access control.

1   Introduction

Raleigh is an object-oriented database system being developed to support applications in software engineering (a dictionary/repository) and in system management (a system configuration database). This paper describes Raleigh's activity model. The activity model, which is based on process modelling concepts, provides a tightly-integrated solution to the requirements for version control, concurrency control, and access control.

The paper starts with a brief summary of background information on Raleigh. It then presents the requirements addressed by the activity model and gives a synopsis of other relevant approaches to meeting these requirements. The activity model is then presented in detail. The paper concludes that the activity model meets the requirements with remarkable economy.

2   Overview of Raleigh

A detailed overview of Raleigh's specification, and an outline of its implementation architecture, are given in [ka91b]. Raleigh uses a functional object model with its roots in Daplex [sh81]; it has similarities with Iris [fi89] and with EFDM [ku86]. In common with FDL [po90] we have extended the functional model to include computationally complete methods. And in common with P/FDM [gr88] and ADAM [pa89] we have implemented the system using a persistent Prolog engine, which in our case is MegaLog [bo90].

The use of object-oriented models to support engineering applications has become widely accepted: the principal benefit is a reduction in complexity achieved through abstraction,

---

1.   Tim Walters is an independent consultant currently working for ICL.

aggregation, and generalisation. But a variety of models can claim to be object-oriented. We chose a functional model because it satisfies the needs of our target applications:

- It provides an excellent canonical form of knowledge representation [ad90]
- It enables information to be transformed between different views [ra91], which helps us to integrate different tools around the dictionary without requiring each tool to conform to a common standard
- It enables queries on complex information to be expressed declaratively

Functions are used to represent both state and behaviour, that is, they may be extensional or intensional. Intensional functions may be written in Raleigh's native persistent programming language called OODL, or in other languages if required.

The Raleigh object model is best illustrated by a simplified class lattice, which is shown in figure 1. Some of the key features of the model are summarised in the following sections.

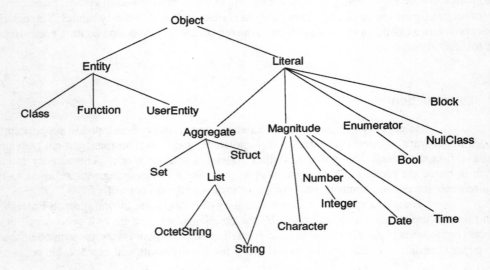

Fig. 1 The Raleigh Class Hierarchy

2.1 Entities and literals

The distinction between entities and literals is well-established, though the terminology varies greatly. Entities are sometimes called surrogates, non-lexicals, or objects, and literals are sometimes called lexicals or values. Different writers also distinguish the two kinds of object in subtly different ways.

In Raleigh, the difference between an entity and a literal is that entities are explicitly created, while literals are drawn from a pre-defined population. The identity of an entity derives from its creation-event, while the identity of a literal derives from its value. On this basis aggregates such as the set {1,3,5} are classified as literals; so, more controversially, are aggregates such as {*Smith*, *Jones*}, where *Smith* and *Jones* are entities. This set is a literal because it does not need to be created; it exists at all times that *Smith* and *Jones* exist, and it has no identity other than its value.

2.2 Classes

Objects belong to a single class; a class may inherit from one or more superclasses. Classes are themselves entities. Inheritance ambiguities are detected with a failure message. In Raleigh, as in most current object-oriented systems, inheritance serves the dual purpose of subtyping and refinement.

2.3 Functions

Like classes, functions are themselves entities. Functions are polymorphic; the appropriate implementation of a function is selected by a run-time binding algorithm. They may be multivalued (that is, they return an aggregate), and they may be partial (that is, they may return the special value *null*).

Functions can take several arguments, and the selection of an appropriate implementation depends on the classes of all the arguments supplied. So, for example, the function *Print(Document, Printer)* may be refined both for subclasses of *Document* (such as spreadsheet) and for subclasses of *Printer* (such as laser printer). This is what the Object Management Group [om91] refer to as a *generalized* object model, and constrasts with classical object models in which functions are uniquely associated with a particular class. Another example of a generalized object model is the Common LISP Object System CLOS [mo89].

Intensional functions may be implemented by means of a block written in the OODL language (or in other languages, but that is less interesting). A block is roughly equivalent to a λ-expression, though we use syntactic notations that commercial programmers will be more comfortable with. Blocks are themselves objects, and they can therefore be used as the arguments or results of functions. This feature allows higher-order functions to be provided such as:

```
Map( Aggregate, Block ) → Aggregate

Restrict ( Aggregate, Block ) → Aggregate
```

The function *Map* returns the aggregate obtained by applying the given block to each component of the supplied aggregate, while *Restrict* returns those components of the supplied aggregate for which the given block returns the Boolean value *true*. Such higher-order functions not only provide the capability of the relational algebra, they also allow recursion. Recursive queries are very common in our two target application areas, which are both dominated by hierarchic assemblies of engineering parts.

2.4 Names

Any object in Raleigh (entities, literals, classes, functions...) can be given any number of names. Names are arranged within hierarchic namespaces as in an operating system filestore. The name of an object can be used to refer to it within OODL programs.

2.5 The OODL language

As we have indicated, OODL has many characteristics of a functional language, but disguised so that commercial programmers will feel comfortable with it. Some aspects of the disguise are:

- An SQL-like *select* statement and a Daplex-like *for each* are provided for manipulation of aggregates, so that it is rarely necessary to use higher-order functions explicitly;
- Infix operators are provided to invoke commonly used functions, for example those used for arithmetic, comparison, and string manipulation;

□ Familiar constructs are provided for conditional and iterative execution;
□ Variables are provided, with conventional assignment semantics, for the benefit of users who feel they cannot cope without.
□ Statements in the language can update the database.

The language currently has no compile-time type checking (all types are checked at run-time), but we intend to change this. The type system of the language is, of course, the Raleigh object model.

To give a feel for the language, the OODL code below calculates the length of a record-type as the sum of the lengths of its components rounded up to a multiple of four. This is typical of the methods that might be found in a data dictionary. The caller of this function need not know whether the length of a record-type is stored explicitly or calculated on demand.

```
implement Length ( RecordType ) as
{ param rec;
  return ((3 + Sum( select Length(c)
                    from c in Components(rec)
                    endselect )) / 4)*4

};
```

Note the recursive call on *Length*. This will invoke a different implementation of the function depending on the class of component within the record-type; it might also invoke the same implementation recursively if record-types may contain further record-types. Also hidden in this code fragment are calls on the functions *Add, Divide,* and *Multiply.* These function calls are written using the conventional infix operators.

3   Requirements on the activity model

The activity model in Raleigh was developed to meet a number of requirements, particularly in the area of version control, access control, and concurrency control. The following sections describe the requirements in each of these areas.

3.1   Version control

The two initial applications for Raleigh are a dictionary/repository [ka91a, ka92] and a system configuration database [wh91]. Both of these applications require multiple versions of information to be maintained. In both cases information is stored at a fine-grained level. For example, a dictionary may be used to hold programs written in a fourth-generation language such as Application Master [br81a, br81b]: each dictionary object then corresponds to a "processing node", which is the equivalent of a few lines of code in a conventional language, or to a "data node" which might be an individual item declaration.

But the user is not interested in version control at this level of granularity. Users may wish to know which data declarations have changed between two versions of a program, but they do not want to concern themselves with the detailed history of each data declaration. In particular, they are not interested in building arbitrary configurations using version V of one data declaration with version W of another. Version control needs to operate at a coarser level than this.

The requirements on version control include the following:
□ It must be easy to define consistent assemblies or configurations of objects

❑ It must be possible to follow various patterns of branching in the development of a single object

These requirements are discussed further in the sections below.

3.1.1 Defining assemblies

Both our application areas are particularly concerned with the maintenance of relationships between objects and the identification of consistent assemblies. Version control schemes such as those of PCTE [ec90], that say a great deal about the history of an individual object but provide very little help in maintaining relationships among objects as they evolve, are therefore of little use.

There are two ways this problem has been tackled in the past. One is to define consistent assemblies bottom-up, the other is to define them top-down.

In the bottom-up approach, each of the component objects has its own version history, and each relationship between objects is effectively tagged, either with a specific version number for the target object, or with an algorithm for selecting a specific version (typically "choose the latest frozen one"). Examples of such schemes are those proposed by [at85], [ab87] and [be88]: in fact, this approach is the conventional wisdom in object-oriented database work.

Defining assemblies bottom-up is extremely laborious and error prone. ICL's larger customers already have dictionaries containing 100,000 objects and half a million relationships, and the volumes predicted for a system configuration database [wh91] are similar. It would be quite impossible to define consistent configurations of these objects by hand.

In Atwood's scheme, creating a new version of a component object may "percolate" up through the whole-part hierarchy to trigger the creation of new versions of assemblies containing that component. But since this would cause far too many incremental changes to the higher-level assemblies, he then introduces the idea of using a version of the assembly as a context for resolving relationships among the lower-level components. This starts to move towards a top-down approach to version control.

In the top-down approach, version control operates at the level of assemblies. Examples of this approach can be found in ICL's current Data Dictionary System DDS [ic91], and in the ISO IRDS standard [is91]. The DDS scheme, for example, has the following characteristics:

❑ A dictionary is divided into a number of assemblies called projects; each project contains a set of objects.

❑ Each project runs in a number of phases called project-versions. The state of the objects within each project-version is assumed to be mutually consistent.

❑ A project-version has read-only access to specified versions of other projects in the dictionary. These might be frozen, or they might be still under development. This set of project-versions is referred to as a project-view. A project-view represents a consistent configuration across projects.

❑ If an individual object is changed several times in the course of developing a project-version, only the last of the changes is retained.

This is illustrated in figure 2. This shows four projects, each with a number of phases; the arrows show how each phase (version) of one project picks up information from different versions of the other projects via a project-view definition.

In this scheme there is still some onus to define consistent configurations manually (by setting up project-views), but for the most part consistency is assured by virtue of

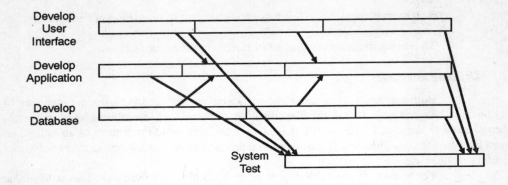

Fig 2 - Example Project-views in DDS

the fact that different objects were changed as part of the same phase of the same project. As we will see, this important insight is carried forward into Raleigh's activity model.

This top-down approach to version control is certainly much more manageable than the bottom-up approach when dealing with very large numbers of fine-grained objects. However, it is important that the user is able to choose the granularity at which version control is applied. Sometimes there is a good reason for keeping track of versions of a few critical objects (for example, the product requirements) at a very fine-grained level to provide detailed traceability of changes. This can be achieved by defining a project whose sole purpose is to maintain such an object.

The DDS scheme does not meet all the requirements. In particular, it does not support branching.

3.1.2 Branching development

We can identify several situations where the line of development of a single object needs to branch. For example:

□ One branch is the mainline development of the next production version of an object; the other is a side-branch concerned with error correction, or "what-if" exploration

□ Two separate mainline developments require changes to be made to different aspects of a single object: for example a compiler is being enhanced both to support new syntax and to include improved error diagnostics; for project scheduling reasons it is necessary to work on both areas concurrently yet independently

□ There is a need to define several variants of a single object, that will each be maintained indefinitely: for example (in the software engineering world), an English variant and a French variant, or a UNIX variant and an MS-DOS variant of an application.

These three scenarios differ in the requirement for branches subsequently to merge. In the first case, changes made on the side-branch may later be merged manually into the mainline development. In the second case, we want to use a locking protocol to prevent the two concurrent activities diverging, so that the changes can be combined later. In the third case, we specifically want to allow divergence, but we want to limit its extent.

There is thus a natural relationship between control of branching versions and concurrency control.

3.2   Concurrency control

It has often been observed [st90] that the conventional transaction model is unsuited to design applications. This is because the unit of work performed by a professional designer lasts longer than the unit of work performed by a clerical worker. There are also requirements for controlled interchange of partially-completed work between one designer and another. Various models of extended transactions have been proposed to meet these requirements: see for example [ha87] and [ru90].

In discussing branching versions, we have seen that we want to support various styles of concurrency control. We want to allow concurrent development from the same baseline either with complete freedom to diverge, or with locking to prevent divergence, or with some control over what is allowed to diverge and what is not. The last requirement suggest that concurrency control needs to be somehow related to access control.

Concurrency is also related to distribution. In design applications it is common to find that users work at individual workstations connected to a server in a network. Many of the design tools run at the workstation. The check-out protocol used to control concurrency is frequently associated with physical migration of the data to the user's workstation; at the end of an extended transaction, the data is returned to the server.

3.3   Access control

Access control models for object-oriented databases are immature, although they have been explored: see for example [di88] and [ra88]. Considerable work has been done on security in the context of PCTE [ec90].

In fact, in the authors' experience access control facilities in most database systems remain largely unused, which suggests some mismatch between the user requirements and the facilities provided. In the case of ICL's existing dictionary system, some of the difficulties have been analysed using a formal methods approach in [su84]. We believe that the vast majority of users have very simple access control requirements, and the system should not impose great complexity or run-time overheads on these users for the sake of satisfying the more specialised requirements of (say) the defence community.

A common assumption of many discretionary access control models is that the person who creates an object is its owner and remains its owner for the rest of its life, controlling who else may access it. It is easy to see that this assumption bears little relationship to commercial reality. The programmer who first writes a module does so because he or she has been assigned that task by the team leader. When the module has been unit tested, it is handed over into a project library. It now belongs to the team, or to the librarian, and the original programmer has no more right to change it than any other member of the team.

When programs are developed the conventional way, using operating system filestore, this difficulty is usually circumvented by copying the object at the point of handover. Typically it is moved to a different library or directory. As a result the object changes its ownership, but in the process it loses its identity and its history. When we use a software engineering database such as a data dictionary instead of operating system filestore, it becomes unacceptable to copy the object merely to reflect a change in ownership, because this would invalidate all references to the object from outside.

There is clearly a need for an access control model that reflects better the way professional workgroups actually behave. The model needs to be very simple (because otherwise it will not be used). We believe that the key to this lies in relating the access control model closely to a process model of what the users are doing. In particular, engineering tasks such as testing a module follow a defined process, and it should be possible for this process to include a standard template for defining the relevant access controls.

4 The Raleigh activity model

In Raleigh we attempt to provide a unified framework for meeting all these requirements using a single model, the activity model. The activity model is based on the premise that many of the problems can be solved more readily if we take a high-level view of what the users are actually trying to do.

In this we have been influenced by the work on process modelling done in the IPSE 2.5 project [wa89a, wa89b], which has developed into the PSS technology [gr92]. The work of the Damokles project [re88] also points in this direction. Our aim is not to include a process support system within Raleigh, but rather to pave the way for integrating the object-oriented database with such a process support system.

An activity, in Raleigh, is an episode of work, which may extend over days or weeks, and which is to some degree isolated from interactions with other concurrent activities. It may involve several people, working either at the same time or at different times; and one user may switch between different activities.

We can consider activities from several perspectives:

□ An activity produces a coherent set of deliverables resulting in a new state of the system: as such it is the basis of version and configuration control

□ An activity is an extended transaction, and as such it is the basis of concurrency and integrity control

□ An activity is associated with people and has a defined scope: it is therefore the basis of access control

□ An activity is an instantiation of a process, and thus provides the link with the disciplines of process modelling and quality control

□ An activity executes a specific task, using specific resources over a specific timescale, and thus provides the link with the discipline of project management.

Raleigh itself has no inbuilt knowledge of the sequence of events within an activity. This will generally depend on the user, though it might be constrained by a process support system.

To provide a link with planning tools, we allow activities to be registered before they actually start; and to provide an auditable record, we maintain information about activities after they have finished. Naturally, therefore, activities are represented as persistent objects within the database.

We recognise that several people may work cooperatively on a task, so we allow a level of concurrency within an activity, with minimal isolation between the different threads.

Within a session a user can break off from one activity and resume another, reflecting the ways users actually operate. Alternatively, of course, a user could run several sessions at once.

Every access to a Raleigh database takes place within the context of a single activity. This is true even for the action of creating or starting an activity. This implies that the system must arrive with a primordial activity already running, ready for the first user to connect to.

5 Activities and version control

Activities can be seen as a generalisation of the project-version concept in DDS described earlier (section 3.1.1), and they can therefore be used to provide a very powerful yet simple version control capability.

5.1 State

To understand version control in Raleigh we must first understand how state is represented in the functional model. In a classical object-oriented system the state of the system is the combination of the states of each object. In a functional system, state can be dispersed among the objects: in fact, the state of the system can be represented as the combination of:

- ▫ the set of entities that currently exist, and
- ▫ the state of each function

In principle we are concerned with abstract state rather than physical state; but since each distinct abstract state is represented by at least one distinct physical state, the distinction is of no practical importance. The physical state, and hence the abstract state, can be changed only when an extensional function is updated: so in practice we are concerned only with the state of the extensional functions.

It is convenient to simplify the model by treating the existence of entities as being itself a function. We do this by imagining a pool of latent objects with undefined class: when the user creates an entity of class C, we select an object E from this pool and set $ClassOf(E):=C$. The set of entities that currently exist can then be deduced from the state of the $ClassOf$ function. In fact, this abstract model closely reflects the implementation.

The state of an extensional function is represented by a set of facts. We can imagine the function $DateOfBirth(Employee)$ as a table, each row containing the internal identifier of an employee and a corresponding date. Each row is one fact. (Aside: facts are *not* objects!)

The principle underlying version control is that each update to the system is associated with the activity that made the update. Because every update changes one or more facts, we can implement this (conceptually) by tagging each fact with the identifier of an activity.

There is thus no explicit concept of an object having a sequence of versions. All we have is the concept of "the state of the system as at activity A". Of course, we can still refer colloquially to "version V100 of XYZ", but it would be more correct to refer to "XYZ as it was on completion of activity V100". Activities, of course, can be named in the same way as any other Raleigh object.

When a function is updated, the new fact is tagged with the current activity. If there is already a fact tagged with this activity, the old value is overwritten and lost. If not, a new version of the fact is stored, and the old version is retained. When a function is evaluated, the fact tagged with the current activity is used if one exists; if not, the system searches for a fact tagged by a previous activity, as described in section 5.2 below.

So successive versions of the state of the system are recorded, corresponding to the state at the end of each activity. The user is free to preserve as many intermediate states as required by breaking up the activity into subactivities.

A consequence of this model is that consistency across relationships is maintained automatically. Because activities are extended transactions, each activity leaves the system in a state that is in some sense consistent; therefore, any subsequent attempt to access the system in that state will see a consistent view.

5.2   Concurrency and branching

Each activity must define a baseline, which specifies the state of the system to be seen within that activity. (This is similar to the project-view concept in DDS.) The baseline is defined as a set of activities that are the logical predecessors to this one. In the simplest case, the baseline of an activity is another activity (typically the previous phase of the same project) that has already finished; in this case the activity sees the database in precisely the state that its predecessor left it. More generally, the baseline of an activity may include several earlier activities; this case is discussed in section 5.3 below. The baseline is used when evaluating a function: if there is no relevant fact tagged with the current activity, a fact will be sought that is tagged with one of the activities in that activity's baseline, and so on recursively.

Two activities may have the same baseline (or more generally, overlapping baselines). We regard such activities as logically concurrent, though they need not overlap in real time. Concurrent activities can create divergent states of the system. As we have seen, in some cases the user will wish to prevent two concurrent activities making conflicting changes. We therefore classify activities as either *coordinated* or *uncoordinated*. Coordinated activities are typically used for the principal line of development, while uncoordinated activities are used for error corrections, or exploratory "what if" changes.

Coordinated activities use a check-out locking mechanism to prevent conflict with other coordinated activities. Uncoordinated activities, on the other hand, operate without applying locks.

There are two kinds of conflict:

□ two activities assert facts that are directly contradictory (that is, they set different values for the same function with the same arguments)

□ the two activities make independent changes which, taken together, violate some integrity constraint involving multiple facts.

Again taking as our guide the way that real projects operate, we provide mechanisms to prevent the first kind of conflict happening in coordinated activities, but rely on subsequent reconciliation to deal with the second kind. This is discussed further in section 5.3. To prevent conflicts, a coordinated activity attempting an update locks the old version of the fact; if it is already locked by another coordinated activity, no suspension takes place, but the user is informed that the information is not available, and is told why. No locks are applied on retrieval.

The check-out lock is held indefinitely. Because the lock prevents divergence between activities that are logically concurrent, irrespective of real time, it cannot be released in the normal way at the end of the activity that claimed it. But since it applies to a particular version of a fact, and only affects other coordinated activities with that version of the fact in their baseline, the lock will decline in importance as time passes.

Where users wish to do so, we allow updates to be released from one activity to another before the first has finished, or after the second has started. Again this reflects common practice: testing frequently starts before coding is finished. This means that one activity A may include another, B, in its baseline even though B is not complete. Changes made subsequently by B can be picked up by A if A has not already updated the same fact.

5.3 Merging

Where an activity includes in its baseline two or more other activities that were running independently, it may be necessary to reconcile inconsistencies. As we have seen, two kinds of inconsistency are possible: contradictory values for the same fact, and mutually inconsistent values for different facts. The second situation is always possible, because we make no attempt to prevent such a conflict. The first situation can happen only when the baseline includes two activities P and Q where the history of P includes an uncoordinated activity that is not in the history of Q. The history of an activity is defined as a set of activities containing that activity together with the history of each activity in its baseline.

In figure 3, for example, activity E may have to cope with inconsistent values for a single fact if any of the activities C, D, M, or N was an uncoordinated activity.

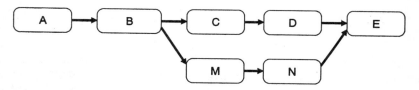

Fig 3 - Example activity lattice

In practice we expect that most consistency checks involving multiple facts will be performed by an application or tool, rather than being defined declaratively at the database level. This is because inconsistency is the norm in design applications while a system is still under development. So the fact that such constraints are not satisfied after a merge presents no unusual problem.

One important exception is a uniqueness constraint. Where two different activities in the baseline have each allocated the same value to a function that is supposedly unique (for example, two employees have been given the same personnel number), we can treat this in the same way as we treat the situation where one fact has contradictory values: the trick is to regard the primary fact as being derived from the inverse fact, "12345 is the personnel number of X".

We offer a default algorithm that decides implicitly which version of a fact to use, and a mechanism that allows the user to override this choice.

The default algorithm is to search the predecessor activities in a defined order. We search the tree of predecessors in a pre-order recursive traversal, except that when a predecessor activity is encountered several times by different routes we take only the last occurrence. This algorithm ensures that we never allow a value set by A to override one set by B if A is a predecessor to B. Consider the example in figure 3. If the baseline of E is [N, D], in that order, then facts required in activity E are sought from activities E, N, M, D, C, B, A, in that order.

To provide more explicit control, we allow a function invocation to be qualified by the activity at which the function is to be evaluated. For example, the OODL construct

```
return F(X) @ A
```

evaluates *F(X)* as at activity *A*. If F is an intensional function, the functions it calls are also evaluated (by default) as at activity *A*. This can be used in a number of ways:

- it can be used to compare the state left by two different activities
- it can be used for historical investigation and audit (for example, to establish when a particular change was made)
- it can be used to select a specific value if it is known, for example, that a particular activity made changes in certain areas to correct a particular problem.

For example, suppose we are translating version V300 of an application P into French. The OODL expression below determines those messages in version V300 that need to be translated, either because they were not present in version V200 or because their text has changed since V200:

```
select m in Messages(P) @ V300
  where m outwith¹ Messages(P) @ V200
    or Text(m) @ V300 != Text(m) @ V200
endselect
```

Merging of states that have been allowed to diverge will always remain a delicate surgical operation. We do not claim to have solved all the problems. In particular, we have not yet addressed fully the problem of branching metadata, that is, reconciling divergent changes to facts about classes and functions.

5.4 Nested activities

Activities correspond to tasks in the project plan, and as such it is natural to allow them to be nested. Once a parent activity has spawned children, it can no longer be active in its own right. But several children of an activity can be running at once.

When an activity starts, its parent becomes part of its baseline, so it will by default see the system in the state its parent left it. Similarly, when the children complete, they are added to the baseline of the parent. This means that for subsequent activities, changes made by a child activity are regarded as if they had been made by the parent.

A completed child activity may form part of the baseline of another activity unrelated to its parent. This situation is perhaps a little unusual, but it is sometimes useful and there is no reason to prevent it. We can refer to such a child activity as being *exposed*.

After an activity has completed, it is possible to *collapse* it. The effect of this is that the state of the system at the start and end of the activity is retained, but intermediate states (the states at the end of its subactivities) are forgotten. This provides an effective way of reducing the overheads of maintaining historical information, by progressively reducing the level of detail. Collapsing an activity may be impossible if it has children that have been exposed.

---

1.   The Scots preposition *outwith*, meaning "not within", has been borrowed here as a user-defined operator.

Similarly, an activity may be abandoned before it has completed. This is analogous to aborting a nested transaction. Again, abandoning an activity will not generally be possible if its children have been exposed. The effect is very similar to that of collapsing the activity, except that the final state as well as the intermediate states are forgotten.

5.5 Deletion

Deletion of entities and of facts poses particular problems.

Where no value is explicitly recorded for a function with certain argument values, the value of the function is considered to be null (or empty, in the case of a multivalued function). A fact is deleted for an activity by setting it to null in that activity.

When an activity has several predecessors in its baseline, we have said that a predecessor that explicitly updates a fact takes precedence over one that makes no change. We apply this rule even when the fact is set to null. We did consider an alternative rule, in which a non-null value for a fact takes precedence over a null value, on the principle that null means "not known", but there is no evidence that this would be an improvement. (This might be an argument for introducing several different flavours of null, as recommended for example by [co86], but we have not felt sufficiently confident to inflict this additional complexity on our users.)

We have already indicated that we can view creation of an entity as taking a latent object from a pool and assigning it a specific class. So we can regard the deletion of an entity as setting its class to null. Since the functions applicable to an object depend on its class, this means that most functions on the deleted entity cease to be available. The identifier of the deleted entity, however, is not returned to the pool, and still refers to that entity unambiguously.

We can thus delve into the past and get an identifier for an entity that once existed, and then return to the present and attempt to use this identifier even though the object no longer exists. Although there are no current facts about this entity, we can use the identifier to enquire into other facts about its past history.

6 Access control

The purpose of access control is to define and control which subjects (such as users) can perform which operations on which objects. As already remarked, we want the controls to be as simple as possible. It appears, surprisingly, that two kinds of access control rule are sufficient:

☐ Which subjects are allowed to participate in a given activity
☐ Which subjects are allowed to establish a new activity with a given activity in its baseline

These are the only rules that are specific to access control. It is also necessary to have rules about which functions can be evaluated and updated under what circumstances, but this can be achieved using general-purpose integrity rules, rather than being specific to access control.

For example, there is a general-purpose function

```
Updatable(Function)  →  Boolean
```

This determines whether or not a particular function can be updated. If we want to ensure that a given activity cannot update a particular function f, we arrange that the baseline of that activity includes the fact *Updatable(f)=false*.

Similarly, we can specify a general mechanism to make checks before an update is performed. We define a multivalued function

```
UpdateChecks(Function)  →  Block
```

Each value of *UpdateChecks* is a block that is to be executed before any update to the given function to check that the update is allowed; the block takes as its parameters the arguments supplied to the function and the new value being assigned. For example:

```
UpdateChecks(Salary) +:=
{ param employee, newsal;
    return newsal > Salary(employee)
}
```

This example allows the salary of an employee to be increased, but not decreased. (The assignment operator "+:=" adds an additional value to a multi-valued function: there can be many update checks applied to each function.) The important point is that this rule is specified in the same way whether it is a general integrity rule or a specific access control rule; the rule is part of the metadata, and it applies to any activity that has that version of the metadata in its baseline.

Of course there will also need to be checks on updates to *Updatable* and *UpdateChecks* as well, to prevent checks being removed. This can be handled by the same mechanism. For example, we can define

```
UpdateChecks(Updatable) +:=
{ param fn, newval;
    return newval==false or Updatable(fn)==null
}
```

This allows the function *Updatable* to be updated provided that the previous value is null or the new value is false.

The guiding principle is that an activity can create a version of the database and of its metadata which is all that its successors (including its children) can see. Objects, classes, and functions that are not to be made available to the successor can simply be deleted, and new constraints can be added to restrict the updates permitted.

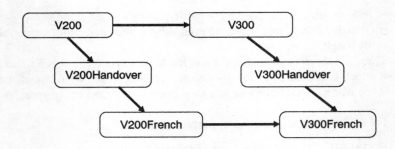

Fig 4 - Handover activities for Access Control

Consider again the example of software translation. We want to define an activity V300French to produce a French translation of the message texts in V300 of application P. The only person entitled to participate in this activity is the translator, and the only things the translator is allowed to change are the message texts. We will also impose a constraint that the translated message must be no longer than the original.

To achieve this we run a preparatory activity V300Handover, with V300 as its baseline, that sets up the data and the rules affecting the translator. Then we define V300French, whose baseline contains V200French and V300Handover. This is shown in figure 4.

The V300Handover activity changes all user-defined functions to be non-updatable, except the function *MessageText(Message)*. This might be done as follows:

```
UpdateChecks(MessageText) +:=
{ param message, newtext;
  return Count(newtext)<=Count(MessageText(message))
};
for each f in ExtentX(Function)
  where UserDefined(f) and f!==MessageText do
    Updatable(f):=false
endfor;
```

Using the activity concept in this way for access control provides great simplification. It means that the definition of access control rules is derived directly from the project plan. It means that applying controls is the responsibility of project management, not of the individual engineers who created the objects. There is no explicit concept of object ownership: rather, access rights are defined by declarative rules. The nature of these rules, and the data maintained to support them, are entirely at the discretion of the application.

As we have presented it, the model is not especially user-friendly. We would envisage adding a layer of software above these primitives to make it more usable.

A glance at figure 4 reveals another characteristic of this model, namely that it is repetitive. The process for translating V200 into French should be reusable when it comes to translating V300. When a process support system is used, the setting-up of appropriate access controls can therefore be automated. This illustrates another benefit of tying access control closely to the activity model.

From the system point of view, access control imposes no additional checks to be applied at each object access, beyond those used for version control and integrity checking; this substantially reduces run-time overhead, as well as giving a welcome saving in implementation effort.

The way permissions between subjects and activities can be allocated in practice is as follows. Subject S initially holds permission both to join activity A and to define a successor to A. (S might be the system manager and A the primordial activity). S then defines a successor activity B, and allows T to join it; S might also allow T to establish a successor activity C. In this case T can define who is allowed to join C and who is allowed to define a successor to C. Authority can thus be delegated onwards as far as required.

7   Summary

We have shown in this paper how the Raleigh activity model, which is essentially an extended transaction model, can be used to meet the requirements of an engineering database in the areas of version control, concurrency control, and access control, in a highly integrated and economical way.

Implementation of this model within the Raleigh system is currently underway, and we hope to report on our experience with it in a later paper.

There remains further work to be done: we have not yet, for example, completed our study of the effects of version control when applied to metadata changes. Results so far, however, indicate that the approach is highly promising in these areas also.

References

[ab87]   ABRAMOWICZ, K., DITTRICH, K.R., GOTTHARD, W., LÄNGLE R., LOCKEMANN, P.C., RAUPP, T., REHM, R., and WENNER, T. *Datenbankunterstützung für Software-Produktionsumgebungen*. Informatik-Fachberichte 136 pp116-131, Springer, 1987.

[ad90]   ADDIS, T.R. and NOWELL, M.C.C. *Knowledge and the Structure of Machines*. In Symbols and Neurons, IOS BV, Amsterdam, 1990.

[at85]   ATWOOD, T.M. *An object-oriented DBMS for design support applications*. Proc COMPINT 1985, pp299-307.

[be88]   BEECH, D., and MAHBOD, B. *Generalized Version Control in an Object-Oriented Database*. Proc 4th Int. Conf. on Data Engineering, 1988. pp14-22.

[bo90]   BOCCA, J. MegaLog – A Platform for developing Knowledge Base Management Systems. ECRC KB Report #75. (1990).

[br81a]   BROWN, A.P.G., COSH, H.G., and GRADWELL, D.J.L. *Development Philosophy and fundamental processing concepts of the ICL Rapid Application Development System RADS*[1]. ICL Tech J. 2(4), pp 379-402. (1981)

[br81b]   BROWN, A.P.G., COSH, H.G., and GRADWELL, D.J.L. *Database Processing in RADS – ICL's Rapid Application Development System*. Proc BNCOD 1981, pp55-79.

[co86]   CODD, E.F. *Missing information (applicable and inapplicable) in relational databases*. SIGMOD Record 15(4). 1986.

[di88]   DITTRICH, K.R., HÄRTIG, M., and PFEFFERLE, H. *Discretionary Access Control in Structurally Object-Oriented Database Systems*. Proc IFIP WG 11:3 Workshop on Database Security. Kingston, Ontario, Canada. Oct 1988.

[ec90]   ECMA (European Computer Manufacturers' Association). Technical Report #149: *PCTE Abstract Specification*. Dec 1990.

[fi89]   FISHMAN, D.H. et al. *Overview of the IRIS DBMS*. In Kim and Lochovsky (ed), Object-Oriented Concepts, Databases, and Applications. Addison-Wesley. ISBN 0-201-14410-7. (1989)

[gr88]   GRAY, P.M.D., MOFFAT, D.S., and PATON, N.W. *A Prolog interface to a Functional Data Model Database*. In *Advances in Database Technology* – EDBT 1988, Schmidt J.W., Ceri S., and Missikof M. (eds), Springer, Mar 1988.

---

1.   The RADS system was subsequently marketed under the name *Application Master*.

[gr92]   GREENWOOD, R.M., GUY, M.R., and ROBINSON, D.J.K *Implementing a Process Support System in a Persistent Language.* ICL Tech J., May 1992.

[ha87]   HAERDER, T., and ROTHERMEL, K. *Concepts for Transaction Recovery in Nested Transactions.* SIGMOD Record 16(3) pp239-248, Dec 1987

[ic91]   ICL. *Data Dictionary System: Additional Dictionary Facilities.* 10397/001. Mar 1991.

[is91]   ISO/DIS 10728. *Information Resource Dictionary System (IRDS) Services Interface.*

[ka91a] KAY, M. H. *Open Repository Technology.* Proc 3rd European CASE Conference. (April 1991). ISBN 0-86353-261-6.

[ka91b] KAY, M.H. and RIVETT, P.J. *An overview of the Raleigh object-oriented database system.* ICL Tech J. 7(4), pp780-798. Nov 1991.

[ka92]   KAY, M.H. *The Architecture of an Open Dictionary.* ICL Tech J. 8(1), May 1992

[ku86]   KULKARNI, K.G. and ATKINSON, M.P. *EFDM: Extended Functional Data Model.* Comp J, 29(1), pp38-46. 1986.

[mo89]   MOON, D.A. *The COMMON LISP Object-Oriented Programming Standard.* In Kim and Lochovsky (ed), Object-Oriented concepts, Databases, and Applications. Addison-Wesley. ISBN 0-201-14410-7. (1989)

[om91]   OBJECT MANAGEMENT GROUP (OMG). *OMA Guide* – ed. Richard Soley. 1991

[pa89]   PATON, N.W. *ADAM: An Object-oriented Database System implemented in Prolog.* Proc 7th BNCOD, Williams (ed), CUP, pp147-161, 1989.

[po90]   POULOVASSILIS, A. and KING, P.J.H. *Extending the Functional Data Model to Computational Completeness.* In *Advances in Database Technology* – Proc. EDBT 90, ed. F. Bancilhon, C. Thanos, and D. Tsichritzis. March 1990.

[ra88]   RABITTI, F., WOELK, D., KIM, W. *A model of authorization for object-oriented and semantic databases.* Proc. EDBT 88, Springer, 1988.

[ra91]   RAMFOS, A., FIDDIAN, N.J. and GRAY, W.A. *A Meta-Translation System for Object-Oriented to Relational Schema Translations.* In *Aspects of Databases*, Proc. 9th British National Conf. on Databases, ed. Jackson and Robinson. Butterworth- Heinemann, 1991.

[re88]   REHM, S., RAUPP, T., RANFT, R., LÄNGLE, R., HÄRTIG, M., GOTTHARD, W., DITTRICH, K.R. and ABRAMOWICZ, K. *Support for Design Processes in a Structurally Object-Oriented Database System.* In Dittrich, K.R. (ed), *Advances in Object-Oriented Database Systems*, Springer, LNCS 334, 1988.

[ru90]   RUSINKIEWICZ, M.E., ELMAGARMID, A.K., LEU, Y., and LITWIN, W. *Extending the Transaction model to capture more meaning.* SIGMOD Record, 19(1), Mar 1990.

[sh81]   SHIPMAN, D. *The functional data model and the language DAPLEX.* ACM TODS 6(1), pp140-173. (1981)

[st90]   STONEBRAKER, M. *Introduction to the Special Issue on Database Prototype Systems.* IEEE Trans. on Knowledge and Data Engineering 2(1), 1990.

[su84]   SUFRIN, B. *Towards a formal specification of the ICL Data Dictionary.* ICL Tech J., 2, pp195-217. 1984.

[wa89a] WARBOYS, B.C. *The IPSE 2.5 project: Process Modelling as the basis for a Support Environment.* Proc 1st Int. Conf. on Software Development, Environments, and Factories, Berlin, 1989.

[wa89b] WARBOYS, B.C. *The IPSE 2.5 project – a Process-Model based Architecture.* Mar 1989.

[wh91]   WHITE, J. *Generation of Configurations – a Collaborative Venture.* ICL Tech J. 7(4), pp 732-740, Nov 1991.

A GRAPHICAL DATA MODELLING PROGRAM WITH CONSTRAINT SPECIFICATION AND MANAGEMENT

Richard Cooper and Zhenzhou Qin

Department of Computing Science
University of Glasgow
Glasgow G12 8QQ

e-mail: rich@dcs.glasgow.ac.uk
          zq@dcs.glasgow.ac.uk

Abstract

Semantic data models are intended to be tools with which database applications can be designed in a relatively intuitive way by a permitting a description of the database which is close to its meaning. For the most part, however, such tools only permit the structure of the data to be described, whereas much of the meaning of the model of data required by the application can only be expressed as constraints. This paper describes how an implementation of the IFO data model has been extended to allow some categories of constraint to be captured. In doing so, constraints become values in the metadata which are therefore amenable to a number of different uses. In order to explore the implications of the work, the paper discusses various issues, including the role of constraints, how they may be specified and how they may be managed.

1/ Introduction

One dominant aspect of recent database research has been the development of models of data which capture the semantics of an application using constructs much closer to those used by human beings to reason about the world. These Semantic Data Models [Hull and King, 1987; Peckham and Maryanski, 1988] claim such constructs create a simpler tool for designing a database for an application than the classical data models. The simplicity arises firstly because the elements of the data model are in one-to-one correspondence with objects in the real world, and secondly because the ways in which the elements are combined are familiar from everyday experience.

Values in the database are categorised into different classes which represent different kinds of object in the real world. These classes are related in meaningful ways such as: all the members of one class are also members of another; all the members of one class are made up of parts, each part being drawn from some other class. In such a way, the structure of the database can be simply defined and this is then used to define a storage structure for the database, by recasting it into an internal data model, such as the Relational Model [Teorey *et al.*, 1986]. Then database access mechanisms are constructed to run against the internal form.

Some of these mechanisms will be constructed to update the database and such programs must be careful not to invalidate certain constraints on the data. For instance, it is usual to constrain salaries to be non-negative and, with more complexity, to constrain employees' salary to be less than their bosses'. These constraints will appear in the database application as lines buried in the code of the programs which implement data input and update. However, these constraints are an essential part of the **meaning** of the database structure. Therefore it seems that they would best be captured at the same time as the other "semantic" information, which properly resides in the metadata.

In fact, the constraints on usage of a database application arise from a number of elements of a DBMS: the nature of the underlying data storage; the nature of the data model presented to the schema designer; the schema of the database being used; and, maybe, particular restrictions on individual data items in the database. One problem with present DBMS is that the ways in which these constraints are implemented is neither coherently organised nor explicitly visible, but rather is an ad-hoc assortment of obscurely structured code fragments.

One approach to managing constraints is that of Frame Based Systems (such as KEE), in which the description of the structure of a "database" includes slots for constraints [Fikes and Kehler, 1985]. Such systems have tended to be implemented in the context of untyped or dynamically typed environments. There is, however, a problem with creating database software which must wait until run-time before discovering that a piece of code is trying to use data of the wrong type. If the code is expected to be used over a long period of time, as is typical of database applications, then typing errors for infrequently used code may take years to show up and be consequently extremely difficult to fix. The present work assumes a strongly typed environment with a maximum amount of static type checking.

In this paper, an initial experiment which attempts to tackle these problems is described. The start point was an implementation of the IFO data model in the persistent programming language, PS-algol. This implementation allows a database structure to be captured graphically. Furthermore, a small amount of database functionality is implemented in the form of minimal data manipulation and retrieval operations, sufficient to populate a database in order to test its structure. This original program was modified so that the constraints implicit in the IFO data model were extracted from the code and made into **values** in the database. Then the program was extended so that some categories of schema constraint could be captured using similar graphical techniques and then be stored uniformly with the model constraints. The data input and update parts were then modified to experiment with different techniques of constraint management - in particular how to handle constraint violations.

In the succeeding sections, the IFO data model and its original implementation are introduced. Then the rôle of constraints in database applications is discussed briefly. The fourth section describes how constraints are specified, while the fifth section describes some techniques for managing constraints. The concluding section summarises and then proposes some potential developments from this work.

2/ The IFO Data Model and Its Implementation

2.1 The IFO Data Model

The IFO data model was introduced by Abiteboul and Hull [Abiteboul and Hull, 1987] to analyse the update semantics in a high order data model. It incorporates the major features of Semantic Data Models, providing a sophisticated taxonomy of types, which will now be discussed with reference to the schema shown in Figure 1.

Firstly, there are three kinds of **atomic** type: **printable** types, such as string, integer, etc.; **abstract** types, which represent the basic entities the schema is modelling, and have "no underlying structure"; and **free** types, which are defined with reference to other types (subtypes are an example of these). Thus *Person*, *Car* and *Boat* represent the fundamental entities being modelled in Figure 1, while *Vehicle*, *VehicleOwner*, *Married* and *Unmarried* are all derived from these. There are also the following complex type constructors: **set** or **collection** creates a multi-valued object (*OwnedVehicles* in the example); while **aggregate** creates single objects out of component parts (*Address* in the example). Using these constructs, the space of objects can be thought of as being partitioned into classes, each of which is controlled by one of the abstract types.

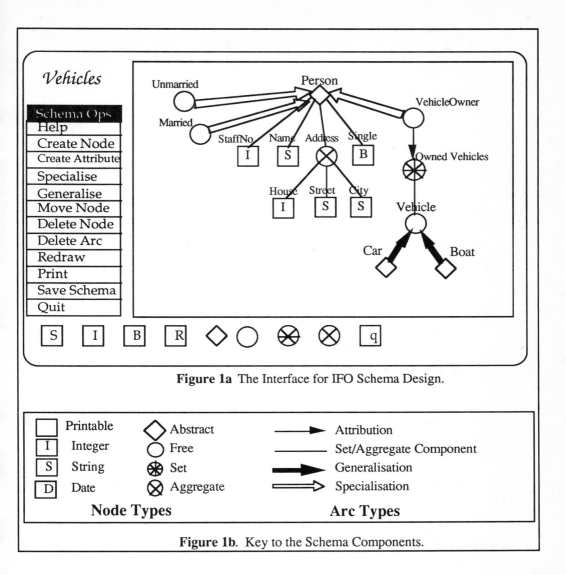

Figure 1a The Interface for IFO Schema Design.

Node Types		Arc Types	
☐ Printable	◇ Abstract	⟶ Attribution	
I Integer	○ Free	— Set/Aggregate Component	
S String	✳ Set	⟹ Generalisation	
D Date	⊗ Aggregate	⟹ Specialisation	

Figure 1b. Key to the Schema Components.

The entity types are connected by a number of different **relationships**. A **fragment** is any graph of types and relationships and a **schema** is the complete graph representing the model. The relationships available in the model are **attribution** (*X* is an attribute of *Y*); **component** (*X* is a **part** of aggregate type *Y* or *X* is an element of set *Y*); and the sub-typing relationships **specialisation** and **generalisation**. Specialisation represents the notion that type *X* is a sub-type of *Y* in the senses that *X* inherits the properties of *Y* and all *X*'s are also *Y*'s. The specialised type, *X*, will be a free type, since it is defined relative to the type being specialised - *Married*, *Unmarried* and *VehicleOwner* are examples of these. Generalisation, on the other hand, creates a free type which is the super-type of a set of other types. It encompasses the notion that every instance of this type must also be an instance of one of the sub-types (thus *Vehicle* is constructed as the union of *Car* and *Boat*).

IFO allows some **constraints** to be specified for the particular schema (in Section 3, these will be termed schema level constraints), such as that a relationship is 1:1, etc. It also allows constraints on specialisation relationships - that the subtypes of *X* must be **disjoint** or that they **cover** *X*. There are also constraints which are enforced on every schema defined using IFO (these will be called model level constraints in Section 3):

- all sub-type sub-graphs must be acyclic;
- no type can be the specialisation of more than one atomic type;
- no free type can have been created simultaneously by generalisation and specialisation.

The first of these is intuitively obvious - it makes little sense to say *X* is a sub-type of *Y*, which is a sub-type of *Z*, which is a sub-type of *X*. If the sub-typing (or subsetting) relationship adds more information at every stage, *X* now has more information than *X*!

The second model constraint means that inheritance from more than one super-type is acceptable as long as these both eventually inherit from the same atomic type. This makes some sense in that whereas a type which specialises both *Married* and *VehicleOwner*, themselves both specialisations of *Person,* seems reasonable, a type which specialises both *Boat* and *Person* does not. (Note however that the type of potential vehicle owners may be the sub-type of both *Person* and *Company*.)

The third constraint is a consequence of the definition of free types. Free types are either created by specialisation or by generalisation and to do both at once suggests that a type gets its defining information from two possibly conflicting sources. Thus *Vehicle* may be created as a specialisation of *MovingThing* or as a generalisation of *Boat* and *Car*, but not both at once. If the model must capture all this, either *MovingThing* must be a generalisation of *Vehicle* (and other types) or *Car* and *Boat* must be a specialisation of *Vehicle*.

2.2 An Implementation of IFO

An implementation of the IFO data model is described in a previous paper [Cooper and Qin, 1990] and only the essential features will be described here. The implementation was carried out in the persistent programming language PS-algol [PS-algol, 1987], since this offers persistent support for numerical, textual and graphical values, as well as first-class functions with parameters of any type, within records whose fields can also be of any type including other records. The IFO program provides two modes of operation: schema definition and data manipulation. The screen for the schema definition phase is shown in Figure 1a.

The screen is divided into a schema diagram window and two menus, one of operations and one of node types, which are used to specify, for instance, which type of node will be created by the *CreateNode* operation. The operations permit the creation and deletion of the schema components as well as saving, printing and redrawing the schema. The operations have a direct manipulation feel to them with nodes being created by dragging icons from the lower menu, arcs being created by clicking over the end points and arcs being deleted by scratching across them.

There is no attempt to support the specification of disjoint, covering or 1-1 relationship constraints, but the three model level constraints are all enforced. Thus it is impossible to create an arc which would create a cyclical sub-typing relationship. Support for these constraints is implemented by lines of code buried in the program at suitable places.

The data manipulation mode provides a similar menu of operations, which permit new data values to be entered, edited, deleted and browsed. Data input consists of selecting a node for which a new value is to be given. Then dependent nodes are visited recursively and, for each, the user may either select an old value using a menu of all the existing instances of the node or a new instance may be created. Thus in the figure, a new address is specified by visiting each of the three dependent nodes in turn. For the city name, for instance, the user may either re-select a city name already in the database or type in a new one. Browsing allows the user to pick an instance from a node and then displays all of the dependent information recursively.

Editing allows parts of a value to be changed, while deleting removes the value from the database. Since there is no way of specifying constraints on the data, none of the data entry or update operations can cause violations and so managing violations did not have to be considered.

3/ The Rôle of Constraints in Database Systems

Use of an application programmed in the context of a general purpose DBMS is constrained by a number of factors which arise either because of the limitations of the system or because of intended restrictions which are a consequence of the meaning of the application. The work described here is part of an attempt to produce a complete categorisation of all such constraints, with a unified specification format (such as that in [Leler, 1988]) and this section summarises the authors' current position which will be more fully developed elsewhere [Cooper and Qin, 1992].

3.1   A Taxonomy of Constraints

All constraints are installed in a DBMS at one of four levels:

i) The global level. It is a limitation of the DBMS that it cannot capture particular information - for instance, the DBMS may be unable to store sounds.

ii) The data model level. Usage of the DBMS is provided via an external data model. This data model will consist of a set of modelling constructs, which have two aspects: they can be mapped onto the globally available structures; and there are constraints on the ways in which they can be combined. For instance, in the ER model, the "attribution" construct is constrained to link an entity type and a base type node. These data model constraints limit the structure of the different schemata that can be produced.

iii) The schema level. The schema of a database defines the nature of the data which it holds. Usually this is restricted to a description of the structure of the data, but a full definition of a database will include constraints on the values that the data can take. For instance, we may wish to constrain all people in a university database to be either staff or students.

iv) The data level - if the DBMS permits more than one database to be created using the same schema, it may be possible to assert further constraints on particular values in the database - such as this particular employee's salary can never rise above a certain ceiling.

How are these constraints implemented? Usually, they are hardwired into programs. The model level constraints are programmed into the system component which provides the data model. The schema and data level constraints appear in application programs. But there is no reason why this should be the case! If constraints are viewed as further data modelling constructs, then the global level could provide structures to house them, so that the model level constraints are described explicitly in terms of these. If constraints are values in the database, then the schema and data level constraints can similarly be made explicit.

In the original IFO implementation, the global level is represented by the PS-algol persistent store [Cockshott *et al.*, 1984]. This is permanent storage in which integers, reals, booleans, strings, images, functions and records (but not sound) can be stored. The structuring is extremely flexible since the parameters of functions and the fields of records can be of any type. The model level is implemented as a PS-algol program in which the data model constraints have been embedded. The schema level constraints described by Abiteboul and Hull are ignored altogether.

3.2   Some Common Constraints

The kinds of constraints which it would be useful to represent are now discussed. For the purposes of this paper, the discussion will be restricted to schema level constraints, although a similar analysis can be given for the other levels [Cooper and Qin, 1992]. For instance, a list of model constraints can be given which either limit the ways in which the modelling constructs can be combined or impose limitations on the data. In IFO, the acyclicity of sub-typing is an example of the former, while the constraint that generalised nodes are covered by their sub-types is an example of the latter.

The following are a list of schema level constraints which it might be useful to allow a schema designer to specify (a longer list appears elsewhere [Cooper and Qin, 1992]):

i) **Uniqueness constraints**. No two instances of a particular node can have the same value. Example: driving license number.

ii) **Non-null constraints**. All instances of a particular node must have a value. Example: name.

iii) **Value range constraints**. The values of instances of a particular node are limited to lie within a particular range. Example: 0 <= Age <= 120.

iv) **Relationship range constraints**. For related nodes, how many instances of one node can be related to an instance of another. Example: every car insurance policy is related to exactly one vehicle.

v) **Cardinality constraints**. The number of values in a multi-valued node must lie in a particular range. Example: number of spouses = 0 or 1.

vi) **Inclusion constraints**. All values of one node are also values of another. Example: drivers are all people.

vii) **Covering constraints**. All values of a particular node are also values of one of a set of other nodes. Example: vehicles are cars or boats or planes.

viii) **Disjointedness constraints**. No pair of a set of nodes have common instances. Example: men and women.

ix) **Referential integrity constraints**. Any reference from one value to another will be guaranteed to exist.

x) **General constraints**. Restrictions on the ways in which which data can populate the nodes not covered above. At its most general, such constraints consist of predicates linking constants and nodes which are related to one another - the linking being performed by the usual boolean operators and connectors. Example: people can only own more than one vehicle if their salary is above £10,000.

Some of these constraints are of such importance that they are embedded in the semantics of the data modelling constructs. Inclusion constraints are virtually always provided in this way and are part of the semantics of the sub-typing relationships in IFO. Some constraints are enforced globally. In persistent systems, referential integrity constraints are always enforced, since if a value containing a reference to another is stored, then the referenced value is dragged into the persistent store as well. In IFO, the generalisation construct always includes the covering constraint, but this may optionally also be enforced on individual instances of specialisation. In the work described here, all of the constraint types are added into the schema specification facilities except inclusion and referential integrity constraints (discussed above) and relationship range constraints (which are not appropriate to the IFO model as relationships are not explicit constructs in IFO).

4/ Constraint Specification in IFO

This section describes the user interface to constraint specification in IFO. To the list of operations seen in Figure 1 are added operations to insert and remove constraints (see Figure 2). The latter works by allowing the designer to select the node at which the constraint is to be removed and then the constraint from all of those defined on that node.

After selecting the "Create Constraint" option, the schema designer must select one of the seven types of constraint and then proceed as follows.

Uniqueness Constraints. Select the node to be unique by clicking on it. In the example, *StaffNo* may be determined to be unique. The node name is underlined in order to provide feedback.

Non-null constraints. Select the node to be non-null by clicking on it. *Name* and *StaffNo* again can be made non-null, which will be indicated by emboldening the name.

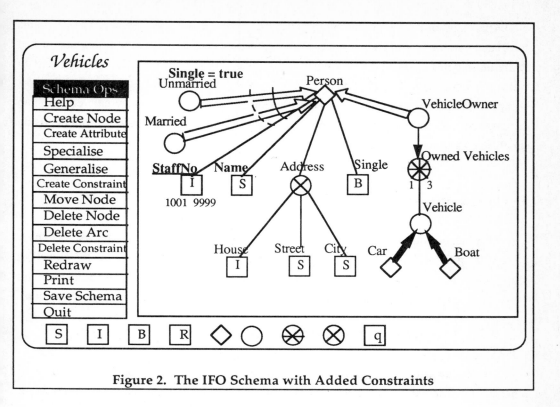

Figure 2. The IFO Schema with Added Constraints

Value range constraints. Select the node (which must be printable) and type in two numbers for the upper and lower bounds. If the node is numerical these are bounds on the values of the nodes. If the node is a string, they are bounds on the length of the string. The staff number can be constrained to lie between 1001 and 9999. The limits appear at the lower corners of the icon representing the node.

Cardinality constraints. The set node to be constrained is selected and upper and lower bounds typed in. Using this, the number of vehicles owned is constrained to be at most 3. Again the limits appear at the lower corners of the set icon.

Covering constraints. The node being covered is selected followed by each of the nodes which cover it. Thus, we can ensure that all people are either married or unmarried. The covering nodes are linked by an arc.

Disjointedness constraints. The node being covered is selected followed by each of the nodes which cover it. Again, we may ensure that no-one is both married and unmarried. The nodes are linked by a broken arc.

General constraints. These are the most difficult to be fully general about. At present, a node is selected to hold a constraint. Then a predicate is built up using relational (<, =, etc.) and logical (and, not and or) operators. The terms of the predicate are constants, which are typed in, the node itself (if a base node) or attributes (including those inherited). To indicate that the constraint *Single* = "true" on the *Unmarried*, the designer would select the *Unmarried* node, then select the *Single* node; choose "=" from a menu of relational operators and then type in "true". The constraint then appears above the node.

The result of such a specification is that each node may have a number of constraints associated with it. Consequently, every time a value of a node is updated, it is possible to find easily those constraints which may have been violated by the update. The revised program thus has integrated the specification of constraints with other elements of schema specification. Using a style which is uniform with the rest of the program, constraints are entered into both the database and the graphical representation of the schema, so that schema design is greatly simplified, as shown in Figure 2.

5/ Constraint Management

The first consideration to be made was how to represent constraints. The goal is to have them as identifiable "values" in the database instead of embedding them in either the modelling program or in application code to having. Once a way of doing this is achieved, methods for using them can be determined. These two concerns are discussed in the next two sub-sections.

5.1 The Representation of Constraints

Having an underlying database with a rich type system gives considerable power in representing different kinds of value. In particular, since functions are denotable values within the database, they can be manipulated in the same way as numbers and strings.

Constraints in the revised IFO implementation are all represented as records containing values which are functions whose arguments are an instance, a node and the schema and whose result is boolean. The functions all return false if the constraint is violated and true otherwise. Often, all three arguments are not required, in which case null values must be supplied. The constraint record also includes sufficient textual information to permit the system to inform the user about violations.

The first revision of the program consisted in extracting the embedded model level constraints (sub-type acyclicity, etc) from the program and replacing them with records of the type given above. They are then stored in the database as a set of data model constraints that must hold for all schemata. Then a general purpose constraint checking module was added as described in the next section. Constraint checks on the structure of the schema are made by calling this procedure at points where schema modifications may cause violations. Notice that with this structure, it becomes much easier to change the model level constraints which hold. It is now possible to change the set of constraints relatively simply and thus change the semantics of the data model if this is desired.

The schema level constraints were added into the overall representation of a schema. In the initial implementation, a database schema is represented as a set of nodes, each node being represented by a record whose fields include the node name, its position in the graphical representation, a set of relationships it has with other nodes and a set of instances. To this is added a set of constraints defined on that node. This means that whenever an update is made to the set of instances at each node, the set of constraints at the node can be checked.

The constraints are added as they are specified using run-time reflection - the ability of PS-algol to create, compile and store program modules during the run of a program [Kirby, 1992]. For each constraint type, there is a string holding the source of a function as a template into which is embedded particular values. For instance, the cardinality constraint template checks the cardinality against two dummy names and these dummy names are replaced by the actual limits before compilation.

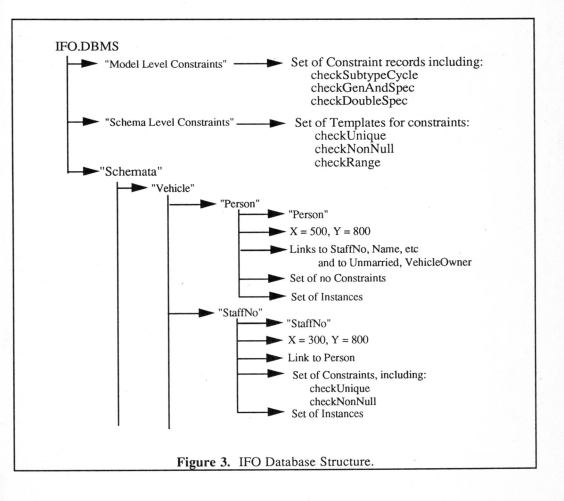

Figure 3. IFO Database Structure.

The database structure which supports all of this is shown in Figure 3, together with some stored values. The DBMS has sets of model level constraints and templates for schema level constraints, which are available to all schemata. Then each schema is stored as a set of nodes with the data as shown.

5.2   The Manipulation of Constraints

Given the storage of constraints in the database described above, it becomes possible to provide system components to a DBMS which implement general purpose constraint handling facilities. The first two of these are:

Single constraint check. This is used to check the model level constraints. As the schema is updated, potential violations are checked and if they occur a warning message is generated, to which the user may respond as described below, and an indication on whether to proceed with the update is returned to the calling program.

Multiple constraint check. This is similar to the above, but all of the constraints in a set are checked. This is used to check potential violation when update to a node instance is made. The set of constraints associated with that node are all checked.

When such checks have been made, there are a number of possible ways in which it is possible to deal with violations:

Forbidding. The update operation is cancelled.

Permitting. The update operation is allowed to proceed, effectively suspending the constraint.

Cascading. The update operation causes further updates which re-validate the constraint.

In the present version of the system, the two constraint checking components, after alerting the user to a violation, give the option of the above three reactions (although cascading is only appropriate with certain constraint types, such as covering or disjointedness). The database is thus able to get into a state which invalidates the constraints.

With the present system as a platform, more sophisticated constraint handling facilities are planned. These are based upon notions of fine control on suspending and re-imposing constraints as the user requires [Sutton, 1991]. To this end, the following facilities are planned.

Check all constraints. Given the possibility of inconsistency in the database already mentioned, this facility will test all constraints for violations, report any of these and seek guidance on repair from the user.

Suspend constraints. This will take two forms: suspending all constraint checking and suspending the checking of selected constraints.

Re-impose constraints. This will have the form of re-imposing selected constraints - the check all constraints has the effect of a general re-imposition.

Begin transaction. Start a log of changes and check constraints only at the matching end transaction. Transactions can be freely nested.

End transaction. Re-impose all constraints which might have been violated in the transaction.

These facilities will be made available as extra items in the data manipulation menu, so that a database user will have complete control on when and how constraint validity is enforced.

6/ Conclusions

The way in which constraints are managed in a standard DBMS is deficient in that a significant portion of the meaning of a database is buried in DBMS components and application code where it becomes difficult to manipulate. It is clear that users wish to express constraints on their data explicitly and then to control how and when those constraints are imposed. Similarly, the constraints which are made on the structure of schemata should also be accessible so that the user can have a clearer understanding of the data model being used and so that the model itself can be modified if required.

A taxonomy of constraints has been briefly described which brings together the different kinds of constraint which affect usage of a database. This taxonomy starts from those constraints which are an intrinsic part of the underlying system; those which are present as part of the semantics of the data model provided to the application builder; and those which are present in the schema and on individual data. All of such constraints can be put on a common footing and thus have general purpose facilities available to them.

The present work has demonstrated that, when this overall taxonomy is understood, it is possible to rescue constraints from the dark dungeons in which they are usually forced to lurk and maintain them as identifiable values in the metadata of the DBMS. Then they become susceptible to user manipulation in an explicit manner.

The current experiment took a program which implements the IFO model as a schema designer tool with a data manipulation component. This was enhanced first of all by extracting the constraints which are inherent to the semantics of the model itself as explicit values. Then facilities were added for the user specification of schema level constraints, which were then stored in the database. By using a common structure for all constraints, general purpose facilities could be added to the system.

The work described here is leading towards the construction of a Configurable Data Modelling System [Cooper, 1990]. The intention behind this is that a DBMS will be constructed which will permit the addition of new access methods (i.e. data models and user interfaces) in a simple way. This will allow a variety of models of data to be available for different categories of user without a significant programming overhead and by embedding these within the same system permit designers and users to move at will between more and less complex access mechanisms as appropriate since all will be accessing the same underlying data.

The initial implementation of such a system covered the constructions of data models which handled the structural component of entity based models. The next step is to add the control of constraints into this system. The management of constraints within a single model system demonstrated here gives considerable encouragement that this can be achieved.

Acknowledgements

The authors would first like to acknowledge Ms. Tan Lay Khim and Ms. Yng Tai for their fine efforts in putting the ideas in this paper into practise. We would also like to acknowledge Ms. Teo Lee Nah, who simultaneously implemented an interface based on automatically generated forms. This work will be reported elsewhere, but Ms. Teo contributed to our overall understanding. Many members of the database group in our department contributed ideas as we presented early versions of this work, including but not restricted to: Malcolm Atkinson, David Harper, Ray Welland, Moira Norrie, Paul Philbrow, David Kerr and Ivan Tabkha. It is always necessary in this work to acknowledge our colleagues at St. Andrews University, led by Ron Morrison. for building persistent systems which work. Without such an elegant platform, the work presented here would soon get lost in implementation detail. We would also like to thank the anonymous reviewers whose comments were extremely useful.

The work was supported by ESPRIT project 2071 (COMANDOS) and by SERC project H17671 (Configurable Data Modelling), whose supported we gratefully acknowledge.

Bibliography

Abiteboul and Hull, 1987
   S. Abiteboul and R. Hull, "IFO: A Formal Semantic Data Model", *ACM TODS*, 12, 4, 525-565, December 1987.

Cockshott *et al.*, 1984
   W.P. Cockshott, M.P. Atkinson, K.J. Chisholm, P.J. Bailey and R. Morrison, "POMS : a persistent object management system", *Software Practice and Experience*, *14*, 1, 49-71, January 1984.

Cooper, 1990
   R.L. Cooper, "Configurable Data Modelling Systems", *Proc. 9th International Conference on the Entity Relationship Approach,* Lausanne, Switzerland, 35-52, October, 1990.

Cooper and Qin, 1990
   R.L. Cooper and Z. Qin, "An Implementation of the IFO Data Model", in *Data Modelling Research at Glasgow University, 1990-91* (R.Cooper, ed.), Technical Report CS 91/R14, *Department of Computing Science, University of Glasgow,* August 1991.

Cooper and Qin, 1992
   R.L. Cooper and Z. Qin, "A Taxonomy for the Specification and Management of Constraints in Database Systems", submitted to VLDB 1992.

Fikes and Kehler, 1985
   R. Fikes and T. Kehler, "The Role of Frame-Based Representation in Reasoning", *Communications of the ACM*, 28, 9, 904-920, September 1985.

Hull and King, 1987
   R. Hull and R. King, "Semantic Data Modeling: Survey, Applications and Research Issues", *ACM Computing Surveys*, 19, 3, 201-260, September 1987.

Kirby, 1992
   G. Kirby, "Persistent Programming with Type Safe Linguistic Reflection", *Proc. 25th Annual Hawaii International Conference on System Sciences,* January 1992.

Leler, 1988
   W. Leler, "Constraint Programming Languages: Their Specification and Generation", Addison-Wesley, 1988.

Peckham and Maryanski, 1988
   J. Peckham and F. Maryanski, "Semantic Data Models", *ACM Computing Surveys*, 20, 3, 153-189, September, 1988.

PS-algol, 1987
   "The PS-algol Reference Manual - Fourth Edition", *Persistent Programming Research Report 12*, Universities of Glasgow and St. Andrews, 1987.

Sutton, 1991
    S.M. Sutton, "A Flexible Consistency Model for Persistent Data in Software Process Programming Languages", to be in *Implementing Persistent Object Bases: Principles and Practise* (eds A. Dearle, G.M. Shaw and S.B. Zdonik), Morgan Kaufmann, 1991.

Teorey *et al.*, 1986
    T.J. Teorey, D. Yang and J.P. Fry, "A logical Design Methodology for Relational Databases Using the Extended Entity-Relationship Model", *ACM Computing Surveys*, 18, 2, 197-222, June 1986.

ASSOCIATION MERGING IN A SCHEMA META-INTEGRATION SYSTEM FOR A HETEROGENEOUS OBJECT-ORIENTED DATABASE ENVIRONMENT

M A Qutaishat [1], N J Fiddian, W A Gray
Department of Computing Mathematics
University of Wales College of Cardiff
Cardiff, U.K.

Abstract

This paper describes a meta-programmed approach for merging class associations during schema integration in a logically heterogeneous Object-Oriented database environment. Association merging represents an important phase in the process of schema integration. Such integration can provide transparency of heterogeneity in two different situations: when pre-existing schemas of separate databases are integrated into a single unified global schema; and when a set of independent user views of the same database are integrated into a global conceptual schema. Here we emphasise the fundamental issues involved in association merging and the meta-programmed realisation of this merging phase in the context of a complete schema integration system we are developing, called the schema meta-integration system (SMIS).

1   Introduction

The increasing use of Object-Oriented (O-O) [ROW87,CAR88,LEC88,ATK90,STO90, ZDO90] and semantic data models for advanced database applications means that many organisations will be faced with heterogeneous sets of databases which will need to be merged and integrated if their potential is to be fully exploited. In fundamental terms, database heterogeneity is a natural consequence of progress and competition over time, as advances in product development are made and different vendors market different alternative systems. In practice, it may occur when data is distributed between autonomous local sections of the same organisation, it may arise out of a requirement for interoperability when different organisations collaborate (e.g. by agreement or merger), or it may result from the choice of different systems as most suitable for different related applications. Independent user views of subsets of data from the same database can also be considered as heterogeneous from the standpoint of integration into a global conceptual schema.

The problem of heterogeneity in such an environment can be solved by constructing an integrated global schema which allows access to all the data held in the databases. In this context we are concerned here with heterogeneity at the logical level [OZS91] (i.e. where different databases are *designed* independently) rather than at the data management level (i.e. involving different data models) which has been dealt with in [HOW87,HOW88,RAM89, QUT90,RAM91].

Our methodology - outlined here - in dealing with the problem of schema integration in general and association merging in particular is a knowledge-based semi-automatic process. This process is guided by an inference engine acting upon the real world data modelling framework which is based on an extended form of the Object Modelling Technique (OMT)

---

[1] on study leave from the Department of Computer Science, University of Jordan, Amman, Jordan.

[LOO87,RUM91], called the Integrated OMT (IOMT), as well as on system-designer interaction. In this context we examine and demonstrate by example several problems relating to the detection and resolution of structural and semantic conflicts in deriving mergeable associations. We formalise this process by discussing the use of meta-programming technology (in particular meta-programming in Prolog [CLO87,MAL87,SCHN89,LUG89, BRA90]) to generalise the efficient production of integrated schemas from the structural components and the semantic contents of logically heterogeneous O-O database schemas.

2   Scope and Objective

2.1   Meta-Programming: Principles and Application in the Area of Database Systems

A meta-program [BRA90] is a program that processes other programs as data. Interpreters and compilers are simple examples of meta-programs. A compiler is a program that reads a program structure written in one language formalism, the source language, and translates it into an equivalent program structure in another language formalism, the target language. Typically, the source language of a compiler is a general-purpose, high level language, such as COBOL or PASCAL, and the target language is the assembly language or machine language of some computer. However, the source and target languages of a compiler may both be any specialised language formalism that has arisen in some specific area of computer application. In this general case the compiler is often referred to as a translator. Just as it is possible to generate conventional compilers automatically by means of a sophisticated meta-program called a compiler compiler, it is also possible to generate such area-specific translators automatically by means of a combination of compiler compiler and code-generator generator mechanisms [AHO86] in a process which we have called meta-translation [HOW87,RAM89].

Application of this meta-programming technology to the generation of language inter-translators in the database systems context has proved in practice to be very efficient and productive [HOW87,RAM91]. Encouraged by this success, we decided to use the same general approach to tackle the schema heterogeneity problem in a heterogeneous O-O database environment. We concluded from our previous experience that it should be possible to develop, in a prototype form, a generalised schema meta-integration system (SMIS) for the construction of a homogeneous global schema from heterogeneous local components, based on the use of a common internal intermediate representation and using Prolog as the system implementation language. This tool would provide a semi-automatic process for global schema production from heterogeneous O-O local schemas. Such a tool would be an asset in a heterogeneous O-O database environment by making it possible to present global users with the illusion of dealing with a single integrated homogeneous global schema, while preserving full autonomy for the underlying local schemas.

2.2   The Schema Integration Problem in an O-O Database Environment

Whenever heterogeneity occurs at the logical level, one solution to the problem of making it viable for users to access data across databases (which are often distributed) is to integrate these databases by constructing a global schema which provides a single unified interface [LAN82,DAY84,BAT86,MOT87,SHE88,BER89a,BER89b,KAU90,OZS91]. An important obstacle in the way of integrating these databases is the problems arising from their independent design. For example, a single concept might have different representations and meaning in different local schemas. Types of heterogeneity occurring in an O-O database environment range from hardware heterogeneity to variations in data management systems. For the purpose of this paper, this diversity can be narrowed down to different perspectives (semantic ambiguity) and incompatible design specifications (structural ambiguity). Differences in perspective are due to different designers adopting their own individual viewpoints in modelling the same objects from the application domain. This can give rise to synonyms, homonyms, different type hierarchies and different associations. Incompatibility in design specifications can be caused by diversities in representation, domain conflicts, type conflicts and conflicts among constraints.

2.3   The Schema Integration Process

The overall task of schema integration can be divided into two main parts; schema analysis followed by schema synthesis. This is begun by the process of establishing correspondences and detecting possible conflicts between structural components or semantic contents of local schemas in the so-called pre-integration phase, where these conflicts are resolved by conforming the different schemas so that they can be compared, merged and restructured, before being integrated to form a global schema. Such activities represent the formal process of designing the global conceptual schema [BAT86,OZS91].

To be able to establish correspondences, e.g. by identifying sets of related objects, classes and associations, a method for comparing structural components and semantic contents has to be determined. Using this the designer of the global schema might want to compare two objects or n objects as equal or related to each other in some other way, with a view to forming an integrated equivalent object at the global level [QUT92]. Having determined the related sets of objects and classes, association integration involves merging the associations in which the classes concerned participate.

To illustrate this, consider a class C1 (Student) in schema S1, and a related class C2 (University-student) in schema S2. Here all the associations in which C1 participates become potentially open to integration with all the associations in which C2 participates. The actual merging of these associations, however, is subject to their semantics, which are determined by (among other factors) the roles of the classes and the associations concerned and the constraints on those associations. In recognition of the importance of this semantic information, we decided to use the real world data modelling approach as a framework for O-O schema integration.

2.4   Real World Data Modelling and Schema Integration

The three-level modelling architecture, shown in figure 1, represents our proposed framework of object modelling, which is similar to the architecture proposed by the ANSI/SPARC committee on DBMS [DAT86]. These three levels consist of the real world level, rO, which represents real world semantics (RWS)/real world objects; the logical level, lO, which represents user-defined classes/objects in DDL formalisms; and the internal level, iO, which represents the internal implementation of the above two levels.

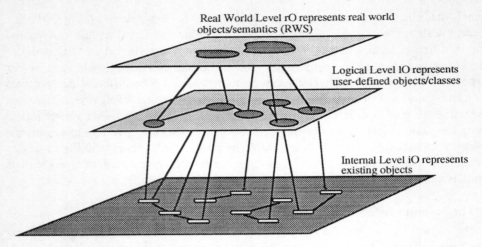

Real World Level rO represents real world objects/semantics (RWS)

Logical Level lO represents user-defined objects/classes

Internal Level iO represents existing objects

Figure 1. The proposed three-level modelling architecture which facilitates the integration of pre-existing objects

Schema integration, against this background, has been identified as the activity of designing a single integrated global schema starting from individual component schemas. When such a design activity is directed towards the detection and resolution of structural and semantic ambiguity, the real world level rO emerges as an important factor, in particular for deriving correspondences among equivalent objects and associations and for semantic ambiguity resolution, while structural ambiguity can be dealt with at the logical level.

2.5   Object Meta-Model

To capture the semantics of the real world precisely and naturally, we decided to adapt the philosophy of the Object Modelling Technique (OMT)[LOO87,RUM91]. OMT consists of a set of object data modelling concepts and a language-independent graphical notation. This notation combines O-O concepts (classes and inheritance) with information modelling concepts (entities and associations) as illustrated in figure 2. There are many advantages in using OMT during the process of schema integration as it represents a high-level conceptual data model which is ideal for modelling objects from the real world, rather than using a specific implementation of O-O database or computer concepts. As such we have developed an extended form of OMT, which we refer to as the Integrated Object Modelling Technique (IOMT), to capture the logic of the RWS level of the real world data modelling framework (see figure 1). This extended form of OMT is our choice for representing the global schema. Such a schema specifies the contents of a database in terms of the semantics and structure of meta-data rather than of data. A semantic interpretation involves a description of what data objects exist, specified in terms of object classes and properties, with the associations among them.

Two types of meta-data have proved to be very useful in schema integration. The source schema in its DDL formalism constitutes the first type, consisting of data descriptions (descriptors) for the data elements that are stored in a database. These include structural and coding information. The second type is contained in a 'data dictionary' consisting of data definitions for the descriptors themselves, i.e. the meaning of the elements stored in the database. The ultimate objective of meta-data exploitation is to allow the RWS level to direct the features and rules of IOMT in the process of integrated schema analysis and construction.

Therefore, we decided to use the three-level architecture shown in figure 1 in developing an interactive tool to assist a designer in constructing a global schema. This tool, the so-called schema meta-integration system (SMIS), is intended to be a prototype front-end interface which facilitates O-O schema integration.

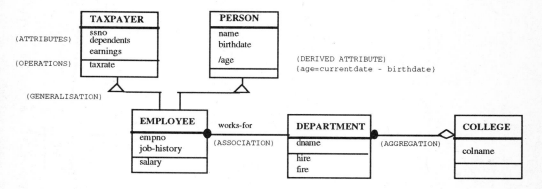

Figure 2. An example of the OMT Object modelling graphical notation

3 The Association Merging Process

An association [RUM91] describes a group of conceptual connections with common structure and common semantics that may exist between object instances. Such associations provide the means for establishing relationships among object classes/types. Aggregation represents a tightly coupled form of association with some extra semantics which represent the "part-whole" or "consists-of" relationship between two objects.

Our approach to carrying out association merging is a knowledge-based semi-automatic process. For the purpose of schema integration, we have developed the classification of associations shown in the graph of figure 3. This figure represents an and/or graph for directing association integration, and uses a supporting inference engine to search its knowledge space to find a solution in a data-driven reasoning approach (i.e. by forward chaining).

As the figure shows, the process begins by reasoning about the type of the associations under consideration for integration. Each path through the graph terminates with a rule base to be triggered at the end of the inference process. In section 3.1 we discuss the criteria which direct this process, while in section 3.2 we discuss a selected subset of the rule bases used to perform merging *per se*.

214

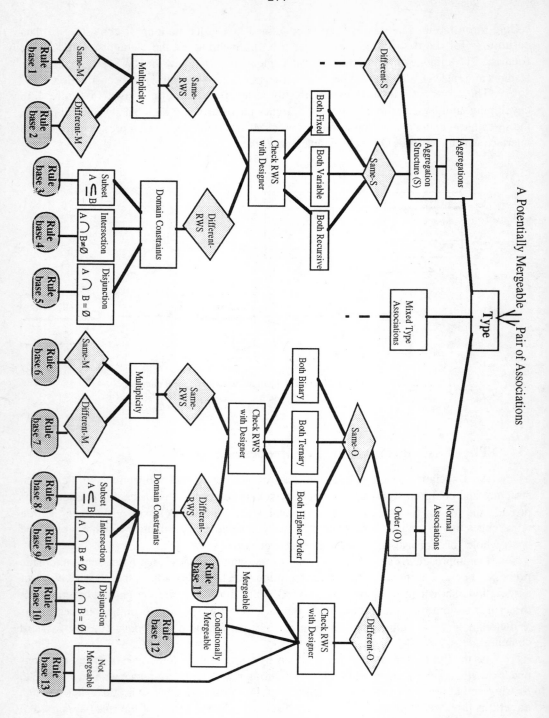

Figure 3. Classification of Potentially Mergeable Associations

3.1 Criteria for Association Merging

There are several criteria which we have found to be important in reasoning about association merging. Some of these have been previously discussed in [NAV86] in Entity-Category-Relationship terms. These criteria are designed to be compatible with our chosen three-level architecture of schema integration which ultimately has to account for all the structural and semantic information involved.

i) Association Type: the type of an association determines whether the association is a normal association or an aggregation. Inference about association types may require designer interaction to provide semantic information by means of a set of assertions.

ii) Association Order: this determines whether an association is binary, ternary or higher order. In practice the vast majority are binary or qualified (a special form of ternary association) [RUM91].

iii) Real World Semantics (RWS): this semantic information is needed to specify the role played by associations. Two associations may have different role names but have the same RWS (i.e. play the same role).

iv) Multiplicity: the multiplicity of an association specifies for its participant classes how many instances of one class may relate to each instance of the other class. It constrains the number of related objects, e.g. to "one" or "many". OMT object diagrams indicate multiplicity by special symbols at the ends of association lines. The complete notation can be found in [RUM91].

v) Domain Constraints: such constraints specify whether a subset, intersection or disjunction relationship holds between one association and another.

vi) Aggregation Structure: this determines whether an aggregation has a fixed, variable or recursive structure. In this way compatibility between aggregations can be determined in preparation for merging.

3.2 Association Merging Rule Bases

These rule bases perform the actual integration of mergeable associations in accordance with the conclusions reached by inference. Due to limitations of space we discuss only a representative subset of the different rule bases available, as follows (those rule bases which are not considered in detail are all variants of those which are). In the figures that follow we use standard OMT notation [RUM91] with two necessary minor extensions, for derived generalisation (e.g. figure 4.c) and virtual class materialisation (e.g. figure 5.c).

• *Rule base 1:* This is the first and simplest case of association merging. If the two associations are both found to be in aggregation form, as shown in schema 1 of figure 4 (a vehicle consists-of one or more parts) and schema 2 of figure 4 (a car consists-of one or more parts), where the aggregations have the same structure, the same real world semantics (RWS) and the same multiplicity, then the integration of these two schemas can be constructed as shown in figure 4.c. Here aggregation merging follows class merging, which is carried out in a semi-automatic process involving designer interaction to specify semantic information. In this case, vehicle represents a super-class of car so the integrated consists-of aggregation is connected to the super-class vehicle and inherited by its sub-class car.

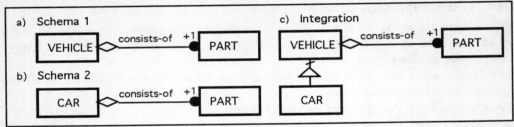

Figure 4. Example for Rule base 1

• *Rule base 3:* This applies if an aggregation association pair are found to have the same structure but have different RWS (i.e. different meanings), with the additional constraint that one of them is a subset of the other as shown in schema 1 and schema 2 of figure 5. Here a domain constraint specifies that the set of planted fields for a particular farm is a subset of the total number of fields of that farm. The integration of these two schemas is shown in figure 5.c, where the farm consists-of fields and the set of planted fields represents a sub-class of field (specialisation of field). This sub-class can be derived and then materialised as shown in figure 5.c.

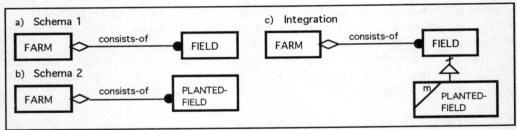

Figure 5. Example for Rule base 3

• *Rule base 6:* This rule base is selected when the two associations under consideration for merging are found to be both normal associations having the same order (e.g. binary), the same RWS and the same multiplicity. Consider for example figure 6, where schema 1 and schema 2 have intersecting classes doctor and consultant (here we are referring to the instances of these classes where the same object is found to be working as a doctor in one schema while working as a consultant in the other). Such schemas can be integrated by generalising the two classes doctor and consultant into a super-class employee by factoring out the commonality between them, then merging the two associations into a single association connected to the super-class, as shown in figure 6.c.

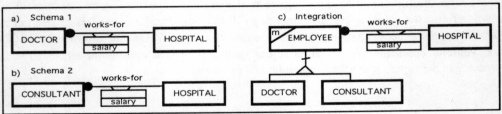

Figure 6. Example for Rule base 6

• *Rule base 7:* This applies if the two associations are found to be both normal associations having the same order and the same RWS, but having different multiplicities. Consider for example the associations in figure 7, where the two classes tutor and laboratory of schema 1 and schema 2 are identical but one of the associations is more restricted than the other. The first schema, held in the department, represents all tutors who may work in laboratories, while the second schema, held in the accounts office, represents those tutors who actually do work in laboratories. The integration of such a situation can be achieved by presenting the integrated schema with a single association connected to a new class employed-tutor derived as a specialisation out of the set of all possible tutors, as shown in figure 7.c.

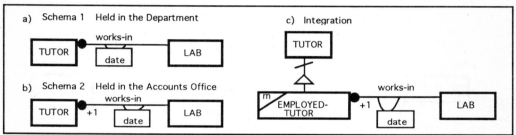

Figure 7. Example for Rule base 7

• *Rule base 8:* In this case RWS plays an important role in deciding the correspondence between associations. The two associations are both normal associations having the same order, but different RWS, with the additional constraint that one of them is a subset of the other (where this has to be decided according to the domain of the associations). This is shown as in figure 8, where the associations can be viewed in the following way: "an employee can't be a chair-of a committee unless he is a member-of it". Such associations can be integrated by drawing a dotted line with the arrow pointing from the sub- to the super- association. The label {subset} should be added to comply with OMT notation, as shown in figure 8.c.

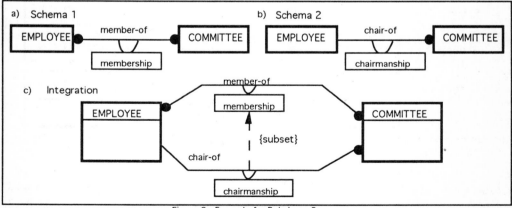

Figure 8. Example for Rule base 8

• *Rule base 9:* In this case the two associations are both normal associations, having the same order, but different RWS, with the additional constraint that some objects are common between the two schemas, as shown in figure 9. Integration can be achieved by deriving two new borrower classes as a specialisation of student which should be connected to the corresponding original associations. A derived super-set association can be added to cover the two original associations, as shown in figure 9.c.

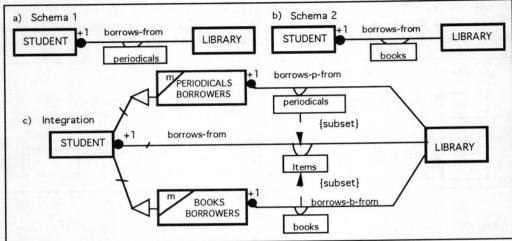

Figure 9. Example for Rule base 9

• **Rule base 10:** If the two associations are both normal, having the same order but different RWS, with the additional constraint that they are disjoint, as in figure 10, then they can be included in the integrated schema as shown in figure 10.c.

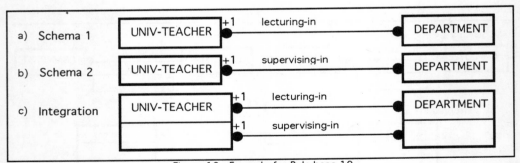

Figure 10. Example for Rule base 10

• **Rule base 11:** Here the two associations are both normal associations but having different orders, as in figure 11 (in schema 1 registration is a binary association while in schema 2 it is of order 1, i.e. the information is represented in a single class). In such a case RWS interaction with the designer can determine if they are mergeable or not depending on the compatibility between these associations. If it has been decided that they convey the same information, where the second schema can be derived from the first, then the integration can be represented as shown in figure 11.c.

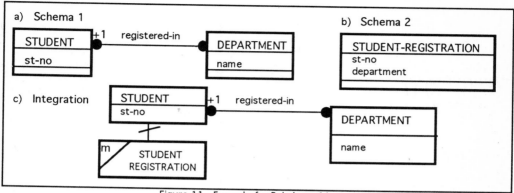

Figure 11. Example for Rule base 11

4   Overview of SMIS: A Schema Meta-Integration System

The complete Schema Meta-Integration System we are developing [QUT92], called SMIS, is defined through identifying its system objectives. These objectives refer both to the external architecture and operation of SMIS, i.e. SMIS as seen and operated by its users, and its internal architecture and operation, i.e. the way in which different Object-Oriented local schemas are processed within SMIS in the course of integration into a global schema. The system has been accorded the prefix "meta" as it uses data about the data it is concerned with in the form of Prolog predicates (meta-predicates) and meta-integration language (MIL) constructs.

The heart of the system, shown in figure 12, is the meta-integration module (MIM), which performs integration via a common internal intermediate schema representation based on the IOMT notation. This module represents meta-knowledge regarding the structural components and the semantic contents of local and global schemas, where we view the IOMT notation in Prolog terms as a description of facts and semantic relationships that hold between classes. The meta-integration module has access to two interpretation schemes, from a source O-O local schema formalism to IOMT and from IOMT to a target O-O global schema formalism, as shown in figure 12.

4.1   System Operation

In operation, the system has three distinct phases. In the first, interpretation specification phase, source and target interpretation scheme specifications are linked into the meta-integration system. In the second, integration application phase, using a binary integration strategy [OZS91] two independently designed local schemas in the source formalism are entered and then combined into an integrated global schema in the target formalism. Application of the system to a pair of local schemas can be repeated cumulatively to achieve integration of n

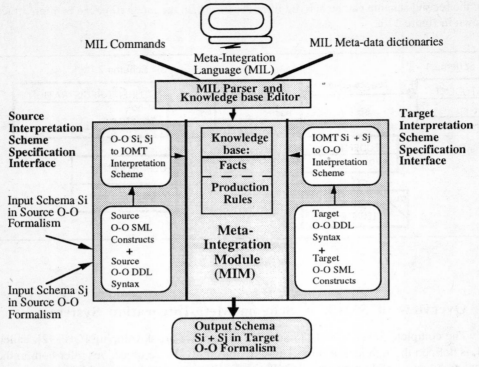

Figure 12. Overview of Schema Meta-Integration System

schemas. The third phase works in parallel with the second phase as an interaction with the database designer to supply the system with semantic information specifying the RWS. As shown in figure 12, this type of semantic information takes the form of MIL commands and meta-data dictionaries. This phase is important as it places an arbitrating layer between the designer and the underlying heterogeneous databases. This layer provides mechanisms for detecting and resolving structural and semantic ambiguity.

4.2   The Meta-Integration Language (MIL)

MIL, a specially designed meta-integration language, drives the knowledge base editor of the system, which handles the addition of designer knowledge. It supports semi-automated detection of different types of conflict, and provides semi-automatic mechanisms for establishing a variety of class relationships corresponding to RWS, such as identicality, containment, intersection, disjunction, referential-equality, arbitrary-equality, role, history and counterpart relationships, which together comprise all the different types of relationship defined in [NAV86,SCH88,MAS90].

The MIL parser was developed in Prolog by using DCG [PER80] as a Prolog-compatible BNF. This parser accepts two types of MIL construct: MIL commands, which can define IS_A relationships and certain other RWS relationships; and MIL meta-data dictionaries, which can be used to define association-related information and to resolve conflicts in units, scales and keys. As an example of the use of a meta-data dictionary in association merging, consider figure 13, which is an extended version of figure 6.

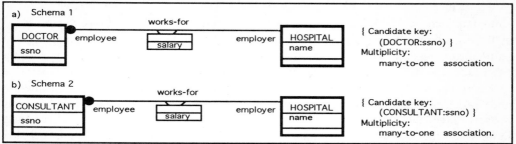

Figure 13. Detailed Association Merging Example

In this context MIL can be used to specify and define the structural and semantic information needed to carry out association merging as follows:

MIL> Dictionary
define works-for association-type(normal) between
DOCTOR : role = (employee), multiplicity = (many - to - one), key = (ssno).
HOSPITAL : role = (employer).
salary : attribute.

This definition states that each doctor (who plays an employee role) working for a hospital (which plays an employer role) receives a salary. The definition also gives the multiplicity of the works-for association which is many-to-one. A many-to-one association needs a single candidate key for the object on the "many" end to uniquely identify each link. Some other situations such as many-to-many association require candidate keys for both related objects; while a one-to-one association has two candidate keys, the key of either of the related objects. The works-for association of schema 2 can be defined in the same way to complete the required merging information.

4.3 Interpretation Scheme Specification Interfaces

SMIS, as a meta-integration system, is able to accept specifications of interpretation schemes for source O-O and target O-O schema formalisms. This is achieved by utilising two separate interfaces for the joint specification of the syntactic and semantic components of source and target DDL interpretation schemes, respectively. The general approach is similar to that used in [HOW87,HOW88,RAM89,QUT90,RAM91], involving syntactic and semantic (SML) meta-languages developed for the purpose in each case. Further details may be found in [QUT92].

4.4 The Meta-Integration Module (MIM)

This module implements the intermediate modelling system at the heart of SMIS. The general usefulness of an intermediate modelling system is based primarily on the capability of the chosen system to assist in mapping between logically heterogeneous local concepts and integrated global concepts. In the context of SMIS we require an intermediate modelling system which is capable of accommodating the rich semantic information content of an O-O schema in a way that is independent of any specific O-O data model implementation, and which is able to manipulate this content throughout the integration process.

As mentioned earlier we have developed an extension to OMT, the IOMT, which is the core component of MIM. We have enhanced OMT with a set of operations which can be applied to facilitate heterogeneous schema integration, in particular during the merging and restructuring phases. The operations concerned address two major issues in schema integration: the definition of (i) a taxonomy, and (ii) a model of integration, where the taxonomy defines a comprehensive set of meaningful schema integration operators and the model provides a framework for specifying schema integration semantics. This model consists of a set of invariants and a set of transformation rules. The set of invariants provides the basis for the specification of schema integration semantics, in that every schema integration operation must preserve all invariants.

The internal knowledge that is processed by MIM is of two types; facts and rules. Facts are represented in primitive or frame-structured Prolog form as appropriate while integration rules are represented in a production rule-based system. This combination provides a suitable organisational form for object meta-knowledge, i.e. knowledge about objects, as derived from schema components and meta-integration language constructs. Schema components consist of class names, property names, data types, keys and associations. MIL constructs consist of command and meta-data dictionary constructs.

4.4.1   Internal Representation of Facts

In principle, the design of MIM facts relies on the familiar concepts of OMT such as generalisation, association and aggregation. The knowledge stored in these facts is the result of schema analysis (interpretation of source schemas into internal intermediate form, IOMT; and the set of semantic assertions provided by the designer through MIL). This knowledge is interactively refined during the pre-integration phase by the designer. We use the frame structure to represent non-primitive knowledge as shown in the following example:

```
frame(  association(ASSOCIATION_NAME),
        ass_type(TYPE),
        connect_between(ASSOCIATION,  CLASS_list),
        role(CLASS_list,  ROLE_list),
        multiplicity(FROM,  TO),
        candidate_key(KEY_list),
        has_attribute(ATT_list)  ).
```

These frames record:
- the associations between classes, including aggregation.
- cardinalities on associations.
- the candidate keys of each class, which must be specified by the designer.
- domain constraints on attributes.
- intersection, union, disjunction and containment constraints on classes and associations.
- the classes in the database, specifying whether they represent primitive or non-primitive objects.

- the properties of these classes, e.g. attributes and operations.
- the class hierarchy between these classes, e.g. generalisation.

4.4.2 Internal Representation of Production Rules

Production rule systems are deductive systems for processing knowledge/facts. They employ specific inference engine techniques whereby they can derive new knowledge from the facts and rules stored in the knowledge base. Unlike procedural knowledge, rules are a form of declarative knowledge[SCHN89,LUG89]. The MIM production rules include invariant enforcement rules, structural transformation rules and semantic interpretation rules which act in concert with the IOMT. Invariant enforcement rules enable MIM to verify and maintain the consistency of the developing global conceptual schema; structural transformation rules enable it to transform source local schema structural components into target global schema constructs; and semantic interpretation rules enable it to transform source local schema semantic contents into target global schema equivalents. This includes an implicit conforming of the target schema to the RWS concepts, the reconciliation of different types of conflict, and the construction of a global query decomposer.

MIM productions consist of a certain number of major rules found in the knowledge base, many of which contain a number of subrules. The application of a subset of this knowledge in association merging (cf. figure 3, right-hand half) is illustrated in following extract (simplified for exposition purposes):

```
/* operator definitions */
:- op(100, fx, if).
:- op(95, xfx, then).
:- op(90, xfy, or).
:- op(85, xfy, and).

/* productions of the knowledge base */
if      compatible_normal_associations
  and   same_order
then    check_real_world_semantics.
if      same_real_world_semantics
  and   same_multiplicity
then    mergeable_association_rule_6.
if      same_real_world_semantics
  and   different_multiplicity
then    mergeable_association_rule_7.
```

```
if      different_real_world_semantics
  and   subset_domain_constraints
then    mergeable_association_rule_8.
.........

/* collected facts from automatic analysis (parsing and
   interpretation ) and designer interaction (a set of assertions ) */
fact(compatible_normal_associations).
fact(same_order).
fact(same_real_world_semantics).
fact(same_multiplicity).

/* knowledge base interpreter - PROLOG clauses */
integrate :-
.........
```

Figure 14. Association Merging Knowledge Base Extract

The complete interpreted results obtained from the above transformations (represented in the target output schema formalism) include a set of base classes; a set of virtual classes combined with definitions of corresponding O-O queries which derive their class mappings from the original local schemas; a set of associations connected to these classes; a set of meta-data dictionaries that enable the reconciliation of different types of conflict, e.g. by conversions between local and global class components; and finally a global decomposition plan which performs query decomposition by associating with each class of the global schema a rule/trigger that reflects the origins of this class in terms of class components of the original local databases. This plan is accumulated incrementally during the integration process. Consequently, when a global query is issued against the global schema, a specific transformation rule will be fired which translates this query over each of the integration operators (MIL commands) that were involved in the construction of the global classes and associations that the global query addresses.

5   Conclusions

5.1   Current Status and Initial Results

Our work is targeted initially on the family of extended relational data models [ROW87,STO90], which exhibit many features of O-O data models. At present our system performs the basic functions of schema integration including class and association integration. A prototype implementation of SMIS has been successfully tested by integrating a set of logically heterogeneous POSTGRES database schemas. We have concentrated initially on integration as it concerns the structural aspects of O-O data modelling and are currently addressing behavioural aspects. The SMIS prototype, which has been implemented in Prolog (Sussex POPLOG v14) on a Sun workstation, includes the MIL parser and knowledge base editor, the source and target interpretation scheme specification interfaces and (partially) the meta-integration module (MIM), cf. figure 12; development of the latter module is still ongoing. The prototype system code is some 3,000 lines of Prolog and growing.

5.2   Conclusion

We have presented a meta-programmed approach for merging class associations during schema integration in a logically heterogeneous O-O database environment. We have described the fundamentals of such integration activity in terms of the three-level modelling architecture and an extended form of OMT, the so-called IOMT.

The development of our schema meta-integration system was considered entirely in terms of logic programming/Prolog language technologies [CLO87,MAL87], where we have emphasised the importance of association merging in the process of schema integration. We have viewed the complete schema integration process as a set of modules which interactively call each other to perform a specific part of the process (e.g. class integration, followed by association integration). Such modules can be combined together into a single comprehensive system which we have called the schema meta-integration system (SMIS) to automate as much as possible of the whole schema integration activity.

In these terms, the heart of the system we are developing consists of an inference engine acting upon a knowledge base of facts and production rules. In parallel with source schema analysis, designer additions to the knowledge base take place interactively by means of a special meta-integration language (MIL). The output of this meta-integration process (MIM) is the integration of the original source schemas as a target global schema in an internal intermediate representation (IOMT). Target schema output is achieved by means of a template-driven intermediate representation traverser, which processes the internal target global schema and, by acting upon the relevant templates, produces corresponding target DDL constructs.

References

[AHO86] Aho, A.V., Sethi, R. and Ullman, J.D., "Compilers: Principles, Techniques and Tools", Addison-Wesley, 1986.

[ATK90] Atkinson, M., Bancilhon, F. and Dewitt, D., "The Object-Oriented Database Manifesto", Proceedings of ACM-SIGMOD International Conference on Management of Data, Atlantic City, 1990.

[BAT86] Batini, C., Lenzerini, M. and Navathe, S., "A Comparative Analysis of Methodologies for Database Schema Integration", ACM Computing Surveys, 18(4), pp. 232-364, 1986.

[BER89a] Bertino, E. *et al*, "Integration of Heterogeneous Database Applications through an Object-Oriented Interface", Information Systems, IS-14(5), pp. 407-420, 1989.

[BER89b] Bertino, E. *et al*, "An Object-Oriented Approach to the Interconnection of Heterogeneous Databases", Proceedings of NSF International Workshop on Heterogeneous Databases, Northwestern University, Illinois, 1989.

[BRA90] Bratko, I., "Prolog Programming for Artificial Intelligence", 2nd Edition, Addison-Wesley, 1990.

[CAR88] Carey, M., DeWitt, D. and Vandenberg, S., "A Data Model and Query Language for EXODUS", Proceedings of ACM-SIGMOD International Conference on Management of Data , Chicago, 1988.

[CLO87] Clocksin, W. and Mellish, C., "Programming in Prolog", 3rd Edition, Springer-Verlag, 1987.

[DAT86] Date, C. J., "An Introduction to Database Systems", Vol. I, 4th Edition, Addison-Wesley, 1986.

[DAY84] Dayal, U. and Hwang, H., "View Definition and Generalization for Database Integration in a Multidatabase System", IEEE Transactions on Software Engineering, SE-10(6), pp. 628-644, 1984.

[HOW87] Howells, D.I., Fiddian, N.J. and Gray, W.A., "A Source-to-Source Meta-Translation System for Relational Query Languages", Proceedings of 13th International Conference on Very Large Databases (VLDB), pp. 227-234, 1987.

[HOW88] Howells, D.I., Fiddian, N.J. and Gray, W.A., "A Source-to-Source Meta-Translation System for Database Query Languages - Implementation in PROLOG", *in* Gray, P.M.D. and Lucas, R.J. (Editors), "Prolog and Databases: Implementations and New Directions", pp. 22-38, Ellis Horwood, 1988.

[KAU90] Kaul, M., Drosten, K. and Neuhold, E., "ViewSystem: Integrating Heterogeneous Information Bases by Object-Oriented Views", Proceedings of 6th International Conference on Data Engineering, 1990.

[LAN82] Landers, T. and Rosenberg, R., "An Overview of MULTIBASE", *in* Schneider H.-J. (Editor), "Distributed DataBases", North-Holland, 1982.

[LEC88] Lecluse, C., Richard, P. and Velez, P., "O2, an Object-Oriented Data Model", Proceedings of ACM-SIGMOD International Conference on Management of Data, Chicago, 1988.

[LOO87] Loomis, M.E. and Rumbaugh, J.E., "An Object Modelling Technique for Conceptual Design", Proceedings of European Conference on Object-Oriented Programming, Paris, 1987.

[LUG89] Luger, G. and Stubblefield, W., "Artificial Intelligence and the Design of Expert Systems", Benjamin, 1989.

[MAL87] Malpas, J., "PROLOG: A Relational Language and Its Applications", Prentice-Hall, 1987.

[MAS90] Masunaga, Y., "Object Identity, Equality and Relational Concept", *in* Kim, W.,

Nicolas, M. and Nishio, S. (Editors), "Deductive and Object-Oriented Databases", Elsevier Science Publishers B. V. (North-Holland), 1990.

[MOT87] Motro, A., "Superviews: Virtual Integration of Multiple Databases", IEEE Transactions on Software Engineering, SE-13(7), pp. 785-798, 1987.

[NAV86] Navathe, S., Elmasri, R. and Larson, J., "Integrating User Views in Database Design", IEEE Computer, January 1986.

[OZS91] Ozsu, M. and Valduriez P., "Principles of Distributed Database Systems", Prentice-Hall, 1991.

[PER80] Pereira, F.C.N. and Warren, D.H.D., "Definite Clause Grammars for Language Analysis - A Survey of the Formalism and a Comparison with Augmented Transition Networks", Artificial Intelligence, 13, pp. 231-278, 1980.

[QUT90] Qutaishat, M., "A POSTGRES to SQL Inter-Schema Translator", M.Sc. Thesis, Department of Computing Mathematics, University of Wales College of Cardiff, UK, 1990.

[QUT92] Qutaishat, M., Fiddian, N.J. and Gray, W.A., "A Schema Meta-Integration System for a Heterogeneous O-O Database Environment - Implementation in PROLOG", Proceedings of 1st International Conference on the Practical Application of Prolog, 18pp., to be published, 1992.

[RAM89] Ramfos, A., Gray, W.A. and Fiddian, N.J., "Object-Oriented to Relational Inter-Schema Meta-Translation", Proceedings of NSF International Workshop on Heterogeneous Databases, Northwestern University, Illinois, 1989.

[RAM91] Ramfos, A., Fiddian, N.J. and Gray, W.A., "A Meta-Translation System for Object-Oriented to Relational Schema Translation", Proceedings of 9th British National Conference On Databases, Wolverhampton, England, 1991.

[ROW87] Rowe, L. and Stonebraker, M., "The POSTGRES Data Model", Proceedings of 13th International Conference on Very Large Databases (VLDB), England, 1987.

[RUM91] Rumbaugh, J., Blaha, M., Premerlani, W., Eddy, F. and Lorensen, W., "Object-Oriented Modelling and Design", Prentice-Hall, 1991.

[SCH88] Schrefl, M. and Neuhold, E., "Object Class Definition by Generalization using Upward Inheritance", Proceedings of 4th International Conference on Data Engineering, 1988.

[SCHN89] Schnupp, P., Nguyen, C. and Bernhard, L., "Expert Systems Lab Course", Springer-Verlag, 1989.

[SHE88] Sheth, A., Larson, J., Cornelio, A. and Navathe, S., "A Tool for Integrating Conceptual Schemas and User Views", Proceedings of 4th International Conference on Data Engineering, 1988.

[STO90] Stonebraker, M. *et al*, "The Implementation of POSTGRES", IEEE Transactions on Knowledge and Data Engineering, March 1990.

[ZDO90] Zdonik, S. and Mair, D., "Readings in Object-Oriented Database Systems", Morgan Kaufmann, 1990.

GENERATING ACTIVE RULES FROM HIGH-LEVEL SPECIFICATIONS

Oscar Díaz†‡, Suzanne M. Embury†

Department of Computing Science†
University of Aberdeen
Aberdeen
Scotland

Facultad de Informática‡
Universidad del País Vasco
San Sebastián
Spain

Abstract

Rules have been proposed as a mechanism for providing active behaviour in databases; some of the most popular uses being the support of integrity constraints, the maintenance of materialised views and security enforcement. However, the difficulty of defining rules discourages end users from taking full advantage of their functionality. What is required is a mechanism for the automatic translation of high-level specifications of behaviour into equivalent sets of rules. In addition to making rules easier and safer to use, such a facility makes the specification of behaviour explicit - rather than having it embedded within rule code - and allows it to be used by other parts of the database management system. For example, if constraints are specified declaratively, they can be used for other purposes such as semantic query optimisation. This paper describes how rules can be generated automatically from declarative specifications of integrity constraints and the operational semantics of relationships. This is borne out by an implementation in ADAM, an object-oriented database written in Prolog.

Keywords Active databases, object-oriented databases, explicit knowledge representation, integrity constraints

1   Introduction

Event-condition-action rules (henceforth referred to as ECA rules) have been proposed in [Daya,89] for enhancing databases with *active behaviour*, i.e. behaviour exhibited *automatically* by the system in response to events generated internally or externally without user intervention [Bauz,90].

ECA rules should not be confused with methods or with situation-action rules. An ECA rule definition includes not only what to do but also when to do it, and can be seen as behaviour exhibited as a result of some event taking place, such as accessing or updating an attribute. As an example, if a *boiler* object has an attribute *temperature* and it is required that, when the value of the temperature rises to 30 degrees, an alarm be raised, an ECA rule would seem to be an appropriate paradigm to represent this event-driven behaviour. Methods, on the other hand, are invoked explicitly, by sending a message to an object, so method invocation can be seen as a kind of procedure call.

The idea of having behaviour triggered by events is not original to the field of databases. It has previously been proposed by researchers in Artificial Intelligence in the context of frame-based systems. *Frames* also follow the object-oriented paradigm but unlike objects in class-based systems, which represent classes and instances, here objects represent the idea of prototypes. Prototypes are described by several *slots* (similar to attributes) to which functions can be attached to be applied when certain operations are performed on a slot. Such functions are know as *demons*. Demons are classified according to the operations that trigger them, namely:

- *if-added demons*, fired when a value is inserted into the slot. They implement a kind of forward-chaining inference by which newly asserted facts can be used to assert other facts.

- *if-needed demons*, fired when the slot value is required and is not available. They implement a sort of backward-chaining inference, where finding the required value is the goal to be satisfied. The demon specifies how this value can be obtained.

- *if-removed demons*, fired when a value is deleted from the slot. They are used to maintain dependencies between the slot values of different frames. In this way, the consistency of certain facts can be made dependent upon the consistency of other facts, the invalidation (i.e. deletion) of which results in the invalidation of all dependent facts.

Thus, demons are triggered by changes in the *data* and their goals can be seen as the maintenance of different kinds of relationships among that data.

ECA rules can be used to mimic the functions of demons in frame-based systems. For example, ECA rules have been used to support derived classes (views) whose instances are obtained on demand and, in this way, are implementing a sort of backward-chaining process [Ceri,91]. Also, ECA rules have been used to support integrity constraints, where insertion of an attribute value fires rules to check the coherence of the new value [Diaz,92].

However, in the context of object-oriented databases (OODBs), ECA rules can have a wider objective. Classes in OODBs describe not only the attributive and structural features of a set of instances but also the behavioural ones. Thus, consistency has to be maintained for both the attributive and the behavioural aspects of the database. This last aspect has hardly been addressed in OODBs, and our experience is that rules constitute a suitable mechanism for the support of such behavioural consistency. As an example, in [Diaz,91b] an approach is presented for supporting behavioural consistency between objects participating in relationships, i.e. whether a message sent to an object is propagated, delegated or just ignored by the relationships in which the object is involved.

Regardless of whether ECA rules are used to support consistency of data or consistency of behaviour, it can be difficult for end users to define ECA rules. Rule definition can be quite complex since the possibility of loops or of undesirable interactions between rules has to be considered. Hence, it would be convenient if users could express their requirements in terms of some high-level specification, from which the system could automatically generate rules to support the required behaviour. Moreover, such a facility would make the specification of behaviour explicit - rather than having it embedded within rule code - and allow it to be used by other parts of the database management system. For example, if constraints were to be specified declaratively, they could then be used for other purposes such as semantic query optimisation.

This paper illustrates how rules can be generated from high-level specifications. Section 2 outlines how rules are defined in ADAM, an object-oriented database implemented in Prolog. In section 3, two examples of how rules have been generated from declarative specification are given. The first example is concerned with integrity constraints, where the user specifies the constraint using a constraint equation approach. The second example illustrates the use of ECA rules in the maintenance of behavioural consistency and shows how the declaratively specified operational semantics of relationships are enforced by system-generated rules. Finally, conclusions are presented.

2 Active Rules

In ADAM, rules are seen as *'first-class'* objects and are described using attributes and methods [Diaz,91a]. Rule structure is essentially defined by the *event* that triggers the rule, the *condition* to be checked and the *action* to be performed if the condition is satisfied. The condition is a set of queries to check that the state of the database is appropriate for action execution. The action is a set of operations and may have a variety of aims, e.g. enforcement of integrity constraints, provision for user intervention, propagation of methods, etc. Information about the operation which caused the rule to fire is available for use in both the condition and action definitions via system-provided predicates. These are *current_object*, which supplies the object to which the rule is being applied, and *current_arguments*, which supplies the arguments of the method that caused the rule to fire.

```
new([OID,[
    active_class([person]),
    active_method([put_age]),
    when([before]),
    is_it_enabled([yes]),
    disabled_for([1@person,23@person]),
    condition([(
        current_arguments([PersonAge]),
        PersonAge > 130
    )]),
    action([(
        current_object(ThePerson),
        current_arguments([PersonAge]),
        get_cname(PersonName) => ThePerson,
        writeln(['The person ',PersonName,
                    'with age ',PersonAge,
                    'exceeds the expected age']),
        fail
    )])
]) => integrity_rule.
```

Figure 1: A rule to prevent people from being older than 130.

The complete context of invocation is described by the **active_method** (i.e. the method firing the rule), the **active_class** (i.e. class of the instances which react to the active method) and the **when** (i.e. *after* or *before* the active method is executed or when this method is *not found*) attributes. In figure 1, an example is given of an active rule that prevents people from being older that 130. This rule will fire *before* executing the *put_age* method. The condition checks whether the argument of the method (i.e. the new age of the person) is greater than 130 or not. If this condition is not met, the rule is not applicable and the action is ignored. Method execution can continue as normal. Otherwise, the rule's action *is* executed. In the case of our example rule, the action displays a message and then fails, preventing *put_age*, and therefore the update, from proceeding. It is also possible, if required, to pass a value from the condition to the action, by using the *condition_result* predicate, the argument of which is instantiated with any value required after condition evaluation. This can be useful in avoiding the need to redo work in the action, that has already been performed during condition evaluation.

In addition to the event-condition-action description, two more attributes are needed to specify the status of the rule itself, i.e. whether it is enabled or disabled. The attribute **is_it_enabled** describes the status at the level of the whole class appearing as the *active_class* of the rule, whereas the **disabled_for** attribute describes the status for specific instances of this class. In the above example, the rule is enabled for all instances of the class *person* (because the value of *is_it_enabled* is *true*) except for those with object identifiers *1@person* and *23@person*. Thus, a rule will not be fired if either the *is_it_enabled* attribute is *false* or the object identifier of the current object appears as one of the values of the *disabled_for* attribute.

3 Generating active rules from high-level specification

Regardless of whether ECA rules are used to support consistency of data or consistency of behaviour, it can be difficult for end users to define ECA rules. Rule definition can be quite complex since the possibility of loops or of undesirable interactions between rules has to be considered. Hence, it would be convenient if users could express their requirements in terms of some high-level specification, from which the system could automatically generate rules to support the required behaviour.

Any declarative specification has to give enough 'clues' to the system to enable it to obtain the event, the condition and the action of the rule(s) to be created. The event consists of the **active_class**, **active_method** and **when** attributes. In most cases, the **when** attribute takes a default value which depends upon the kind of behaviour that is being specified.

Rule interactions can be detected by checking existing rules. Remember that rules are objects and thus their attributes can be as easily retrieved or modified as the attributes of any other object. Rules whose active method appears in the condition or action of some other rule, can produce undesirable cascade effects. Often, such interactions can be avoided by temporarily inserting the current object as a value of the *disable_for* attribute (or an attribute playing a similar role). When rules are generated, temporary deactivation of other rules can be achieved by inserting the appropriate deactivation command in the condition or action of the rule. In this way, undesirable interactions can be prevented at execution time, by avoiding having certain combinations of rules active at the same time.

The following examples show how ECA rules have been generated from high-level specifications.

3.1 Deriving rules for constraint maintenance

One approach to the enforcement of integrity constraints is to enlarge method definitions with checks to verify the correctness of the operations they perform. However, such an approach jeopardises proper constraint maintenance, since methods and constraints have different functionalities. Whereas constraints represent invariant states of the database, method definitions can sometimes be legitimately overridden. Hence, in ADAM, constraints are explicitly represented as additional facets of attributes and are independent of method definitions. As an example, the following is a definition of the attribute *age* in ADAM:

```
attribute(attribute_tuple(age,global,single,optional,integer,
    [age of person > 0, age of person < 130]))
```

Here, the standard set of facets, i.e. name (*age*), visibility (*global*), cardinality (*single*), status (*optional*) and type (*integer*), has been enlarged with a facet containing a list of constraints specified in a constraint equation (CE) language. CEs consist of chains of relationships, called *paths*, where the last item in each chain is the class which represents the origin, or *anchor* of the path (e.g *person*).

Once a constraint has been introduced by the user, the system must generate a set of rules to enforce it. The rule attributes *when* and *is_it_enabled* take *before* and *yes* as their respective default values. Values for the *active_method*, *active_class* and *condition* attributes can be obtained from the declarative specification of the constraint. In many cases, the *action* attribute of the rule will take the default value of *fail*, which has the effect of preventing the execution of any operation that would violate the constraint. However, it is sometimes possible for the system to use the information given in the constraint specification to work out how database integrity might be restored, if the operation were allowed to go ahead. In this case, the action is generated from 'clues' provided by the user within the definition of the constraint, by means of the so-called *weak-bond*, i.e. the attribute "more readily modified in response to an initial change to the other side of the CE" [Morg,84]. A more extensive account of this process can be found in [Diaz,92]. For simplicity's sake, we will here consider the situation where no restorative actions are taken and the system will just reject operations that would violate a constraint.

3.1.1 Active_method and active_class generation

The **active_method** attribute must contain the names of the methods which are to fire the rule. To obtain these method names, the approach described in [Nico,78] for deductive databases is followed. This approach is based on the Horn Logic counterpart of CEs: class names can be seen as predicates with a single argument and attributes (i.e. the rest of the links in the path) as binary predicates. Attributes are viewed as required properties, i.e. it is essential that attributes involved in a constraint have known values, if that constraint is to be satisfied. This is know as a *strong translation*, which contrasts with a weak translation where the attributes are not required properties [Urba,89]. As an example, consider a constraint similar to the one given in [Morg,84] which demands that the set of *projects* for which a *lecturer* is responsible, is to be the same as the set of *projects* that his/her *research_assistants* work on. This can be expressed as the CE:

```
projects of lecturer  ::  projects of research_assistants of lecturer
```

This can be translated into a set of equivalent Horn rules, such as the following:

$$\text{lecturer(M)} \wedge \text{research\_assistants(M,S)} \wedge \text{projects(S,P)} \rightarrow \text{projects(M,P)}$$

P	Q	P $\longrightarrow$ Q
T	T	T
T	F	F
F	T	T
F	F	T

Figure 2: Truth table for the implication operator

From these Horn rules we can obtain the names of the methods that could violate the constraint, based on the properties of the implication operator. The truth table for this operator is shown in figure 2, from which we can note the following points:

1. If Q is false, P must also be false to make the implication true. Delete operations on predicates appearing in the head of the Horn rule (i.e. Q) can falsify the head. To maintain the validity of the implication, delete operations can be necessary to falsify the body of the Horn rule (P).

2. If P is true, Q must also be true to satisfy the implication. Insert operations on predicates appearing in the body of the Horn rule can satisfy the body. Therefore, insertions may be needed in the head of the Horn rule to make it true, so that the entire Horn rule can be satisfied.

3. If P is false, the implication evaluates to true regardless of the value of Q. The Horn rule is *trivially satisfied* [Urba,91]. This means that delete operations on the body of the Horn rule do not need any compensating action to make the implication true.

4. If Q is true, the implication is evaluated to true regardless of what P evaluates to. Therefore, compensating actions are not required when insert operations are made on the head of the Horn rule.

So the approach in [Nico,78] is used not only as a way of detecting the operations that can violate a constraint but also as a mean of indicating the changes to be made to satisfy it. As an example, consider the Horn rule given above and the conclusions that can be drawn from it. When a new *research_assistant* is assigned to a *lecturer*, the body of the Horn rule can become true, forcing the head of the Horn rule to become true also (i.e. to assign a project to the new inserted research assitant). On the other hand, the head of the Horn rule can become false when a *project* of a *lecturer* is deleted. To make the whole implication true, deletion of the *project* from this *lecturer's research_assistants* or deletion of the *research_assistant* itself may be necessary.

Since the path of a CE is translated into a conjunction of existentially quantified predicates (i.e. using a strong translation), every link in the path (excluding the anchor, of course) will appear on both the left and right sides of Horn rules within the conjunction. Hence, insertions and deletions to every attribute occurring within the CE path have to be checked to verify that the constraint will still be satisfied after the update has taken place. Therefore, two event objects must be created for each of these attributes; one triggered

```
event(before,put_projects,lecturer)
event(before,delete_projects,lecturer)
event(before,put_research_assistants,lecturer)
event(before,research_assistants,lecturer)
event(before,put_projects,person)
event(before,delete_projects,before)
```

Figure 3: Set of *before events* generated for the projects-of-lecturer constraint.

by a *put* method and the other by a *delete* method. As an example, figure 3 shows the set of *before* events that would be generated for the *projects-of-lecturer* constraint given above.

Values for the **active_method** attribute are obtained from the names of the attributes by adding the prefixes *'put_'* and *'delete_'*. The **active_class** attribute is obtained from either the CE anchor or the domain of each attribute. The active method and the active class, together with the *when* attribute, define the events that can potentially invalidate the constraint. It would be possible to create a single ECA rule, invoked by the occurrence of any one of these events, to maintain the constraint but this would not be very efficient, for the following reason. The occurrence of one of the triggering events signals only *potential* violation of the constraint. It is then the role of the rule *condition* to decide whether violation will actually occur. The condition of a rule triggered by many events must examine the effects of all those events on all the objects which they involve. In most cases, this will be a waste of effort since, in reality, only one of those events has occurred and the condition need check only those objects affected by that one event.

A more efficient scheme, then, is to define a separate ECA rule for every potentially dangerous event so that each rule's condition and action need consider only the changes produced by that event. Notice that this assumes that the database is in a valid state before the update. Since ECA rules are indexed by class, an increase in the number of rules does not lead to a significant system slow-down. In our proposal, a rule-based version of the algorithmic solution for CE maintenance proposed in [Morg,84] is adapted to an object-oriented environment.

3.1.2 Rule condition generation

Rule conditions are used to check whether a constraint will be violated by a given update. If the condition is satisfied the action is executed and will either restore the database to a valid state or reject the update.

In contrast to a deductive approach, where relationships are represented as predicates whose arguments stand for the entities related, in the object-oriented paradigm an attribute-based view of relationships is more popular. Whereas a predicate view provides a *non-*

directional representation (i.e. the same predicate is used regardless of the argument being instantiated), in an object-oriented system attributes representing relationships are seen as pointers to the related objects. In this case, the method invoked depends on the direction in which the relationship is traversed. As a result, the constraint, declaratively stated by the user, cannot be directly translated to the rule's condition as in [Urba,90]; we must also consider the direction in which the constraint is checked. For example, in the *projects-of-lecturer* constraint the *research_assistants* link is transformed to the *supervised_by* link (i.e. its inverse) if the constraint is traversed backwards.

The process of generating a rule's condition can be better understood if paths are seen as function compositions. In this way, a constraint such as:

$$r_m \text{ of } r_{m-1} \text{ of } \dots r_2 \text{ of } r_1 \text{ of anchor} :: l_n \text{ of } l_{n-1} \text{ of } \dots l_2 \text{ of } l_1 \text{ of anchor}$$

can be seen as a comparison of functions S and T:

$$\underbrace{r_m \circ r_{m-1} \circ \cdots r_2 \circ r_1}_{S}(anchor\_instance) = \underbrace{l_n \circ l_{n-1} \circ \cdots l_2 \circ l_1}_{T}(anchor\_instance)$$

When an insertion occurs, for instance the object O_1 is inserted[1] as an r_i of the object O_2, the equality between functions S and T must be maintained if the constraint is to be adhered to. Since r_i is the modified link, the condition takes into account only the change produced in r_i. Let LS be the set of r_m_range *objects* that have been affected by the update:

$$LS = r_m \circ r_{m-1} \circ \cdots r_{i+2} \circ r_{i+1}(O_1)$$

Let AS be the set of *anchor objects* that have been affected by the update:

$$AS = r_1^{-1} \circ r_2^{-1} \circ \cdots r_{i-2}^{-1} \circ r_{i-1}^{-1}(O_2)$$

where r_i^{-1} denotes the inverse function of r_i.

As a result of the above insertion, function S has been enlarged with the set of pairs obtained from the Cartesian product of AS and LS, except for those already in S [2]:

$$\triangle S = (AS \otimes LS) - S$$

The rule's condition must be able to deal with the following cases:

1. **if** $LS = \emptyset$ **or** $AS = \emptyset$ **then** the constraint is trivially satisfied

2. **if** $\triangle S = \emptyset$ **then** the constraint is satisfied

3. **if** $\triangle S \neq \emptyset$ **then** the constraint is violated

---

[1] The message $put\_r_i([O_1]) => O_2$ would achieve this insertion in ADAM.
[2] Once the update has been made, the original value of S can be obtained from T.

```
new([RuleOid,[
   active_class([lecturer]),
   active_method([put_projects]),
   when([before]),
   is_it_enabled([yes]),
   condition([(
      condition_result([ConstViolPairs]),
      current_object(InstanceOid), % This is O₂
      current_arguments([NewValue]), % This is O₁
      findall(Anchor, (Anchor = InstanceOid), Anchors),
      findall(Leaf, (Leaf = NewValue), Leaves),
      .....
      ((Anchors = [] ; Leaves = []) − >
         % first case: constraint trivially satisfied
         fail
      ;
         findall([AAnchor, ALeaf], (
               member(AAnchor, Anchors),
               member(ALeaf, Leaves),
               \+ (
                  get_research_assistants(Emp) => AAnchor,
                  get_projects(ALeaf) => Emp
               )
         ), ConstViolPairs),
         (ConstViolPairs = [] − >
            fail % second case
         ;
            true % third case
         )
      )
      .....
   )]),
   action([[(fail)]])
]]) => integrity_rule.
```

Figure 4: A constraint maintenance rule.

In cases 1 and 2 the condition evaluates to false and the rule does not fire. In the third case the action is executed since the constraint has been violated, i.e. the equality between S and T no longer holds. In figure 4 the rule generated for an insertion to the *projects* relationship in the *projects-of-lecturer* constraint is shown. Functions AS and LS are obtained as compositions of the methods given in the specification of the constraint. In this case *(Anchor = InstanceOid)* and *(Leaf = NewValue)* represent such compositions for AS and LS respectively. Once these functions have been calculated, the rule's condition ascertains which of the above cases (1, 2 or 3) has occurred. It is worth noticing that the set of pairs violating the constraint, i.e. $\triangle S$, is passed to the action part as the result of condition evaluation. In re-establishing the constraint, the action can focus on this set of pairs rather than considering the whole of S.

When a deletion occurs, e.g. the object O_1 is deleted as an r_i of the object O_2, the function S is reduced to the set of pairs:

$$\triangledown S = \{AS \otimes LS\} - S'$$

where S' is the function S after the deletion has taken place. As before, three situations are possible; namely, the constraint is trivially satisfied, the constraint is satisfied or the constraint is violated.

3.2 Deriving rules for supporting the operational semantics of relationships

Semantic Data Models provide a set of structural constructs for representing the UoD in a more direct way. These constructs refer mainly to abstract relationships such as generalisation, aggregation, classification and association. For each of these a clear semantics must be defined, specifying how insertion, deletion and modification operations made at higher levels of abstraction (e.g. *person*) can affect the object abstracted (*student, lecturer*, other subclasses) and vice versa. Whereas the abstract relationships provided by Semantic Data Models come with an operational semantics built-in, no mechanism is provided for describing the semantics of user-defined relationships.

ADAM has been extended to represent relationships as *'first-class'* objects [Diaz,91] with their semantics collected within a single class. Amongst other things, it is now possible to describe the operational semantics of user-defined relationships in terms of how they behave in response to operations performed on the objects which they relate. As an example, consider the *parent-child* relationship between the class *grown-up* and the class *child*, both being subclasses of the class *person*, which has a method *moves* attached to it. The designer may be interested in modelling the situation where the 'movement' of the parent involves the movement of his/her children, i.e. when the message *moves* is sent to a *grown-up* participating in a *parent-child* relationship, this message is propagated to his/her children *through the parent-child relationship*.

This leads to a new mechanism for sharing behaviour. However, unlike previous approaches where sharing is defined solely at the class level, now relationship-based sharing can be specified. Hence, the behaviour of an object is defined not only by the class to which it belongs but also by the classes to which it is related. This is, after all, quite realistic!

In [Diaz,91a] we have explored two kinds of sharing, namely

- *propagation* whereby a message is sent to other objects *in addition to* the one which receives the message in the first place, and

- *delegation* whereby a message is sent to another object *instead of* being answered by the object which receives the message in the first place. In the example below, the method *legal_responsibility* is not defined for instances of the class *child* and, in this case, it can be automatically delegated, by the system, to the parents of the child (but only, of course, if this child has some parents).

As an example, the operational semantics of the *parent-child* relationship can be declaratively specified by the user as follows:

```
propagating   moves              from   the_parent   to   the_child
propagating   moves              from   the_child    to   the_parent
delegating    legal_responsibility from the_child    to   the_parent
```

where *the_parent* and *the_child* are the roles played by each *person* participating in the relationship. If a message *moves* is sent to *the_parent*, besides moving himself/herself, the message *moves* has to be propagated to the *person* playing the role of *the_child*[3]. The reverse situation occurs if the message *moves* is sent to *the_child*. Notice that the system has the responsibility of preventing infinite loops. Such loops arise when cyclic graphs are formed by the relationships. A simple example is illustrated by the *parent-child* relationship just described, in which the same message (i.e. *moves*) can be received and also propagated by both the participants. Hence, the participant objects can keep on propagating the message *moves* in turn for ever. To prevent this, the system must ensure that the same message is never sent to an object more than once in any propagation cycle.

The mechanism is available to any relationship class so that the user can *declaratively* specify whether messages sent to either of the related objects are to be propagated, delegated or ignored by the relationship. In the next section, we describe how rules are generated from these specifications to support the required behaviour.

---

[3]This can be retrieved using the *get_children_of* method, which, when sent to a *grown_up*, will retrieve all his/her children in turn. Similarly, the parents of a *child* can be obtained using the *get_parents_of* method. The *children_of* attribute and its inverse, the *parents_of* attribute, have been declared as part of the semantics of the *parent-child* relationship object. See [Diaz,91] for further details.

3.2.1 Rule generation

In essence, the principle used to translate specifications of operational semantics is much the same as that described above for constraints: the information given in the declarative constraint is used to 'fill in' predefined templates to create the various parts of the rule. In this case, however, the generation of the condition and the action is a much simpler process, due to the more restricted nature of the specifications being translated.

Propagation of a message occurs before the initial receiver is allowed to respond to it. To implement this behaviour we give the **when** attribute of the triggering event the value of *before*. Delegation, on the other hand, occurs only when an object *cannot* respond to a message. In this case, we give the value *not_found* to the **when** attribute. This is the only respect in which the process of rule generation differs for propagation and delegation. Although, to simplify the description of the remainder of this process, we will refer only to propagation, we ask the reader to bear in mind that the principle is equally valid in the case of delegation.

The value for the **active_method** attribute of the rule can be taken directly from the specification, as it is simply the name of the method which is to be propagated (e.g. *moves*). The **active_class** is the class of the object that is to propagate the method (e.g. *grown-up* - the class of the objects playing the role of *the_parent*). The **is_it_enabled** attribute takes the default value of *yes*.

The **condition** for propagation is that there exists at least one object to which the message must be propagated. The value of this attribute consists, therefore, of a piece of Prolog code which generates a list of the identifiers of *all* objects to which the message must be sent and then checks that this list is not empty. If the **condition** is satisfied then the rule **action** has the job of sending the message out to all the appropriate objects. Rather than waste time rebuilding this list within the **action**, we can reuse the version generated during **condition** evaluation by specifying it as the *condition_result*.

Unfortunately, there is a further complication to be considered. As we mentioned earlier, a perfectly innocent-looking combination of specifications can result, in practice, in an infinite sequence of propagations. Something must be done to prevent such undesirable effects. In our approach this is achieved by adding a new attribute - the **already_propagated** attribute - which records the identifiers of those objects which have received the message at the current stage in the cycle of propagations. In building the list of candidate objects for propagation we must now take care to exclude objects *which have already received the message*, i.e. those whose identifiers are stored in the **already_propagated** attribute.

There are two points to note about the maintenance of the **already_propagated** attribute:

- Objects are added to the attribute within the rule **action**, immediately before the message is propagated to them. Unfortunately, this does not insert the first object, the one to which the message was originally sent, and so this must be added separately, within the rule **condition**.

- At the end of each propagation cycle the **already_propagated** attribute must be cleared, in readiness for the next, which may involve a different set of objects. The end of the cycle is recognised by the fact that the current object is the object to which the message was originally sent, i.e. the first object contained in the **already_propagated** list.

The rule generated from the specification for the propagation of *moves*, given above, is shown in figure 5. Notice that both specifications (i.e. from *the_parent* to *the_child* and vice versa) are dealt with by a single rule. This is because of the importance of maintaining a complete list of objects which have received the message being propagated. For any given event there must be **one** *comprehensive* version of the **already_propagated** attribute and the easiest way to achieve this is to ensure that, for any given event, only one propagating rule exists. Therefore, whenever a new propagating rule is created, the system checks whether a rule already exists with the same event. If one does, the conditions of the two rules are merged to form a single, dual-purpose piece of code. This is what has happened to the rule in figure 5.

4   Conclusions

Active rules have proved to be a useful mechanism for the support of a wide range of mechanisms in databases. However, the definition of such rules can be quite cumbersome due to their flexibility and the difficulty of predicting how they will interact with one another. This makes rules a less than popular mechanism with end users.

High-level specifications can make life easier. The user can focus on the desired functionality rather than on how to support that functionality. Moreover, declarative specifications can be used for purposes other than those initially envisaged. These specifications must give enough 'clues' to the system to enable it to generate the appropriate rules. Special attention must be paid to rule interaction and the responsibility for managing this should lie as much with the system as is practicable.

In this paper an approach has been presented and two examples have been discussed. The experience of the authors is that both ease of use and reuse of specifications is greatly increased by the use of high-level specifications.

```
new([RuleOid,[
    active_class([grown_up, child]),
    active_method([moves]),
    when([before]),
    is_it_enabled([yes]),
    condition([(
        condition_result(ToObjects),
        current_object(FromObject),
      % Store the object which originated the cycle
        ( get_already_propagated(_) => 0@propagating_rule
        ; put_already_propagated([FromObject]) => 0@propagating_rule )
      % Obtain list of objects to be propagated to
        findall(ToObject, (
            is_it_instance_of(FromObject, child),
            get_parents_of(ToObject) => FromObject,
            is_it_instance_of(ToObject, grown_up),
            \+ get_already_propagated(ToObject) => 0@propagating_rule
          ;
            is_it_instance_of(FromObject, grown_up),
            get_children_of(ToObject) => FromObject,
            is_it_instance_of(ToObject, child),
            \+ get_already_propagated(ToObject) => 0@propagating_rule
        ), ToObjects),
        !, \+ ToObjects = []
    )]),
    action([(
        condition_result(ToObjects),
        current_object(FromObject),
        current_arguments(Arguments),
      % Propagate the message to each object identified in the condition
        ( member(ToObject, ToObjects),
        put_already_propagated([ToObject]) => 0@propagating_rule,
        moving => ToObject,
        fail ; true),
      % At end of cycle, clear already_propagated list
        (get_already_propagated(FirstReceiver) => 0@propagating_rule,
        FromObject = FirstReceiver - >
          (get_already_propagated(DisableObject) => 0@propagating_rule,
          delete_already_propagated([DisableObject]) => 0@propagating_rule,
          fail ; true)
        )
    )])
]]) => integrity_rule.
```

Figure 5: A rule implementing propagation.

Acknowledgements

The authors would like to thank to Peter Gray and Norman Paton for useful discussions during the implementation of these ideas. Oscar Díaz was supported by a grant from the Spanish Government. Suzanne Embury was supported by a grant from the SERC Biotechnology Directorate.

References

[Bauz,90] C. Bauzer Medeiros, P. Pfeffer *A mechanism for Managing Rules in an Object-oriented Database*, Altair Technical Report

[Case,89] Y. Caseau *A Formal System for Producting Demons from Rules in an Object-Oriented Database* in Proc. 1st. DOOD (Deductive and Object Oriented Databases), Kyoto, 1989, pp.188-204

[Ceri,90] S. Ceri, J. Widom *Deriving Production Rules for Constraint Maintenance* in Proc. 16th VLDB, Brisbane, 1990, pp. 567-577

[Ceri,91] S. Ceri, J. Widom *Deriving Production Rules for Incremental View Maintenance* in Proc. 17th VLDB, Barcelona, 1991, pp. 567-577

[Daya,89] U. Dayal *Active Database Management Systems* SIGMOD RECORD, Vol. 18, No 3, 1989, pp. 150-169

[Diaz,91] O. Diaz, P.M.D. Gray *Semantic-rich User-defined Relationship as a Main Constructor in Object Oriented Databases* in *Object-Oriented Databases: Analysis, Design and Construction (DS-4)* Meersman, Kent and Khosla (eds), North-Holland, 1991, pp. 207-224

[Diaz,91a] O. Diaz, N.W. Paton *Sharing Behaviour in an Object-Oriented Database using a Rule-Based Mechanism* in British National Conference on Databases (BN-COD), Wolverhampton, Butterwarth Publishers, 1991, pp. 17-37

[Diaz,91b] O. Diaz, P.M.D. Gray, N.W. Paton *Rule Management in Object Oriented Databases: a uniform approach* in Int. Conf. on Very Large Data Base, Barcelona, 1991, pp. 317-326

[Diaz,92] O. Diaz, *Deriving Rules for Constraint Maintenance in an Object-Oriented Database*, Submitted for publication

[Morg,84] M. Morgenstern *Constraint Equations: Declarative Expression of Constraints with Automatic Enforcement*, Proc. Inter. Con. on VLDB, 1984, pp. 153-299

[Nico,78] J.M. Nicolas, K. Yazdanian *Integrity Checking in Deductive Data Bases, Logic and Data Bases*, Gallaire and Minker (Eds.), 1978, pp. 325-346

[Pato,89] N.W. Paton *ADAM: An Object-Oriented Database System Implemented in Prolog* , Proc. 7th BNCOD, M.H. Williams (edt), CUP, 1989, pp. 147-161

[Rumb,87] J. Rumbaugh *Relations as semantic Constructors in an Object-Oriented Language* OOPSLA, 1987, pp. 466-481

[Ston,90] M. Stonebraker, A. Jhingram, J. Goh and S. Potamianos *On rules, procedures, caching and views in database systems* in Proc. ACM SIGMOD, 1990, pp. 281-290

[Urba,89] S.D. Urban *ALICE: An Assertion Language for Integrity Constraint Expression* in Proc. Fifth Int. Con. on Computer Software and Applications, Los Angeles, 1989

[Urba,90] S.D. Urban, M. Desiderio *Translating Constraints to Rules in CONTEXT: A CONstrainT EXplanation Tool*, in Proc. IFIP DS-4 Intl. Workshop on *Object-Oriented Databases: Analysis, Design and Construction*, Kent and Meersman (Eds.), 1990

[Urba,91] S.D. Urban, L.M.L. Delcambre *Constraint Analysis: A Design Process for Specifying Operations on Objects*, Transactions on Knowledge and Data Engineering, 1991

Employing Integrity Constraints for Query Modification and Intensional Answer Generation in Multi-database systems

M.M. Fonkam & W.A.Gray,
Dept. of Computing Mathematics, University of Wales College of Cardiff,
Cardiff CF2 4AG, email : mmf@uk.ac.cf.cm.

ABSTRACT

A significant number of database (DB) users today lack complete knowledge of the semantics of the DB(s) they desire to query. This is a very common phenomenon in the Multidatabase System (MBS) type of distributed database systems (DDBSs). In MBSs, a number of DBs, are loosely linked without creating a global schema in order to enable occasional sharing of their information contents. As some cost is normally associated with querying any particular site in this system, a lack of complete knowledge of the DB semantics can often result in fruitless but costly searches. The aim of the work described in this paper is to provide a tool which can assist Multidatabase users gain an understanding of the semantics of DBs accessible to them. Specifically, we use the explicit integrity constraints(ICs) of the database intension in two essential ways to elicit the semantics of those views of the DB addressed in the user's query; firstly to ascertain the relevance of a user query at a particular site and thus to advise the user in case of any constraint violations, suggesting a modification for the query in the process, and secondly to provide abstract or intensional answers to a user request.The first goal aims to provide a system free of the ambiguities associated with an empty response to some retrieval request while the second goal aims to improve the user's understanding of the semantics associated with the data values generated as answers by providing with the tuples of the answer the general rules that they obey.

INTRODUCTION

Integrity constraints express intensional information (or knowledge) that applies to multitudes of real-world objects stored in the database(extensional database). They represent logical restrictions on data that are expected to hold true if the DB objects (the extension of the database) actually conform to the existing knowledge about them. Constraints are required for both semantic and integrity reasons[TSIC82]. In terms of *semantics*, they permit the data model to more accurately reflect the real-world situation. In terms of *integrity*, they permit the DBMS to restrict the possible DB states that can be generated from a given schema to those that meet the conditions expressed by the constraints. In current relational systems, constraints are usually expressed as formulae in predicate logic that assert the required relationships among the data values and their enforcement is normally achieved by a process of query modification [STON75].

Current relational systems use ICs to monitor changes made to the database relations. Assuming that the relations initially satisfy the constraints, any subsequent update requests are only accepted if they do not violate any of these constraints. Usually only a subset of the constraints (those that could be violated by the update) need be used for such monitoring and approaches have been described in the literature for isolating the relevant set, [BRY88, KIN81a,

KOW87]. Enforcement of certain types of constraints can be very costly thus, most current systems do not allow constraints that are arbitrary first-order predicate formulae. Usually only very specific types of constraints such as range(domain) constraints and referential constraints are allowed. Apart from their use for monitoring updates to the extensional DB, ICs have also been widely used for semantic query or transaction optimisation [KIN81a, WAN90]. This is a technique of query or transaction optimisation based on the use of ICs to transform a query or transaction to an equivalent query or transaction that can be more easily and cheaply executed. In [WAN90], we also looked at how such constraints can be used to delete those update requests that do not affect the DB contents. In part, the work described in this paper extends the ideas presented in [WAN90] to the MBS environment, but we use ICs mostly for a different purpose; namely, to enhance the user's understanding of the semantics of the DB being queried.

Much recent research has been undertaken on intensional query processing, primarily for deductive databases [CHOL87, CHOL88, MOT89, PIR89, SONG90]. The aim of this research is to provide answers that are independent of any database state representing conditions that any tuples of data must fulfil to be an answer to the query. Although most of this research has been undertaken in the domain of deductive databases the ideas of this research need to be developed for the relational systems primarily due to their semantic limitations[KENT79] and their dominance in the commercial scene. With the arrival of Prolog-DBMS interfaces [CERI90] that allow the use of Prolog for DB querying, it even becomes possible to treat the overall system as a deductive database where the ICs form the rule base. Even without such an interface, Motro [MOT89] has shown how ICs can be employed to provide an intensional answer to characterise the set of DB values that serve as an answer to the query. His approach is that of arranging the relevant constraints in meta-relations (one for each relation of the database) and evaluating these meta-relations for an intensional answer whenever those relations are accessed. Motro's approach is model-theoretic, our own described in this paper is proof theoretic and thus we assume some deductive capabilities of the system.

The aims of the work described in this paper are twofold; firstly we investigate how ICs can be employed in an MBS to isolate (locate) the relevant sites and relations for some user request and secondly how an intensional response can be generated from the relevant sites to accompany the data values that serve as answers to the query. The second goal serves as an enhancement to our earlier work on *reverse modelling* concerned with deriving a conceptual model for an existing DB from its given relational DB schema, in an attempt to provide the users with a better means of understanding the intension of the database. The results of that work are reported elsewhere [FONK92].

This paper is organised as follows. In section 1 we survey and classify the different types of ICs found in a relational system. In section 2, we introduce through a Proof-theoretic view point, the notion of an intensional answer to a query. Section 3 briefly discusses the MBS approach and the problems therein. In section 4, we present an approach for generating an intensional response for sites guaranteed to produce a null response to some user query and also show how the overall Multidatabase query could be modified. Section 5 illustrates an approach by which an intensional response can be generated from those relevant sites yielding some answer tuples. Section 6 discusses the implementation of our system using the Arity Prolog programming language. In Section 7 conclusions are drawn and future directions for this work are identified.

1. Integrity Constraints in Relational Systems

At an abstract level two types of constraints are distinguishable in databases; *inherent* (or structural) constraints and *explicit* (behavioural) constraints. Inherent constraints are part of the data model and as such can be automatically enforced by the system, e.g. the relational model being based on the concept of the mathematical set has the inherent constraint that duplicate tuples are not allowed in the extension of a relation and hence the concept of a tuple identifier (key) is valid. Explicit constraints are those constraints that are tangential to the data model and serve to augment the structure specification of the database[TSIC82].We only consider explicit constraints since inherent constraints cannot be separated from the structure of the database.

Explicit constraints can be further classified into *state constraints* which characterise valid database states and *transition constraints* which impose restrictions on certain possible changes of state. Our discussion is again limited to *state constraints* due to difficulties involved in handling transition constraints [WAN90], problems which are closely related to the frame problem in Artificial intelligence[REIT84].

Two types of state constraints are distinguished in [CODD90], namely ; *column integrity* (C-type) which further restricts the range of the basic type (D-type) upon which some attribute is defined, each C-type constraint being automatically linked by the DBMS with a D-type constraint by logical AND, e.g. the constraint that Employee ages lie between 16 and 65 years; and *User-defined integrity* (U-type) which is a constraint defined in terms of one or more C-type constraints and/or other U-type constraints, usually involving arithmetic operators, and primarily used to enforce company regulations; e.g. the constraint for some employee DB that the sum of the salary and the commission being received by each employee must be less than the salary value of that employee's manager is a U-type constraint. Most operational relational DBMSs such as Ingres and Oracle store the definitions of integrity constraints in specified system tables in the data dictionary that can be accessed by a user or program using the query language. Some of these systems, such as Oracle version 6.0, actually support the syntax of most constraints even if they cannot automatically enforce all of them.

2. The Concept of an Intensional Answer

We adopt a Proof-theoretic view of relational DBs [REIT83,FROS86,HOGG90]. In this approach the DB is viewed as a theory with its ICs and queries being theorems of this theory. This view provides a uniform treatment of both the DB queries and its ICs. It also provides a more efficient computational method for carrying out deductions on the database. ICs are expressed as closed first-order formulae that a DB must satisfy. For our own purposes, we take the theory to be made up of both the DB and its ICs. We assume familiarity with the terminology of first-order logic as defined in most texts on the subject [GRAY84, FROS86, CHAN73, HOGG90, CERI90, AMB87, KOW79, WOS84, BUN83].

According to Cholvy and Demolombe [CHOL87], who first proposed and formalised the concept of intensional answers for deductive databases, an intensional answer is simply those conditions which must be satisfied by any tuple to belong to an answer to the query, rather than the tuples themselves. An intensional answer characterises the extensional answer, providing more insight into the nature of the set of values retrieved; the qualification in the user's query being the first source of intensional information. Intensional answers provide a more stable answer to a query than the extensional answer and since their construction does not need any accessing of the usually much larger extensional database, they can be constructed much faster and more cheaply than the extensional answers. For example, assume a personnel DB with the following relation scheme :

$$Employee(Name, Title, Salary, Department)$$

and two constraints, one states that all the employees in the design department are guaranteed a salary of at least £20,000 and the other states that all employees in research positions are in the design department. The horn-clause specifications of these constraints are given respectively by IC1 and IC2 :

$$IC1 : Employee(N,T,S,D) \ \& \ D='design' \rightarrow S >= 20,000$$

$$IC2 : Employee(N,T,S,D) \& T='research' \rightarrow D ='design'$$

We would like the intensional answers (stated here in English for expository reasons) given by IA1 and IA2 below to accompany the extensional answers for the query: "retrieve all employees in the 'design' department".

IA1 : "All employees retrieved earn at least 20,000 pounds".

IA2 : "All employees in research positions have been retrieved".

If we denote by $T \vdash F$ the theorems F of the first-order theory T, by Q(X) our query where X is a tuple of free variables and by Ansi the answers we require, then we can formalise the definition of an intensional answer to Q, Ans(Q) by :

$$Ans(Q) = \{Ansi(X) : T \vdash \forall X(Ansi(X) \rightarrow Q(X)$$

$$\underline{OR} \ \forall X(Q(X) \rightarrow Ansi(X))\}$$

Within the context of deductive DBs the emphasis has been on the first type of answers, i.e. answers restricted by :

$$Ans(Q) = \{Ansi(X) : T \vdash \forall X(Ansi(X) \rightarrow Q(X)\}$$

We henceforth refer to this type of answer as Type 1 answers and those answers restricted by:

$$Ans(Q) = \{Ansi(X) : T \vdash \forall X(Q(X) \rightarrow Ansi(X))\}$$

as Type 2 answers. As our example shows, when we use integrity constraints to provide intensional answers, both types of answer are necessary for eliciting the semantics of the DB. In fact, considering the actual tuples generated as answers, the latter type of answers seem more reliable. IA2 above may only apply to a subset (not necessarily the whole set) of the tuples generated as answers. As will be seen in Section 5, a refutation technique is sound and complete for Type 1 answers whereas we need to reason forwards with the query to generate answers of Type 2. Type 1 intensional answers are typically obtained by replacing, in the query or in already obtained intensional answers, a virtual predicate by its definition in the deduction rules.

3. Multidatabase Systems (MBS)

The *Multidatabase Systems* (MBSs) are the logically decentralised and either physically centralised or decentralised class of distributed databases [CERI87 ,HEIM81, HEIM85, LIT88, LIT84]. This class of databases is made up of a non-integrated set of autonomous DBs with the sole objective of *occasional sharing* of their information contents. No global schema exists in these systems against which users can make queries, but the independent DBs are simply loosely linked to each other by a communication network with each database having its own schema. As pointed out in [LIT88] most commercial distributed systems under the label of

Distributed Databases (DDBs) are actually MBSs; examples of which include Ingres/star, Sybase, Oracle's SQL*Plus etc. Thus in comparison with the other types of Distributed Database systems (DDBSs), most of which only exist as prototypes, the MBS approach seems to be the furthest along in current implementations. The example commercial systems cited above may not provide an MBS language with the features described below but their operations are basically the same as those of systems that provide such features. The classical MBS approach, [LIT87], provides a common language by which the DBs can be queried together. An MBS user is expected to use the features of this language to define the *interdatabase dependencies* that exist across the DBs, in effect creating a temporary global schema (which however, only exists for the duration of a single multidatabase query), and then to make queries that reference the dependencies defined. It is these dependencies that an MBS system uses in translating a user's request to a set of requests over the databases involved.

To define these dependencies and to be able to use the underlying systems effectively, the users need to have a proper understanding of the semantics of the DBs in the system. Because MBS users only occasionally use remote databases it is unlikely that they will ever possess complete knowledge of their semantic contents. Such knowledge can only be gained through frequent interactions with the system. The usual approach to providing such users with some assistance in understanding the semantics of any particular database in the system has been to attempt to regain the conceptual model of the DB schema using one of the semantic data models like the Entity-Relationship model to display its schema. This process of reverse engineering has been the subject of much research[DAVI87,KAT91,FONK92]. As noted in [FONK92] where we reported on our own work in this area of reverse modelling and as discussed in Section 1 of this paper, only the *inherent constraints* are captured by the data model and thus only these constraints can be portrayed in the graphical output which usually represents the conceptual model. The relational model however, is rather weak on inherent constraints [TSIC82] and as such most restrictions on the actual DB states are often stated as *explicit constraints*. A further problem is that while such graphical presentations may actually indicate descriptions of some objects of interest to the user, a further analysis of the explicit constraints may lead to their rejection as they may not fall within the requirements of the user. Users' confidence in the system thus needs to be regained in this case by showing them those constraints that caused the particular rejection. Our work in this paper is concerned with using ICs to filter out the relevant sites in an MBS as well as to provide intensional answers that can serve to improve the user's understanding of the semantics of the DB.

4. Employing ICs to Isolate Relevant Sites in an MBS

As discussed in Section 3, to make MBS queries that reference more than a single site, the user needs to define *interdatabase dependencies* which the MBS system uses in breaking up the query into sub-queries to be executed at the relevant sites. Normally, all the user has at his disposal for making such definitions are the names of relations and their attributes in the accessible databases of the MBS system. Without complete knowledge of the other semantics of the database(s) being queried in an MBS, the user's query may inevitably include those relations and sites from which an empty response will result due to the fact that the qualification in the user's query (which forms the first intensional answer) violates one or more of the constraints on the data of those sites or relations. The normal response by a conventional DBMS to a query whose qualification violates an IC is to return no tuples. This is rather ambiguous because a null response is also the case for when no value actually exists in the system meeting the query restrictions but which could potentially exist. An intensional answer in this case thus serves to clarify this ambiguity and ICs help in isolating such empty answers and queries. As a side effect of this intensional answer generation process it becomes possible, in an MBS in this case, to reframe the query so that the irrelevant sites and/or relations are ignored, thus yielding some cost savings.

In our subsequent discussion, we consider the three DBs shown together with their consistent set of ICs in Fig.1 as forming the Multidatabase (MDB), REST-GUIDES, given in MSQL by :

CREATE MULTIDATABASE

REST-GUIDES ={MICHELIN,KLEBER,GAULT-M}

The Integrity Constraints (ICs) are given in English and expressed in the standard prenex normal form [CHAN73].

DB MICHELIN : Site A

R(R*,RNAME,STREET,TYPE,STARS,AVPRICE,TEL)	RESTAURANT
C(C*,R*,CNAME)	COURSE
M(R*,C*,PRICE)	MENU
ENDDB	

ICs DB MICHELIN

ICA-1 : The average price of each meal is at least £10

$\forall(t,u,v,w,x,y,z)$ R(t,u,v,w,x,y,z) $\rightarrow$ y >= 10

ICA-2 : All Chinese restaurants are on 'China street'.

$\forall(t,u,v,w,x,y,z)$ R(t,u,v,w,x,y,z) & w = 'Chinese' $\rightarrow$ v = 'china street'

ICA-3 : Restaurants with a star rating above 3 are on 'High Street'

$\forall(t,u,v,w,x,y,z)$ R(t,u,v,w,x,y,z) & x > '***' $\rightarrow$ v = 'High street'

ICA-4 : All restaurants on 'china street' sell 'pizzas'

$\forall(t,u,v,w,x,y,z)\exists(r)$R(t,u,v,w,x,y,z) & v='china street' $\rightarrow$ C(r,t,'pizzas')

ICA-5 : All restaurants with the name 'yan' are 'Chinese'

$\forall(t,u,v,w,x,y,z)$R(t,u,v,w,x,y,z) & u='yan' $\rightarrow$ w='Chinese'

DB KLEBER : Site B

REST(REST*,NAME,STREET,TYPE,FORKS,TEL*,MPRICE)	RESTAURANT
C(C*,REST*,CNAME,NCAL)	COURSE
MENU(REST*,C*,PRICE)	MENU
ENDDB	

ICs For DB KLEBER

ICB-1 : No restaurant has a star rating greater than '***'

$\forall(t,...,z)$ R(t,...,z) $\rightarrow$ x $\leq$ '***'

ICB-2 : Only restaurants with a star rating of '***' sell meals costing above £8.0

$\forall(n,t,q,r,s)$ $\exists(u,..,z)$ C(n,t,q,r) & MENU(t,n,s) & s > 8.0

$\rightarrow$ REST(t,u,...,z) & x = '***'

Fig. 1. Sample Opened sites in a MBS (Continued)

DB GAULT-M : Site C

R(R*,RNAME,STREET,QUAL,TEL,TYPE,AVPRICE)   RESTAURANT

C(C*,R*,CNAME,NCAL)   COURSE

M(R*,C*,PRICE)   MENU

ENDDB

ICs For DB Gault-M

ICC-1 : The only known restaurant types are Indian,French and Italian.

$$\forall(t,...,z)\ R(t,...,z) \rightarrow y=\text{'Indian'} \vee y=\text{'French'} \vee y=\text{'Italian'}$$

ICC-2 : Only French restaurants have average prices above £10.0

$$\forall(t,...,z)\ R(t..,z)\ \&\ z > 10 \rightarrow y =\text{'French'}$$

ICC-3 : All restaurants that sell meals costing less than £10 have a star rating less than '****'.

$$\forall(t,n,m,p,q)\ \exists(u,..,z)\ C(n,t,p,q)\ \&\ M(t,n,m)\ \&\ m < 10$$

$$\rightarrow R(t,...,z)\ \&\ w < \text{'***'}$$

Fig. 1. Sample Opened sites in a MBS

In each case the first set of variables in brackets appearing before the formula are assumed to be universally quantified (denoted by the quantifier $\forall$) while the second set, if it exists, are assumed to be existentially quantified (denoted by $\exists$). An MDB query such as : "retrieve all the restaurants from REST_GUIDES that a guide considers 'Chinese'", is represented in MSQL by the following sequence of statements:

        USE REST-GUIDES

        LET X BE R REST

        SELECT * FROM X WHERE TYPE='Chinese'

This MDB query makes use of 2 novel features of an MDB language[LIT87,LIT84], namely Multiple Identifiers, and Semantic Variables. The query statement -LET X BE R REST declares a semantic variable X, which is a designator ranging over other designators, R and REST. One of the designators of this semantic variable R, is a Multiple Identifier since it occurs more than once in the scope of the query (in the databases MICHELIN and Gault-M).

      This query would be split by the MBS system into 3 sub-queries, two of the sub-queries attempting to retrieve tuples from the relations named R in DBs MICHELIN and Gault-M, while the other sub-query will attempt to retrieve tuples from REST in the DB KLEBER. An analysis of the qualification in the query against the ICs at each site in turn would however, show that the result from DB Gault-M is guaranteed to be empty since ICC-1 would be violated by this qualification.The three sub-queries that result from the above MDB query are :

    subQ1 : For DB MICHELIN

         SELECT *

         FROM R

         WHERE R.TYPE = 'Chinese'

    subQ2 : For DB KLEBER

         SELECT *

         FROM REST

         WHERE REST.TYPE = 'Chinese'

    subQ3 : For DB Gault-M

         SELECT *

FROM R

WHERE R.TYPE = 'Chinese'

It can be seen that the same qualification applies for all the sub-queries. Thus it is possible to employ the qualification in a user's query to identify those relations and/or sites from which a null response will be derived owing to a violation of one of its constraints and thus employ the definitions of the involved constraints to appropriately advise the user. It also becomes possible to rewrite the MDB query so as to ignore those sites. The appropriately modified MDB query which excludes the site Gault-M is given by :

- LET X BE MICHELIN.R REST
- SELECT X WHERE TYPE = 'Chinese'

Here we have employed the site name as a prefix (another capability of an MBS system) to resolve ambiguities in relation names. The result of this modification is that only two sub-queries are generated and shipped to the appropriate sites instead of the three derived above. Thus some cost savings (communication costs and the cost of processing queries at the site in question) are made by determining and ignoring those sub-queries that are guaranteed to yield a NULL response. This may also help counteract problems of site failure which may halt the system even though the faulty site could not produce any results. Some overhead would be incurred in processing ICs to isolate and ignore irrelevant sites and/or relations but this would be small compared to communication cost and processing time (especially when sites are some distance apart). Sites may typically also charge some price for processing queries from remote locations whether such queries yield some result or not. It may be helpful to make such modification of the query visible to users together with the reasoning behind the modification as an initial step to eliciting the semantics of the DB.

By treating the qualification in the query as another integrity constraint to be included in the already existing set of ICs at a site it is easy using the resolution process [GRAY84, AMB87, CHAN73, HOGG90, CERI90] to prove inconsistency. Resolution is an automatic theorem proving procedure which combines the *modus ponens* inference rule with *unification*. The modus ponens inference rule states that given proposition A and a rule that A *implies B*, we can deduce the proposition B. This is denoted by the expression $\{A, A \rightarrow B\} \vdash B$. Unification is a general pattern-matcher used for matching sentences with similar patterns. Resolution is used mostly to carry out refutation proofs due to its completeness for refutation proofs. Using resolution, in order to prove that some formula ω, is a theorem of some theory Ω, denoted by $\Omega \vdash \omega$, one tries to show that Ω and $\sim\omega$ are not simultaneously satisfiable. As resolution preserves satisfiability, if one can by applying resolution on the clausal forms of Ω and $\sim\omega$ derive the empty clause, then Ω and $\sim\omega$ cannot simultaneously be satisfied. Thus ω must be derivable from Ω and as such is a theorem of Ω To investigate if the qualification in a certain query violates one of the existing ICs and as such is bound to yield a null answer, we adopt a forward-reasoning strategy similar to that in [KOW87]. As in that work, the particular resolution strategy used is an extended SLDNF strategy of resolution where the top clause can be a denial or any definite clause. This species of resolution is extended so that it can recognise those derivations which are bound to fail since relying merely upon the derivation of finite failure is no longer guaranteed when reasoning forwards with this strategy. Our extended version recognises mutually unsolvable conjunctions of calls and loops.

To illustrate how applying resolution on the ICs of Gault-M together with the qualification in our query above leads to a contradiction we re-express the relevant ICs and the qualification as clauses and try to resolve the clauses using the qualification clause(s) as top clause (s).The relevant IC in this case is ICC-1, which is obviously not a definite clause. As explained in [KOW79] we can transform this clause into a horn-clause by renaming. *ICCd-1* below represents the definite clause equivalent of ICC-1:

$$ICCd\text{-}1 : \sim R(t,u,v,w,x,y,z) \lor \sim uneq(y,\text{'Indian'}) \lor \sim uneq(y,\text{'French'}) \lor eq(y,\text{'Italian'})$$

where the predicate 'uneq' represents the positive equivalent of ~eq.The query qualification in clause form is given by :

$$QC : R(t0,u0,v0,\text{'Chinese'},x0,y0,z0).$$

where t0,u0,v0,x0,y0,z0 are Skolem constants introduced to remove the existential quantifier in the query clause. A refutation is obtained by resolving the query clause, QC with ICCd-1; all the literals in the resolvent obtained are false.. The constraint, ICC-1 would thus need to be shown to the user as reason for a null response to his query from the particular site involved.

5. Using ICs to generate an Intensional Answer to a MDB Query

We formalise the derivation of Intensional answers as follows :
For Type 1 answers discussed in Section 2 :

$$T \vdash \forall X(Ansi(X) \rightarrow Q(X)) \quad \textit{iff}$$

$$T \cup \sim \forall X(Ansi(X) \rightarrow Q(X))$$

is refutable by a resolution strategy, where U denotes the set union operator.

$$\sim \forall X(Ansi(X) \rightarrow Q(X))$$

leads to the two clauses

$$\{Ansi(x0),\sim Q(x0)\}$$

where x0 is a tuple of Skolem constants introduced to remove the existential quantifier. Thus we can adopt as the basis for our resolution the set given by :

$$T \cup \sim Q(x0)$$

If we denote by $R(x0,y)$, all the resolvents of this, where y denotes the tuple of all free variables derived, then as proved in [CHOL87,CHOL88] our intended Type 1 answers are given by :

$$Ansi(X) = \exists Y \sim R(X,Y).$$

For answers of Type 2, our theorem is given by

$$\forall X(Q(X) \rightarrow Ansi(X))$$

Thus we require that

$$T \cup \sim \forall X(Q(X) \rightarrow Ansi(X))$$

be refutable by a resolution strategy. Applying the same manipulations as for Type 1 answers leads to the two clauses :

$$\{Q(x0),\sim Ansi(x0)\}$$

So we can adopt as the basis for our resolution the set given by

$$T \cup Q(x0).$$

Again, if we consider $R(x0,y)$ as the resolvents, then we can take as a potential answer all ansi(x0) such that

$$\sim Ansi(x0) = \sim R(x0,y).$$

Thus we can simply take as Ansi(x0) the resolvents R(x0,y). However, because of the nature of our particular forward-reasoning strategy, some of the resolvents will be redundant and need to be deleted. Examples of redundant answers are those that are syntactically redundant or that are subsumed by others; e.g. given formulas F1 and F2; F2 is redundant to F1 & F2 and F1 v F2 is subsumed by F1. Redundant answers are not generated when formulas are in the form of horn-clauses and the top-clause is a denial (as for Type 1 answers).

As an example, suppose the following mono-query (single site query) is made on the DB MICHELIN : "Retrieve all the 'Chinese' restaurants". In SQL this query is :

SELECT *
FROM R
WHERE R.TYPE = 'CHINESE'

This query can be expressed in the generalised logic form as :

$Q : R(t,u,v,w,x,y,z)$ & $eq(w,'Chinese')$.

From our formalisation for Type 1 answers

$\sim Q(X0) : \sim R(t0,u0,v0,w0,x0,y0,z0)$ v $\sim eq(w0,'Chinese')$.

Adopting this as our centre-clause in a SLDNF-resolution strategy, we obtain, upon resolving with ICA-5 the single resolvent given by :

$R(X0,Y) : \sim R(t0,u0,v0,'Chinese',x0,y0,z0)$ v $\sim eq(u0,'yan')$.

As this is the only resolvent obtainable from our set of ICs, its negation forms the only intensional answer for answers of Type 1.

$\exists Ys \sim R(Xs,Ys) : R(T,U,V,'Chinese',X,Y,Z)$ & $eq(U,'yan')$

where Ys denotes the tuple of free variables encountered within the resolution process (which is empty for the intensional answer derived) and Xs denotes the tuple of variables originating from the Skolem constants introduced at the start of the resolution process, given by $\{T,U,V,X,Y,Z\}$. This asserts that the answer(tuples) derived includes all the restaurants with name 'yan'.

Using our formalisation to derive intensional answers of Type 2, we have to generate resolvents from the set (T U Q). In this case we take the compact form of the query clause given by:

$Q(X0) : R(t0,u0,v0,'Chinese',x0,y0,z0)$.

Using SLDNF, the top-clause can only be a denial, so we need to extend it to handle our definite clause and reason forwards with our query clause as the top-clause. Resolving $Q(X0)$ with ICA-1 leads to a resolvent of this type; $gtoreq(y0,10)$. All the intensional answers generated by this process after deleting redundant answers (i.e. those subsumed by others and those that evaluate to true) are given by IA1,IA2,IA3,and IA4 together with their English interpretations.

$IA1 : gtoreq(y0,10)$ - from ICA-1

"All restaurants retrieved have average price greater than or equal to 10" .

$IA2 : eq(v0,'china\ street')$ - from ICA-2

"All restaurants retrieved are on 'china street'".

$IA3 : \sim gt(x0,'***')$ v $eq(v0,'high\ street')$ - from ICA-3

"If the star rating is greater than '***' then the street is 'high street'".

$IA4 : 'C'(n,t0,'pizzas')$ - from ICA-2 and from ICA-4

"All the restaurants retrieved sell 'pizzas'".

From these results we see that our approach derives some answers that must be interpreted in the context of the query as well as from our knowledge of the relational model to make them more meaningful (e.g. IA3). From IA3 we would like to be able to derive the intensional answer IA3'.

IA3' : ~gt(x0,'***')   meaning

"All restaurants retrieved have a star rating not greater than '***'".

We need to interpret this resolvent within the entire set of Integrity constraints and our query. IA3 actually says: "If the number of stars is three then the street is 'high street'", but there is no way of proving that the number of stars is three. However, one of our intensional answers asserts unconditionally that all the restaurants derived are on 'china street'. From our knowledge of the relational model an attribute cannot have more than one value, so further constraints need to be derived (which we shall appropriately call implicit constraints) which embody these semantics. The derived constraints attempt to complete (taking the closed-world assumption[HOG90]) the semantics of each constraint already existing in the system. For ICA-2 we can derive the implicit constraint given by, DICA-2 to complete its semantics :

DICA-2 : ~R(t,u,v,w,x,y,z) ∨ ~eq(w,'Chinese') ∨ ~eq(v,'high street')

and for ICA-3, DICA-3 completes its semantics for our given set of constraints

DICA-3 : ~R(t,u,v,w,x,y,z) ∨ ~ gt(x,'***') ∨ ~eq(v,'china street').

As Fig.3 shows, by adding these two constraints to our initial constraint set, we are able to derive our intended answer, namely that, *"all restaurants retrieved have a star rating not greater than three"*.

6. Implementation Considerations

Our prototype system has been implemented in the Arity Prolog system on an IBM PC machine. We briefly discuss the various modules of this system in the same order as presented so far in the paper.

$$Q(X0) : R(t0,u0,v0,'chinese',x0,y0,z0)$$

$$\mid ICA\text{-}3$$

$$(\sim gt(x0,'***')\; ^{\vee}\; eq(v0,'high\ street'))$$

$$\mid DICA\text{-}2$$

$$(\sim gt(x0,'***')\; _\vee\; \sim R(t,u,'high\ street',w,x,y,z)\; _\vee\; \sim eq(w,'chinese')$$

$$\mid Q(X0)$$

$$\sim gt(x0,'***')$$

Fig. 2 A New More Meaningful Resolvent Due to the Derived Constraint

The first sub-system of our system deals with analysing the MDB query in an attempt to isolate irrelevant sites and if any are found, to rewrite the query and advise the user of such modification. An MDB query such as the example in Section 4 is typed in as:

    let x be 'R' or 'REST'

    select * from x where type = 'Chinese'.

This query is suitably modified to aid development of its syntax analyser in Prolog since developing such an analyser is not one of our major objectives. This modification makes it extremely easy to develop a simple syntax analyser and to directly employ Prolog's built-in reader for reading in the query. In our system, the keywords (i.e. the invariants of a query) of

the general MDB retrieval statement, namely; 'let','be','or',select','where',and 'and', are
declared as Prolog operators making a suitable choice of operator precedences, thus:

:-

    op(970,fx,let),
    op(960,xfx,be),
    op(1,xfx,':'),
    op(952,xfy,and),
    op(955,xfy,or),
    op(972,xfx,from),
    op(980,xfx,select),
    op(975,xfx,where).

This definition leads to the internal form given by :

$select(let(be(x,and('R','REST'))),where(from(*,x),=(type,'Chinese')))$

and has the advantage of easy reading and writing of terms as well as allowing the use of simple
expressions in manipulations [Li84]. All MDB retrieval statements can be made to have the 'let'
prefix which is somewhat analogous to the range statement in the Ingres query language,
QUEL. Our system assumes this more general form of an MDB retrieval statement.

    Using the schemes of the relations mentioned in the 'let' part of the MDB query, our
system generates the logic equivalent of the query needed for each site. Specifically, given the
schema of the DB at each site our system automatically generates a template for each relation
scheme in which the attributes are replaced by variables. These templates are used together with
the relation scheme to generate the logic equivalent of the query for that site. Considering the
query above and the relation schemes for the relations 'R' and 'REST' in Fig. 1, three logic
equivalents are derived for the 3 sites, given in their more general forms by:

    'R'(T,U,V,W,X,Y,Z) & eq(W,'Chinese')   - for site A;
    'REST'(T,U,V,W,X,Y,Z) & eq(W,'Chinese')   - for site B;
    'R'(T,U,V,W,X,Y,Z) & eq(Y,'Chinese')   - for site C.

The integrity constraints (ICs) for each site are converted into Prolog-type clauses (horn-
clauses) and stored in a special two argument predicate with the following schema:

    $integrity(Site\_name,clause(Clause\_id,Conse\_list,Ante\_list))$

The first argument designates the site to which the constraint belongs and the second holds the
details of the clause representing the constraint. This latter argument is itself a three argument
predicate with its first argument bearing the identifier for the clause, the second, a list denoting
the consequent of the horn-clause while the last argument is a list holding the literals for the
antecedent part of the horn-clause. Employing lists for both antecedent and consequent of the
horn-clause ensures a uniform representation for all types of clauses (i.e. denial, the general
horn-clause, a fact and the empty clause). Evaluable predicates such as the inequalities <, =<,
>, >=, =, and ≠ are represented by named predicates lt., ltoreq, gt, gtoreq, eq and nt_eq
respectively as in [WAN90] Our implementation supports the equality axioms through the
paramodulation inference rule and the reflexivity axiom [BUD83].

    Once the logic equivalents of the query have been generated for the sites involved, a
Prolog goal is invoked which succeeds when a refutation is derived using the logic equivalent
of the query for that site as a top-clause in a forward-reasoning strategy with the ICs of that site.
This goal is iterated over the sites and sites yielding a refutation are shown to the user together
with the ICs used in their refutation. A modified form of the query that excludes the sites from
which a refutation was derived is also derived and presented to the user. The intensional answer
generation phase then considers only the logic equivalents of the query at sites not listed as

yielding a refutation. To generate answers of Type 1, the extended form of the logic query is negated and used as the top-clause in a pure SLDNF-resolution (i.e. one where the top-clause is a denial). In this case all the resolvents derived are simply presented to the user as intensional answers for that site. No checks are needed to remove redundant resolvents because none are derived in this case. However, evaluable literals are evaluated whenever their variable parts become instantiated and deleted if need be. The algorithm for deriving Type 1 answers works in a depth-first strategy similar to Prolog's built-in theorem-prover. In fact, it takes advantage of this built-in depth first strategy. The top-level Prolog predicates for this algorithm are given by 'int_ans_type1' and 'int_ans' defined thus:

```
int_ans_type1(Tc,X,_) :-
        int_ans(Tc,X),
        fail.
int_ans_type1(_,X,L) :-
        reap_ans(X,L).

int_ans(Tc,X) :-
        ic(X,C),
        [! resolvent(Tc,C,C1),
           assert(new(X,C1)),
           int_ans(C1,X)
        !],
        fail.
   int_ans(_,_).

reap_ans(X,[H|T]) :-
        retract(new(X,H)),
        reap_ans(T).
reap_ans(_,[]).
```

int_ans_type1(X,Y,Z) means that Z is the list of intensional answers for the site Y using the top-clause X. *int_ans(X,Y)* means that X is the top-clause to be used at site Y for generating Type 1 answers. It is this predicate that implements the depth-first strategy. At the start of the process, the query clause is used to derive a resolvent which is in turn used to derive a further resolvent and so on (through recursion) until no further resolvent can be derived on this path; at which point backtracking is forced using Prolog's built-in 'fail' predicate. All resolvents derived along any path are asserted into Prolog's internal database. When no further resolvents can be derived, then *int_ans_type1* uses the *reap_ans* predicate to collect all the asserted answers. The definition of this predicate is self-explanatory. The '[!' and '!]' constructs in the definition of *'int_ans'* is a built-in performance-oriented feature of Arity Prolog (called the sniff) used for preventing backtracking over the predicates enclosed within the two constructs.

For Type 2 answers, its top-level predicate, initially generates for the site involved all the implicit constraints necessary for interpreting all the resolvents derived. This top-level predicate is given by 'int_ans_type2' which is defined thus:

```
int_ans_type2([H|_],X,_) :-
          gen_imp_constraints(X),
          int_ans(H,X),
```

```
          fail.
int_ans_type2([_|T],X,L) :-
          reap_ans(X,L1),
          del_redundant(L1,L2),
          filter(L2,T,L).
```

int_ans_type2(X,Y,Z) means that Z is the list of interpretable resolvents derived using the ICs at site Y using the list of clauses for the query in X. Where X is made of more than one clause, the first is employed to derive resolvents using the same int_ans predicate as for answers of Type 1. The set of resolvents derived are then resolved with the remaining query clause to generate the required intensional answers needed in Z. The predicate *gen_imp_constraint(X)* generates all implicit constraints at the site X using the existing set of ICs and asserts the results as further constraints of that site. *filter(X,Y,Z)* means that Z is the list of resolvents generated from resolving the set of resolvents with the remaining query clauses in Y. This is defined by the following Prolog clauses :

```
filter(X,[],Y) :-
          del_redundant(X,Y).
filter(X,[H|T],Y) :-
          del_redundant(X,X1),
          forward_resolve(H,X1,L),
          filter(L,T,Y).
```

forward_resolve(X,Y,Z) means Z is the set of resolvents derived using X as top_clause and Y as the list of base clauses while *del_redundant(L1,L2)* means L2 is the list of resolvents obtained by removing redundant resolvents from the list L1.

7. Conclusions and Future Directions

Our position in this paper has been that the explicitly defined integrity constraints of a relational system embody a significant part of its semantics and that any front-end system built for the purpose of eliciting the semantics of such DBs to users must take these constraints into consideration to be complete. Most of the previous systems built for this task have only dealt with the structures and the inherent constraints that can be captured by these structures of the relational systems. Since the relational model is rather weak in capturing inherent constraints, it follows that such previous works have fallen far short of achieving their goals.

Our approach, described in this paper, to eliciting the said semantics of the DB has been through employing the explicitly defined integrity constraints firstly to advise the user of any constraint violations and suggest a modification of the query and secondly to provide intensional answers to queries which are made by users without much further knowledge of the implications in the system. One can envisage providing a system that would allow users to directly query such explicitly defined constraints but such a system would undoubtedly pre-suppose the users' familiarity with at least the form of the constraints as well as dictate some new interface for making such queries. Our approach of generating intensional answers is system initiated as the generation of intensional answers does not make any additional demands on the user.

Our approach for deriving intensional answers differs significantly from Motro's where he developed an algorithm for evaluating meta-relations holding the constraints. His algorithm, though sound is not complete. Our theorem proving strategy inherits its soundness and completeness for answers of Type 1 from the proof given in [CHOL87]. It is also proved in [KOW87] that reasoning forwards with an extended SLDNF resolution strategy such as the one described in this paper (which is obviously a subset of their extended version) is sound in general and complete when the DB contains no negative conditions. As we have shown, answers of Type 2 are relevant when using integrity constraints to provide intensional answers, thus some of the derivations in our work are different from those for deriving intensional answers within the context of deductive databases [CHOL87, PIR89, SONG90].

We showed in Section 5 that for answers of Type 2 certain implicit constraints are needed before all derived answers can be interpreted. Redundant resolvents also need to be deleted when generated in resolvents of Type 2 answers. We have also shown how constraints can be used to isolate relevant sites in an MBS and hence provide some cost savings for queries ranging over the DBs comprising the MBS. This, together with the concept of intensional responses will provide an MBS user with a very convenient means of understanding the semantics of the underlying DBs.

At present our implementation only considers MSQL queries of the form shown in Section 6. It needs to be extended to handle all forms of MDB retrieval statements. The conditions of the 'where' part of our query are also assumed to be conjuncts only and as such need extending to include disjuncts and a mixture of the two. The intensional answers of each site are also treated independently. For certain MDB queries these answers need to be combined. The system does not support integrity constraint definitions that are recursive and only employs a limited implementation of the paramodulation inference rule to support the equality axioms due to the potential recursion and combinatorial effect inherent in these axioms. Further investigations are needed on these aspects of the system.

Acknowledgements
We are grateful to the referees for their helpful comments on an earlier version of this paper. We would also like to thank Prof. P.M.D. Gray for his helpful suggestions.

References

[AMB87]. T. Amble, *"Logic Programming and Knowledge Engineering"*, International Computer Series - 1987.

[ARI87]. Arity Corporation, *"Arity/Prolog Programming Manual"* - Arity Corporation -1987.

[BRAT90]. I.Bratko, *"Prolog Programming for Artificial Intelligence"*, 2nd Edition, Addison-Wesley, -1990.

[BRY88]. F. Bry, H.Decker & R.Manthey, *"A Uniform Approach to Constraint Satisfaction and Constraint Satisfiability in Deductive Databases"*, In Procs. of the Conf., EDBT, Venice -1988.

[BUN83]. A. Bundy, *"Computer Modelling of Mathematical Reasoning"*, Academic Press Inc. 1983.

[CERI87]. S.Ceri & G.Pelagatti, *"Distributed Databases: Principles and Systems"*, McGraw Hill Int.- 1987.

[CERI90] S. Ceri, *"Logic Programming and Databases - surveys in Computer Science"*, Springer- Verlag - 1990.

[CHAN73] C-L. Chang & R-CT. Lee, *"Symbolic Logic and Mechanical Theorem Proving"*, Academic Press Inc. -1973.

[CHOL87]. L. Cholvy & R. Demolombe, *"Querying a Rule Base"*. In Procs. of the 1st International Conf. on Expert Database Systems, Pp365-371, S. Carolina - L. Kerschberg (Etd) - 1987.

[CHOL88]. L. Cholvy & E. Pascual, *"Answering Queries Addressed to the Rule Base of Deductive Database"*, In Procs of the 2nd Int. Conf. on Info. Processing and Management of Uncertainty in Knowledgebased Systems, pp 138-145. Springer-Verlag. Lecture Notes in Computer Sciences 313. - 1988.

[CLOC84]. W.F.Clocksin & C.S. Mellish, *"Programming in Prolog"*, 2nd Edition - Springer-Verlag - 1984.

[CODD90]. E.F.Codd, *"The Relational Model of Data for Database Management Systems version 2"*, Addison Wesley Pub.Co. 1990.

[DATE90]. C.J. Date, *"An Introduction to Data Base Systems"*, Vols 1(5th Edition) & 2, Addison Wesley Pub.Co. -1990 (Vol I) and -1984 (Vol II).

[DAVI87]. K.A.Davis & A.R Arora, *"Converting A Relational DB model into anEntity-Relationship Model"*, - Proc. 6th Inter. Conf. on Entity Relationship Analysis - 1987.

[FONK92]. M.M. Fonkam & W.A. Gray, *"An Approach to Eliciting the Semantics of Relational Databases"*, To appear in the Fourth International Conference on Advance information Systems Engineering (CAiSE '92) - 1992.

[FROS86]. R.A.Frost, *"Introduction to Knowledge Base Systems"*, - Collins Professional & Technical Books, 1986.

[GARD90]. G.Gardarin & P. Valduriez, *"Relational Databases and Knowledge Bases"*, Adison-Wesley Pub-Co -1990.

[GRAY84]. P. Gray, *"Logic, Algebra and Databases"*, Ellis Horwood Series, -1984.

[GRAY87]. P.M.D. Gray, G.E. Storrs & J.B.H. du Boulay, *"Knowledge representations for database Metadata"*, -AI review Vol.2, pp. 3-29, 1988.

[HEIM81]. D. Heimbigner & D. McLeod, *"Federated Information Bases - a preliminary report"*, Infotech State of the Art Report on Databases, Pergamon Infotech Ltd, Maidenhead,U.K., 1981.

[HEIM85]. D. Heimbigner & D.McLeod, *"A Federated Architecture for Information Management"*, ACM Trans. on Office Information Systems-1985.

[HOG90]. C.J. Hogger, *"Essentials of Logic Programming"*, Clarendon Press.Oxford - 1990.

[IMI87]. L. Imielinski, *"Intelligent Query Answering in Rule Based Systems"*,Journal of Logic Programming, 4(3):229-258, Sept, -1987.

[JOHN84]. R.G. Johnson; *"Integrating Data and Meta-data to enhance the user interface"*, Procs. of the 2th British National Conf. on Databases,-1984.

[KENT89]. W.Kent, *"Limitations of Record-Based Information Models"*, ACM Trans. on Database Systems, 1989.

[KAT91]. Katalin Kalman, *"Implementation and Critique of an Algorithm which maps a Relational Database to a Conceptual Model"*, Procs. of the 3rd International Conference on Advance Information Systems Engineering, Trodheim, Norway, May 1991, Springer Verlag.

[KIN81a]. J.J. King, *"QUIST: A System for Semantic Query Optimisation in Relational Databases"*, Procs. of the 7th VLDB Conf., Cannes France, 1981.

[KIN81b]. J.J. King, *" Modelling Concepts for Reasoning about Access to Knowledge"*,

Procs.Workshop on Data abstraction, Databases and Conceptual Modelling, 1981.

[KOW79].   R.A. Kowalski, "Logic for Problem Solving", Elsvier North Holland, 1979.

[KOW87a]. R. Kowalski, F. Sadri & P. Soper, "Integrity Checking in Deductive Databases", Procs. of the 13th VLDB - 1987.

[KOW87b]. R. Kowalski & S. Sadri, *"An Application of General Purpose Theorem-Proving to Database Integrity"*, Procs. of the Workshop on Foundations of Deductive Databases and Logic Programming, Morgan Kaufmann, Los Altos, Ca, 1987.

[LI84].   D. Li, *"A Prolog Database System"*, Research Studies Press, 1984.

[LIT88].   W.Litwin, *"From Database Systems to Multidatabase Systems : Why and How?"*, In Procs. of The British National Conference on Databases,Ed.by W.A. Gray Cardiff - 1988,.

[LIT84].   W.Litwin, *Concepts for Multidatabase Manipulation Languages"*,- JCIT - 4, Jerusalem, (June,1984) pp433-442.

[LIT87a]. W.Litwin &, "An Overview of the Multi-database Manipulation Language MSDL", Procs of the IEEE,Vol. 75, NO. 5, May 1987.

[LIT87b]. W.Litwin,A.Abdellatif,B.Nicolas,Ph.Vigier & A.Zeroul, "MSQL : Un Langage Multibase", INRIA - Research Rep. 695, June, 1987. Also in Info. Science - An international Journal, Special Issue on Databases, 1987.

[MOT89].   A. Motro, *"Using Integrity Constraints to Provide Intensional Answers to Relational Queries"*, Procs. of the 15th International Conf. on VLDBs, Amsterdam, - 1989.

[PIR89].   A. Pirotte & D.Roelants. *Constraints for Improving the Generation of Intensional Answers in a Deductive Answer"*. In the Procs. of the International Conf. on Data Engineering, Los Angeles, California - 1989.

[REIT84]. R. Reiter, *"Towards a logical reconstruction of Relational Database Theory"*, in On Conceptual Modelling: Perspectives from Artificial Intelligence, Databases and Programming Languages, Springer-Verlag, New York, 1984.

[STON75]. M. Stonebraker, *"Implementation of Integrity Constraints and Views by Query Modification"*, Procs. ACM SIGMOD,-1975.

[SONG90]. I-Y.Song,H-J.Kim & P. Geutner, *"Intensional Query Processing: A Three-Step Approach"*,   Procs. 1st International Conf. on Databases and Expert Systems Applications, Vienna - 1990.

[TSIC82]. D.C Tsichritzis & F.H. Lochovsky, *"Data Models"*, Published by Prentice Hall Inc. - New Jersey - 1982.

[TULP90]. A.J. Tulp, *"Concepts for Intelligent Database front-end Systems"*, Procs. of the 1st International Conf. on Databases and Expert Systems Applications, Vienna, - 1990.

[WAN90].   X.Y.Wang,N.J.Fiddian & W.A.Gray, *"Semantic Transaction Optimisation in Relational Databases"*, Procs. of the 8th British National Conference on Databases - Edited by A.Brown & P. Hitchcock. - 1990.

[WOS84].   L. Wos,R.Overbeen,E.Lusk & J.Boyle, *"Automated Reasoning: Introduction and Applications"*, Prentice-Hall, Inc.1984.

Lecture Notes in Computer Science

Further Volumes on Databases

Vol. 580: A. Pirotte, C. Delobel, G. Gottlob (Eds.)
Advances in Database Technology – EDBT '92
1992. ISBN 3-540-55270-7

Vol. 566: C. Delobel, M. Kifer, Y. Masunaga (Eds.)
Deductive and Object-Oriented Databases   (DOOD '91)
1991. ISBN 3-540-55015-1

Vol. 554: Gösta Grahne
The Problem of Incomplete Information in Relational Databases
1991. ISBN 3-540-54919-6

Vol. 525: O. Günther, H.-J. Schek (Eds.)
Advances in Spatial Databases   (SSD '91)
1991. ISBN 3-540-54414-3

Vol. 504: J.W. Schmidt, A.A. Stogny (Eds.)
Next Generation Information Sytems
1991. ISBN 3-540-54141-1

Vol. 503: P. America (Ed.)
Parallel Database Systems
1991. ISBN 3-540-54132-2

Vol. 495: B. Thalheim, J. Demetrovics, H.-D. Gerhardt (Eds.)
MFDBS 91   (Mathematical Foundations of Databases)
1991. ISBN 3-540-54009-1

Vol. 479: Helmut Schmidt
Meta-Level Control for Deductive Database Systems
1991. ISBN 3-540-53754-6

Vol. 474: D. Karagiannis (Ed.)
Information Systems and Artificial Intelligence: Integration Aspects
1991. ISBN 3-540-53557-8

Vol. 470: S. Abiteboul, P.C. Kanellakis (Eds.)
ICDT '90   (International Conference on Database Theory)
1990. ISBN 3-540-53507-1

Springer-Verlag Berlin Heidelberg New York London Paris Tokyo Hong Kong Barcelona Budapest

Lecture Notes in Computer Science

For information about Vols. 1–529
please contact your bookseller or Springer-Verlag

Vol. 530: D. H. Pitt, P.-L. Curien, S. Abramsky, A. M. Pitts, A. Poigné, D. E. Rydeheard (Eds.), Category Theory and Computer Science. Proceedings, 1991. VII, 301 pages. 1991.

Vol. 531: E. M. Clarke, R. P. Kurshan (Eds.), Computer-Aided Verification. Proceedings, 1990. XIII, 372 pages. 1991.

Vol. 532: H. Ehrig, H.-J. Kreowski, G. Rozenberg (Eds.), Graph Grammars and Their Application to Computer Science. Proceedings, 1990. X, 703 pages. 1991.

Vol. 533: E. Börger, H. Kleine Büning, M. M. Richter, W. Schönfeld (Eds.), Computer Science Logic. Proceedings, 1990. VIII, 399 pages. 1991.

Vol. 534: H. Ehrig, K. P. Jantke, F. Orejas, H. Reichel (Eds.), Recent Trends in Data Type Specification. Proceedings, 1990. VIII, 379 pages. 1991.

Vol. 535: P. Jorrand, J. Kelemen (Eds.), Fundamentals of Artificial Intelligence Research. Proceedings, 1991. VIII, 255 pages. 1991. (Subseries LNAI).

Vol. 536: J. E. Tomayko, Software Engineering Education. Proceedings, 1991. VIII, 296 pages. 1991.

Vol. 537: A. J. Menezes, S. A. Vanstone (Eds.), Advances in Cryptology – CRYPTO '90. Proceedings. XIII, 644 pages. 1991.

Vol. 538: M. Kojima, N. Megiddo, T. Noma, A. Yoshise, A Unified Approach to Interior Point Algorithms for Linear Complementarity Problems. VIII, 108 pages. 1991.

Vol. 539: H. F. Mattson, T. Mora, T. R. N. Rao (Eds.), Applied Algebra, Algebraic Algorithms and Error-Correcting Codes. Proceedings, 1991. XI, 489 pages. 1991.

Vol. 540: A. Prieto (Ed.), Artificial Neural Networks. Proceedings, 1991. XIII, 476 pages. 1991.

Vol. 541: P. Barahona, L. Moniz Pereira, A. Porto (Eds.), EPIA '91. Proceedings, 1991. VIII, 292 pages. 1991. (Subseries LNAI).

Vol. 542: Z. W. Ras, M. Zemankova (Eds.), Methodologies for Intelligent Systems. Proceedings, 1991. X, 644 pages. 1991. (Subseries LNAI).

Vol. 543: J. Dix, K. P. Jantke, P. H. Schmitt (Eds.), Non-monotonic and Inductive Logic. Proceedings, 1990. X, 243 pages. 1991. (Subseries LNAI).

Vol. 544: M. Broy, M. Wirsing (Eds.), Methods of Programming. XII, 268 pages. 1991.

Vol. 545: H. Alblas, B. Melichar (Eds.), Attribute Grammars, Applications and Systems. Proceedings, 1991. IX, 513 pages. 1991.

Vol. 546: O. Herzog, C.-R. Rollinger (Eds.), Text Understanding in LILOG. XI, 738 pages. 1991. (Subseries LNAI).

Vol. 547: D. W. Davies (Ed.), Advances in Cryptology – EUROCRYPT '91. Proceedings, 1991. XII, 556 pages. 1991.

Vol. 548: R. Kruse, P. Siegel (Eds.), Symbolic and Quantitative Approaches to Uncertainty. Proceedings, 1991. XI, 362 pages. 1991.

Vol. 549: E. Ardizzone, S. Gaglio, F. Sorbello (Eds.), Trends in Artificial Intelligence. Proceedings, 1991. XIV, 479 pages. 1991. (Subseries LNAI).

Vol. 550: A. van Lamsweerde, A. Fugetta (Eds.), ESEC '91. Proceedings, 1991. XII, 515 pages. 1991.

Vol. 551: S. Prehn, W. J. Toetenel (Eds.), VDM '91. Formal Software Development Methods. Volume 1. Proceedings, 1991. XIII, 699 pages. 1991.

Vol. 552: S. Prehn, W. J. Toetenel (Eds.), VDM '91. Formal Software Development Methods. Volume 2. Proceedings, 1991. XIV, 430 pages. 1991.

Vol. 553: H. Bieri, H. Noltemeier (Eds.), Computational Geometry - Methods, Algorithms and Applications '91. Proceedings, 1991. VIII, 320 pages. 1991.

Vol. 554: G. Grahne, The Problem of Incomplete Information in Relational Databases. VIII, 156 pages. 1991.

Vol. 555: H. Maurer (Ed.), New Results and New Trends in Computer Science. Proceedings, 1991. VIII, 403 pages. 1991.

Vol. 556: J.-M. Jacquet, Conclog: A Methodological Approach to Concurrent Logic Programming. XII, 781 pages. 1991.

Vol. 557: W. L. Hsu, R. C. T. Lee (Eds.), ISA '91 Algorithms. Proceedings, 1991. X, 396 pages. 1991.

Vol. 558: J. Hooman, Specification and Compositional Verification of Real-Time Systems. VIII, 235 pages. 1991.

Vol. 559: G. Butler, Fundamental Algorithms for Permutation Groups. XII, 238 pages. 1991.

Vol. 560: S. Biswas, K. V. Nori (Eds.), Foundations of Software Technology and Theoretical Computer Science. Proceedings, 1991. X, 420 pages. 1991.

Vol. 561: C. Ding, G. Xiao, W. Shan, The Stability Theory of Stream Ciphers. IX, 187 pages. 1991.

Vol. 562: R. Breu, Algebraic Specification Techniques in Object Oriented Programming Environments. XI, 228 pages. 1991.

Vol. 563: A. Karshmer, J. Nehmer (Eds.), Operating Systems of the 90s and Beyond. Proceedings, 1991. X, 285 pages. 1991.

Vol. 564: I. Herman, The Use of Projective Geometry in Computer Graphics. VIII, 146 pages. 1992.

Vol. 565: J. D. Becker, I. Eisele, F. W. Mündemann (Eds.), Parallelism, Learning, Evolution. Proceedings, 1989. VIII, 525 pages. 1991. (Subseries LNAI).

Vol. 566: C. Delobel, M. Kifer, Y. Masunaga (Eds.), Deductive and Object-Oriented Databases. Proceedings, 1991. XV, 581 pages. 1991.

Vol. 567: H. Boley, M. M. Richter (Eds.), Processing Declarative Kowledge. Proceedings, 1991. XII, 427 pages. 1991. (Subseries LNAI).

Vol. 568: H.-J. Bürckert, A Resolution Principle for a Logic with Restricted Quantifiers. X, 116 pages. 1991. (Subseries LNAI).

Vol. 569: A. Beaumont, G. Gupta (Eds.), Parallel Execution of Logic Programs. Proceedings, 1991. VII, 195 pages. 1991.

Vol. 570: R. Berghammer, G. Schmidt (Eds.), Graph-Theoretic Concepts in Computer Science. Proceedings, 1991. VIII, 253 pages. 1992.

Vol. 571: J. Vytopil (Ed.), Formal Techniques in Real-Time and Fault-Tolerant Systems. Proceedings, 1992. IX, 620 pages. 1991.

Vol. 572: K. U. Schulz (Ed.), Word Equations and Related Topics. Proceedings, 1990. VII, 256 pages. 1992.

Vol. 573: G. Cohen, S. N. Litsyn, A. Lobstein, G. Zémor (Eds.), Algebraic Coding. Proceedings, 1991. X, 158 pages. 1992.

Vol. 574: J. P. Banâtre, D. Le Métayer (Eds.), Research Directions in High-Level Parallel Programming Languages. Proceedings, 1991. VIII, 387 pages. 1992.

Vol. 575: K. G. Larsen, A. Skou (Eds.), Computer Aided Verification. Proceedings, 1991. X, 487 pages. 1992.

Vol. 576: J. Feigenbaum (Ed.), Advances in Cryptology - CRYPTO '91. Proceedings. X, 485 pages. 1992.

Vol. 577: A. Finkel, M. Jantzen (Eds.), STACS 92. Proceedings, 1992. XIV, 621 pages. 1992.

Vol. 578: Th. Beth, M. Frisch, G. J. Simmons (Eds.), Public-Key Cryptography: State of the Art and Future Directions. XI, 97 pages. 1992.

Vol. 579: S. Toueg, P. G. Spirakis, L. Kirousis (Eds.), Distributed Algorithms. Proceedings, 1991. X, 319 pages. 1992.

Vol. 580: A. Pirotte, C. Delobel, G. Gottlob (Eds.), Advances in Database Technology – EDBT '92. Proceedings. XII, 551 pages. 1992.

Vol. 581: J.-C. Raoult (Ed.), CAAP '92. Proceedings. VIII, 361 pages. 1992.

Vol. 582: B. Krieg-Brückner (Ed.), ESOP '92. Proceedings. VIII, 491 pages. 1992.

Vol. 583: I. Simon (Ed.), LATIN '92. Proceedings. IX, 545 pages. 1992.

Vol. 584: R. E. Zippel (Ed.), Computer Algebra and Parallelism. Proceedings, 1990. IX, 114 pages. 1992.

Vol. 585: F. Pichler, R. Moreno Díaz (Eds.), Computer Aided System Theory – EUROCAST '91. Proceedings. X, 761 pages. 1992.

Vol. 586: A. Cheese, Parallel Execution of Parlog. IX, 184 pages. 1992.

Vol. 587: R. Dale, E. Hovy, D. Rösner, O. Stock (Eds.), Aspects of Automated Natural Language Generation. Proceedings, 1992. VIII, 311 pages. 1992. (Subseries LNAI).

Vol. 588: G. Sandini (Ed.), Computer Vision – ECCV '92. Proceedings. XV, 909 pages. 1992.

Vol. 589: U. Banerjee, D. Gelernter, A. Nicolau, D. Padua (Eds.), Languages and Compilers for Parallel Computing. Proceedings, 1991. IX, 419 pages. 1992.

Vol. 590: B. Fronhöfer, G. Wrightson (Eds.), Parallelization in Inference Systems. Proceedings, 1990. VIII, 372 pages. 1992. (Subseries LNAI).

Vol. 591: H. P. Zima (Ed.), Parallel Computation. Proceedings, 1991. IX, 451 pages. 1992.

Vol. 592: A. Voronkov (Ed.), Logic Programming. Proceedings, 1991. IX, 514 pages. 1992. (Subseries LNAI).

Vol. 593: P. Loucopoulos (Ed.), Advanced Information Systems Engineering. Proceedings. XI, 650 pages. 1992.

Vol. 594: B. Monien, Th. Ottmann (Eds.), Data Structures and Efficient Algorithms. VIII, 389 pages. 1992.

Vol. 595: M. Levene, The Nested Universal Relation Database Model. X, 177 pages. 1992.

Vol. 596: L.-H. Eriksson, L. Hallnäs, P. Schroeder-Heister (Eds.), Extensions of Logic Programming. Proceedings, 1991. VII, 369 pages. 1992. (Subseries LNAI).

Vol. 597: H. W. Guesgen, J. Hertzberg, A Perspective of Constraint-Based Reasoning. VIII, 123 pages. 1992. (Subseries LNAI).

Vol. 598: S. Brookes, M. Main, A. Melton, M. Mislove, D. Schmidt (Eds.), Mathematical Foundations of Programming Semantics. Proceedings, 1991. VIII, 506 pages. 1992.

Vol. 599: Th. Wetter, K.-D. Althoff, J. Boose, B. R. Gaines, M. Linster, F. Schmalhofer (Eds.), Current Developments in Knowledge Acquisition - EKAW '92. Proceedings. XIII, 444 pages. 1992. (Subseries LNAI).

Vol. 600: J. W. de Bakker, K. Huizing, W. P. de Roever, G. Rozenberg (Eds.), Real-Time: Theory in Practice. Proceedings, 1991. VIII, 723 pages. 1992.

Vol. 601: D. Dolev, Z. Galil, M. Rodeh (Eds.), Theory of Computing and Systems. Proceedings, 1992. VIII, 220 pages. 1992.

Vol. 602: I. Tomek (Ed.), Computer Assisted Learning. Proceedigs, 1992. X, 615 pages. 1992.

Vol. 603: J. van Katwijk (Ed.), Ada: Moving Towards 2000. Proceedings, 1992. VIII, 324 pages. 1992.

Vol. 604: F. Belli, F.-J. Radermacher (Eds.), Industrial and Engineering Applications of Artificial Intelligence and Expert Systems. Proceedings, 1992. XV, 702 pages. 1992. (Subseries LNAI).

Vol. 605: D. Etiemble, J.-C. Syre (Eds.), PARLE '92. Parallel Architectures and Languages Europe. Proceedings, 1992. XVII, 984 pages. 1992.

Vol. 606: D. E. Knuth, Axioms and Hulls. IX, 109 pages. 1992.

Vol. 607: D. Kapur (Ed.), Automated Deduction – CADE-11. Proceedings, 1992. XV, 793 pages. 1992. (Subseries LNAI).

Vol. 608: C. Frasson, G. Gauthier, G. I. McCalla (Eds.), Intelligent Tutoring Systems. Proceedings, 1992. XIV, 686 pages. 1992.

Vol. 609: G. Rozenberg (Ed.), Advances in Petri Nets 1992. VIII, 472 pages. 1992.

Vol. 610: F. von Martial, Coordinating Plans of Autonomous Agents. XII, 246 pages. 1992. (Subseries LNAI).

Vol. 612: M. Tokoro, O. Nierstrasz, P. Wegner (Eds.), Object-Based Concurrent Computing. Proceedings, 1991. X, 265 pages. 1992.

Vol. 613: J. P. Myers, Jr., M. J. O'Donnell (Eds.), Constructivity in Computer Science. Proceedings, 1991. X, 247 pages. 1992.

Vol. 614: R. G. Herrtwich (Ed.), Network and Operating System Support for Digital Audio and Video. Proceedings, 1991. XII, 403 pages. 1992.

Vol. 615: O. Lehrmann Madsen (Ed.), ECOOP '92. European Conference on Object Oriented Programming. Proceedings. X, 426 pages. 1992.

Vol. 616: K. Jensen (Ed.), Application and Theory of Petri Nets 1992. Proceedings, 1992. VIII, 398 pages. 1992.

Vol. 617: V. Mařík, O. Štěpánková, R. Trappl (Eds.), Advanced Topics in Artificial Intelligence. Proceedings, 1992. IX, 484 pages. 1992. (Subseries LNAI).

Vol. 618: P. M. D. Gray, R. J. Lucas (Eds.), Advanced Database Systems. Proceedings, 1992. X, 260 pages. 1992.